SUPERFREAKS

SUPER FREAKS

KINK, PLEASURE, AND THE PURSUIT OF HAPPINESS

ARIELLE GREENBERG

BEACON PRESS
BOSTON

BEACON PRESS
Boston, Massachusetts
www.beacon.org

Beacon Press books
are published under the auspices of
the Unitarian Universalist Association of Congregations.

Printed in the United States of America
26 25 24 23   8 7 6 5 4 3 2 1

This book is printed on acid-free paper that meets the uncoated paper
ANSI/NISO specifications for permanence as revised in 1992.

Text design and composition by Kim Arney

Library of Congress Cataloguing-in-Publication
Data is available for this title.
Hardcover ISBN: 978-0-8070-2021-0
E-book ISBN: 978-0-8070-2022-7
Audiobook: 978-0-8070-1277-2

For the one I call Daddy.
From the very start, you have been
the embodiment of my deepest, kinkiest desires,
and my ideal partner for every kind of adventure.
I love you so hard.

CONTENTS

INTRODUCTION

She's a Very Kinky Girl: Why I Wrote This Book   1

*What this book holds in store—reclaiming the term
"pervert"—who am I to write about this—my central
fetish—kink in kiddie cartoons—sexual superheroes.*

CHAPTER I

Let's Talk About Sex, Baby: The Ins and Outs of Erotic Desire   15

*Defining "normal" sexual desire and where eros
might come from—strong preferences—the tangled
web of sexual compatibility—everyone needs an escape
pod—the fallacy of "spicing up a relationship."*

CHAPTER 2

Take a Walk on the Wild Side: A Primer on Kink, BDSM, and Fetishes   36

*Defining kink, fetishes, and other deviant practices—is it
kink if you're not aroused?—consent at the center—the
spectrum of fetishistic desire—some handy acronyms.*

CHAPTER 3

Heaven Help Me for the Way I Am: Taboos as the Heart of Kink   61

*The four P's (categories of taboo)—kinks you can't try
in real life—objects that are closer than they appear—
some controversial thoughts on pedophilia.*

CHAPTER 4

Chains and Whips Excite Me: On Sadomasochism   **76**

*Pain as a conduit of pleasure—sadism and masochism and
the perverts who gave those terms their names—BDSM
contracts, an origin story—what do we do when we do
S/M—the controversy around "topping from the bottom."*

CHAPTER 5

Let's Play Master and Servant:
On Dominance and Submission   **97**

*The fantasy of the rape fantasy—power exchange (and the
importance of consent in sexual non-consent)—a fetish for
stability?—what it means to be leather—"queer 1950s household."*

CHAPTER 6

She's Got Legs: On Fetishes   **122**

*The spectrum of fetishistic desire—partialism, including but
not limited to feet and shoes—sensory paraphilias—smoking,
spanking, and other obsessed-over activities—when your
thing is "atypical situations"—the love of bodily fluids.*

CHAPTER 7

I Will Be Your Father Figure: On Role Play   **137**

*The possibilities of role play—race play, age play, and other
fascinating scenarios—Littles and ABDL—a Daddy/girl age play
mixtape—how much is that doggie in the window?—furries:
a que(e)ry—a call for a new word for "nonsexual kink."*

CHAPTER 8

Caught Up in You:
On the Kinks of Attention and Neglect   **157**

*The eros of attention—voyeurship and exhibitionism—the art of sex
in public—hotwife and other ways to turn jealousy on its head—
in the realm of no senses—a case for reverent objectification—
hypnosis, bimbofication, feeding, and other forms of control.*

CHAPTER 9

Super Freaky: Kink History and Icons   **176**

Icons and milestones of kink history—sexual deviance
and the birth of the Internet—a highly personal
roundup of representations of kink in the movies.

CHAPTER 10

Thank U 4 a Funky Time:
Forging Your Path and Community   **198**

Resources for finding community—can
perversion really make you happy?

APPENDIX

We're Going Down to Alphabet Street:
An A-to-Z of Kinky Stuff   **209**

An abecedarium of gear, from anal hooks to zentai
suits, including but not limited to blindfolds, collars,
handcuffs, urethral sounds, and violet wands—alternately,
#buynothing, an argument for psychological kink.

Acknowledgments   **231**
Works Cited   **232**
Index   **253**

SHE'S A VERY KINKY GIRL

Why I Wrote This Book

What this book holds in store—reclaiming the term "pervert"—who am I to write about this—my central fetish—kink in kiddie cartoons—sexual superheroes.

What a time to be alive. I remember when one had to slip into the back room of an adult bookstore to find the rack of niche materials, and then treasure one's single, well-worn copy of an underground magazine. There was something romantic and exciting about that arcane experience: the thrill of the hunt, and the sense of being special and unusual are all much harder to capture when all we need to do is open up a browser window and type in a few key words to see our innermost desires splashed all over PornHub. Now, even in a little city in my rural state, there's a terrific feminist sex shop with bookshelves offering a wide assortment of sexy how-tos, short fiction, essays, and more.

But even with all the books out there now, as a lifelong fetishist and avid researcher, I have always been hungry for one that takes a wide view of kinky identities, beyond the ones most typically represented: a work that looks not just at the expected bondage enthusiasts, Dominants, and masochists, but also at fetishists, furries, and Littles. Furthermore, I wanted a book that looks not at just *how* people participate in these practices and communities, but *why* we do: where do these desires come from? What do they *mean?* Finally,

I wanted to read about these things in a book that felt friendly and enthusiastic, not academic or prescriptive.

I couldn't find such a book. So I've tried to write one.

I've always felt that our individual sexualities, and the way we enact them with ourselves and one another, are important, powerful—and even magical. (Maybe it's because I'm a Scorpio?) Luckily, no less than the brilliant writer and thinker Audre Lorde agrees, and in her essay "The Uses of the Erotic: The Erotic as Power" she writes, "The erotic is a measure between the beginnings of our sense of self and the chaos of our strongest feelings. It is an internal sense of satisfaction to which, once we have experienced it, we know we can aspire. For having experienced the fullness of this depth of feeling and recognizing its power, in honor and self-respect we can require no less of ourselves."

In my own experiences and in community, I've found that our deviant desires—our "strongest feelings"—can become a pathway to deep satisfaction and achieving our highest selves. Since we are required to navigate a society that doesn't currently honor our nonnormative sexualities, we can learn to be more creative in our daily lives, not to mention in finding our bliss. (In this way, kink community is similar to queer community, disabled community, neurodivergent community, and other groups that problem-solve to make our way through spaces that are too often uncomprehending, intolerant, and inaccessible.) I also believe that learning to access and embrace our strangest erotic urges can open our hearts and minds to living with more tolerance, empathy, and compassion. I hope that as you read this, you will feel beautifully connected to a long history and global citizenry of kinky fuckers of every possible race, ethnicity, age, gender, body type, and so on—and that this, in turn, will help you feel less lonely, less isolated, and less unsure of where to turn.

Another thing that unites humans across space and time is music, and music is probably as important to me as sex. So I've named the chapter titles after my favorite song lyrics, which I hope will help to keep the mood playful, even when some of the things discussed get pretty heavy. After all, an intentional mix of songs is called a *playlist*, and when we do kinky shit with other people, we call it *playing*. Come play along!

PERVERT, FREAK, AND OTHER "BAD" WORDS

Let's begin, shall we, with some of these words I'm putting on the cover of this book and the tops of these pages. "Pervert"? "Deviant"? *Really?*

Am I those things? Do I want to call myself those things? Some days, claiming these terms scares the hell out of me. They *should* scare me: as a writer, I believe full-heartedly in the power of language, and as a kinky person who enjoys role playing with dominance and submission, I have enormous respect for—and therefore a healthy fear of—power. Words like "pervert" and "deviant"—even when detached from any specific person, place, or thing—are powerful, in both abstract and tangible ways.

When I'm at a sexuality conference or among friends who proudly identify as queer, kinky, sex-positive, ethically nonmonogamous, and/or just plain slutty, we cheerfully call one another "pervs" and "sickos" as inclusive terms of endearment. As historian Peter Tupper writes, ours is "a story of misfits, hustlers and visionaries," a space where we can celebrate our difference and our outsider status.

But beyond my participation in those communities, I am also a mother, a professional, an employee, and a stand-up member of my community. In those circles, such words are not understood the same way. As writer Annaliese Griffin notes, "The word 'pervert' has long been used to marginalize, silence, and victimize certain communities."

Those most at risk of persecution for their sexual identities are also those who are most at risk of harm of any kind. Because American culture has such deeply rooted prejudice against and fear of Black, indigenous, and other people of color; feminine and femme-identified people; gay men; and trans people (especially trans women of color), these groups are more likely than white, cisgender, and masculine-identifying and -presenting people to be the victims of violence, harassment, and discrimination—not just by their fellow citizens but also by institutions such as law enforcement and schools. From the Human Rights Campaign: "Fatal violence disproportionately affects transgender women of color—particularly Black transgender women. . . . The intersections of racism, sexism, homophobia, biphobia, transphobia and unchecked access to guns conspire to deprive them of employment, housing, healthcare and other necessities."

Although I identify as queer, I am also a middle-class white cis woman currently married to a white cis man, and thus am in a very privileged position and enjoy relative security. Many others are not afforded the same levels of agency, and that's important for those of us with more privilege to note and work to change.

And truth be told, none of us in the kink community are completely safe from the danger of ridicule or exposure. When an adult is outed as participating in legal and consensual but "abnormal" sexual behavior such as sadomasochism or urine play, we can be at risk of arrest, eviction, losing custody of our children, being fired from our jobs, and enduring public humiliation and scandal.

As sociologist Elisabeth A. Sheff points out in a 2014 article for *Psychology Today*, anyone considered sexually nonnormative is "at particular risk in legal settings." She explains, "With sexuality, whatever is the current social norm often passes as . . . absolute. The sense of moral taint or even revulsion that can inflect any variation from conventional sexualities or gender roles means that being seen as a 'pervert' can be the kiss of death in the courtroom." All of which is to say that I do not want to use these terms lightly, or without regard to the long history of persecution and prosecution that is attached to them.

Other days, though, I worry that I'm not pervy *enough* to claim this identity. I'm really such a good girl, a responsible citizen. I never even got detention in high school. The truth is, I spend a lot more time making wholesome, nutritious family meals than I do bent over a spanking bench.

And yet. On my left wrist, I wear a discreet chain bracelet that I never take off. So every time I make a meal for my family, I do it while wearing a chain that signifies, to me and my primary partner, something about my erotic identity. And more important than this piece of jewelry is the mindset that goes with it, which can transform even a completely normal, vanilla task like making dinner into an erotic game of power exchange.

And most nights, once the kids are safely tucked into bed, my primary partner and I play out all manner of taboo acts in the privacy of our own bedroom, things that would no doubt be seen as weird or disturbing by many who know us but that are the very core of our sexual relationship.

So when I use terms like "pervert" or "deviant," it is an act of reclaiming. I am trying to seize the negative charge back from these words, subvert that negativity into something playful and delightful and equally powerful, and then harness that force for myself and those like me.

This act of reclaiming is parallel to some aspects of coming out as LGBTQ+. Coming out as kinky isn't *the same* as coming out as queer, of course. There are countless nuanced differences, but one that I think about a lot is how, while coming out as pansexual or gay or lesbian or trans or nonbinary implies some things about who we're attracted to, it doesn't necessitate that we reveal the exact details of our innermost fantasies to strangers. Coming out as a sexual deviant, on the other hand, means that we *are* bringing the details of our erotic lives into a public sphere. We are choosing to center not just our sexual orientations but also our sexual *behaviors* as part of our identities.

This is itself not without controversy. In recent years, there has been a good deal of pushback from LGBTQ+ folks who seek to distance themselves from our community's kinky factions and even ban expressions of kinky identity at Pride parades. People who adopt this stance tend to want to assimilate into mainstream society, with the idea that queer and trans folks will face less discrimination, if, over time, their identities become seen as "normal" and therefore nonthreatening: this is the definition of "respectability politics." People on the other side take issue with the corporatization and general co-opting of Pride, and feel that to exclude kink from Pride is to ignore and erase the very kinds of freedoms that Pride has fought for. As culture reporter Alex Abad-Santos puts it in a 2021 article for *Vox*, "Queer history is often about resistance to norms and embracing radical existence, so engaging in respectability politics . . . flies in the face of those goals." Abad-Santos goes on to say, "Instead of broadening mainstream culture to accommodate the humanity of the LGBTQ community as a whole, respectability politics asks a community to change itself for mainstream sympathy. . . . Queerness, at its core, is a rejection of that respectability."

I suppose you can guess which side I'm on. But my decision to be out as kinky is informed by both my desire to be respected and my desire to resist. Both come together when I choose to call myself a pervert, in part, as a means of getting ahead of any potential criticism or gossip. If I am out as a member of this sexual minority, owning that identity, and waving it defiantly in public, I am also engaging in a risk-reduction exercise, taking control of my narrative before someone else can.

Like being openly LGBTQ+, identifying as sexually nonnormative is an act of self-love, of pride, and of solidarity. I am very fortunate to currently live in a progressive community that values privacy and independence; I am also fortunate to work mostly in the arts and academia, where freethinkers are highly regarded and many sexual misfits have paved the way before me. (See chapter 9 to read about important pervy groundbreakers.) Even my family of origin is relatively unfazed by the weird things they know I think and write about and do (though when I first told my parents that I am ethically nonmonogamous, they refused to stay in my household for a few years). There have been moments (luckily few) when I've been worried because someone has threatened to expose me, but since a quick Internet search of my name returns the essays and poems and interviews in which I openly discuss my sexuality, there's not much a bully can hold over me. Because I enjoy relative security due to my whiteness, my cis gender, my marriage to a man, and my middle-class status, I feel it's my responsibility to promote positive attention and thoughtful discourse around erotic deviance. I'm hoping that actions I take can help the world become slightly safer and more tolerant for those who don't have the privileges that I have. But there are other, far less high-minded reasons I like to call myself a pervert, too.

First of all, I like the word. It sounds like the best parts of the 1970s as seen through the sunset haze of my early childhood memories: "pervert" is like the delicate music of walking through a beaded curtain on a wood-paneled basement rec room where someone is hosting a key party. Or it sounds naughty, like a secret Victorian bookcase doorway that leads to a luxuriously outfitted dungeon with satin blindfolds and hand-crafted torture equipment. Or it sounds joyous and wild, like pagan-inflected sex rituals performed outdoors by a bonfire under a full moon. It sounds like *fun*. (Confession: I have participated in a pagan-inflected sex ritual performed outdoors by a bonfire under a full moon. My partner and I and two other couples were with a group of people of varying genders and were surrounded by live drumming and dancing. It was *exceedingly* fun.)

I also like the inherent subversion of the term and the oppositional stance it takes. *Pervert*: to alter course or meaning. *Subvert*: to turn under or go below. These interconnected terms smack of the less taken, of nonconformity, of political radicals and art-makers and wild-eyed geniuses who defy norms and change history. James Baldwin wrote, "Freaks are called freaks . . . because they are human beings who cause to echo, deep within us, our most profound terrors and desires." I believe that living a life that provokes others to reconsider their own is sacred, impactful work. I admire art that is deeply, intentionally unsettling, provocative, and hard to take. I am drawn most to work that risks offensiveness, while also being playful and witty and honest. The word "pervert" links me to artists like these and to denizens of underground cultures throughout time: ancient Roman bacchanalias, Dashwood's Hellfire Club, pre-war Berlin cabarets, Andy Warhol's Factory. (See chapter 9 for more on some of these, too.)

WHERE ONE OF MY FAVORITE BANDS, THE VELVET UNDERGROUND, GOT ITS NAME

My love of alternative sexuality runs parallel to my love of music (which, again, is why all the chapters in this book are taken from song lyrics). Sometimes these two loves intertwine. One of my favorite bands, the Velvet Underground, has a long association with kink. Their song "Venus in Furs," with its "shiny shiny boots of leather," was inspired by kinky forefather Leopold von Sacher-Masoch's novella of the same name (the term "masochism" is derived from this work). The band did indeed wear a lot of shiny black leather. And their name is taken from a smarmy 1963 best-selling paperback by Michael Leigh that purported to be a document of a "burgeoning demi-monde of sado-masochism, transvestism . . . paedophilia, bestiality and pornography" in suburban America.

Like so many other passwords of underground culture, "pervert" is a term that defines a tribe, a space outside the mainstream, a fringe place for those of us who never quite fit in.

I think I will always find the most kinship and pleasure in gatherings of marginalized people. And at this phase of my life, as a respectable middle-aged wife and mother whose days are full of responsibility and good decisions, I hungrily hang on to any shred of underground shadow I can.

Mostly through sex.

Which brings me to a couple of very intimate confessions.

First, I want to tell you that I have been masturbating to orgasm (using a hands-free method some scientific literature calls "knee-chest") since infancy. My mother's accounts confirm that I started masturbating long before I can remember, literally in my crib, before I had language, and I have never stopped. As an anxious person, I have used orgasm to self-soothe, for emotional release, and as a sleep aid.

I have spent so many years exploring and learning how to get myself off and fantasizing, that I know exactly what turns me on. I have therefore always been an arousal factory, a lube factory, an orgasm factory. And I believe this has given me an unusual degree of agency, control, and self-awareness in my erotic life, one that I wish more people were able to access.

I didn't set out to teach myself to get off as an infant. It feels like dumb luck that I happened upon this little parlor trick. Dumb luck, but powerful luck. A perverse luck, if you will.

Second, I want to tell you that although, like many of us in the alternative sex community, I have multiple and overlapping kinks, I most identify as a pretty hardcore fetishist: someone who finds sexual arousal in objects or body parts that aren't normally considered erotic. (Foot and shoe fetishists are the most well-known and notorious of our tribe.)

AND WHAT *IS* MY FETISH?

So sweet of you to ask! Unfortunately, I'm not aware of a term that exists for exactly what I'm into. But I'm glad to tell you about it, because it illustrates the extremely individual nature of fetishistic sexuality—and maybe that will resonate for some of you reading this, even if my specific fetish does not.

My fetish overlaps with some other fetishes out there that do have names, like "weight gain," "feederism," and "gainer/encourager," all of which have to do with getting turned on by a person—either yourself or someone you're attracted to—consuming a lot of calories and getting physically bigger. The communities around these fetishes are huge (ha ha), and, like all fetish communities, include people with specific and differing interests: some people love watching someone else (or themselves) go from very thin to not quite as thin; some people are into others of truly epic proportions; some people are into gaining that intersects with humiliation or force-feeding; others are into affectionate and admiring support.

But though gaining/feeding/encouraging fetishes are the most aligned with my own, they don't fully encompass what I'm into. My fetish, the one that has been with me since I was a little girl, is an intricate tangle of attitudes, psychological situations, and sensual experiences. It has multiple facets, not all of which are about weight gain. The best way for me to put it is to say that I'm into when people I find appealing (of various genders and ages) overindulge in food and/or alcohol (preferably beer, because it is both filling and intoxicating) for their own pleasure, not mine, and have an attitude of being really proud of and defiant about their hedonistic behavior—and have round, firm bellies as a result.

As you can see, like many fetishists, what I like is very specific. In fact, I'd theorize that my fetish is for a whole *style*, wherein style, as defined by sociologist Mike Brake, has three components: image (how it looks), demeanor (its attitude), and argot (its slang or terminology). For me to get really turned on and feel like my needs are being completely satisfied, I require the object of my affection to possess a specific body type (a firm, round belly on an otherwise average-sized body), accompanied by a specific attitude (eager indulgence and smug pride), and a specific way of talking about it (e.g., "I'm so full, but I'm gonna drink even more tomorrow").

It's not easy having a fetish that is unusual even within the unusual world of fetishists. When I want to access erotic material, I find my fetish porn by searching the Internet for really particular key terms (my go-tos have included "stuffed belly drunk erotic" and "ball belly beer")—and even then, I inevitably turn up videos and stories that won't quite work because some minor element is off. In this way, we fetishists are like any vanilla person searching for porn: it can be difficult to find the exact combination of tone and look and scenario that we need. For example, many beer-drinking videos for fetishists feature a lot of burping, and I'm turned off by that. But judging from the number of such videos on YouTube, a lot of other fetishists are really turned *on* by it. (These videos don't get flagged as porn since they contain no nudity or "sexual content"—they are often videos of fully dressed individuals eating pasta or drinking liter bottles of soda. Which is also why the comment sections on such videos are filled with non-fetishist viewers completely baffled by what they've just seen.)

Assuming you don't share my fetish, would you find anything erotic about a video in which someone drinks multiple cans of beer and thrusts their distended stomach into the camera? Probably not. (If you *do* share my fetish, please get in touch and let me know!)

While lots of feeders/encouragers want to see someone indulging to the point of pain or unhappiness, I don't want the object of my affection to feel bad about themselves in any way: I want to see them wholly delighted, with lots of reveling. Their shameless pleasure and indulgence—again, the *demeanor*—is a huge part of what's erotic to me. I'm sure the multi-layered cultural taboos involved—we are supposed to be moderate! and responsible! and thin! and never greedy!—are part of what I find so hot. (Kink expert and podcaster Tina Horn told me I have an "enabler" fetish, or maybe a "seven deadly sins"/gluttony fetish, and I think she's onto something there.)

How does this fetish get fulfilled in actual, partnered encounters? Mostly it looks like me passively or actively encouraging a partner to eat or drink too much . . . or, more often, me getting quietly aroused as I watch them go to town. There's something about just being near a big round belly that makes me feel excited, safe, and blissful. When I'm lucky, though, I get to rub my face all over my lover's packed mid-section while they brag about how much they ate and/or drank and how good they feel. I don't even have to be witness to the act of overdoing it: I am often even more turned on if my lover goes off to a bar and comes home to me drunk and full and pleased with themself. It's the "I feel so good" part, usually accompanied by me licking their taut skin, that usually sends me over the edge to orgasm.

In communities of gainers and other fetishists, this kind of sexual experience—of reveling in the physical presence of the fetish object (body part or otherwise)—is often referred to as *worship*. "Worship" is an apt term: a fetishist encountering their beloved object of lust feels something akin to a religious experience.

Sometimes, right after I cum from a particularly exciting and kinky play session, I say out loud, almost involuntarily, *I'm a fetishist!* It sounds like a confession at a 12-step meeting, but I'm saying it because I am astounded, still, after all these years living with it, by how powerful it is. It colors my entire worldview and sense of self.

MY THING FOR TEMPLETON, OR WHY IS THERE SO MUCH KINK IN KIDDIE SHOWS?

Hypnosis. Inflation. Being eaten. Rope bondage. Furries. Tickling. Force-feeding. Quicksand. Sploshing. Giants. Kids' cartoons and shows are full of scenarios that also happen to be the stuff of many fetishists' fantasies.

Are artists and animators playing out their own kinks safely within this "wholesome" form? Are cartoons, with their ability to depict extremes of behavior and bodies, simply one of the few media formats in which more exceptional desires can be manifested? Do kids see something on a cartoon when they're young, get excited, and extrapolate it into a fetish?

I have no idea. What I do know is that many young kinksters discover their preferences while watching a program that isn't supposed to be remotely sexual—and then continue to go to those family-friendly cartoons for their "porn" well into adulthood.

My own fetish is on display in any number of kiddie cartoons, but can perhaps be best defined through one scene in particular. It's the scene in the 1973 animated film of *Charlotte's Web* when Templeton the rat visits the fairground at night and gorges on leftover junk food, singing an ode to his shameless self-indulgence as he goes.

Here's the thing: I am *not* attracted to anything about rats, cartoon or otherwise. I am in fact repulsed by rats. And I'm not attracted to Templeton. He's a jerk (albeit a jerk fascinatingly voiced by a campy gay actor). I don't like him and am not aroused by him in any other moment of the movie (or book!). But from the very first time I saw it, Templeton in that fairground scene turned me on like nothing else.

I can break down just why this scene epitomizes my core fetish. But before I do, I want to recognize that for people without this fetish, this blow-by-blow account might sound bizarre, unrelatable—even boring. And that's the thing about fetishes: they are an eroticization of things that other people don't find appealing at all. Doing research for this book, I read about a lot of fetishes that eluded—or even repelled—me. So if you want to skip this part (or any part of the book), go ahead. Just try not to "yuck on someone else's yum," as we say in the kink community. "Your kink is not my kink, and that's okay" is a tenet of our world.

Anyway, here is my fetish, explained through a gay cartoon rat singing a song:

He indulges himself, doing exactly what he wants. The psychology of this is really important: what turns me on is someone who engages in indulgent, taboo behavior with pride and joy, doing exactly what they damn well please. Templeton celebrates his "night to remember" before it even begins, singing with gusto about the "gobs of gorgeous goop" he's going to eat.

He's "overdoing it." It excites me when someone goes beyond a reasonable limit and does "more than they should," whether that's in eating, drinking, or other pleasure-driven activities. (Sex counts, too.)

He gets a noticeably big belly. When the scene begins, Templeton has no heft, but he gets visually bigger by the second: the hot dogs and watermelon go in and the belly expands (in a way that can only happen in animation, which is part of why weight-gain fetishists rely so heavily on porn rendered in comics and cartoons). A round, full belly is verrry erotic to me.

He gets drunk. Toward the end of the scene, already quite full, Templeton plunges into a pitcher of beer. His belly gets even more enormous and sloshy, and his expression shifts from frenzied food-fueled desire to blissful relaxation. He hiccups (movie shorthand for "drunk"), and the whole song slows down and slurs along with him as he ingests a final treat. I find this kind of happy drunkenness incredibly arousing.

He's smug and unembarrassed about his appetites. Templeton ends his song staggering around, stroking his own belly. Dopey and still buzzed, he stumbles back to his friends in the morning, gloating about how "rich" the whole experience was. Pragmatic Charlotte scolds him, "You ought to be ashamed of yourself!" But he is not. And that shamelessness is so hot to me. It's also what is perhaps hardest to source in real life. Finding a lover who willingly eats or drinks to excess isn't that hard. But finding one who does so without any remorse or self-loathing—and, rather, pridefully boasts about it—is quite another.

And lest you now think that I am indeed a singular freak and nobody else is into anything this weird, I can tell you that a simple Internet search for "charlotte's web templeton fetish" turned up over half a million hits. On the very first page of results, I found other people posting things like:

> There was a Disney cartoon where Goofy's clothes got filled with water and it made him look fat ["The Big Wash," 1948], and I loved that part. I also liked the part of Charlotte's Web where the rat eats and eats at the fair until his belly gets huge. I never really thought of it as a sexual thing until much, much later (after all, I am a straight male, so being attracted to males would have been weird; I was just attracted to the weight gain).

Noted feeder-erotica writer Molly Ren said in an interview that her "earliest memory is seeing the cartoon version of *Charlotte's Web*, where Templeton the Rat goes a little nuts on the fairground trash and gets a huge belly. I can't even tell you why I liked it so much, except there was happy and color and swelling. I've since learned a lot of people into feederism had a similar 'awakening' with this cartoon or others."

SEXUAL SUPERHEROES

Is all of this cartoon rat stuff completely bizarre to you and not at all what you think of when you think of sexual deviance? That's OK. No matter if you are just a little kinky or a full-blown fetishist, I want you to come away from this book knowing that being a sexual minority makes you special, and that—as long as you practice enthusiastically consensual sex—having a kinky life is like a superpower.

I'm borrowing the comic book–superhero analogy from sex workers I admire, who talk about their professions in this way. Like Superman or Batman, escorts and strippers have secret alter egos, complete with different names and costumes, in which they do powerful, amazing, extraordinary things. Like comic book heroes, sex workers have to keep this identity hidden from the everyday world.

Sexual minorities are a kind of nonprofessional erotic superhero. We, too, keep a cherished part of ourselves hidden from our colleagues, families, and friends: many of us use "scene names"—alternate names—online and at events to ensure our privacy. We too have extraordinary skills and adventures that we can't safely reveal. But in every waking moment of our day, we know we are not just Clark Kent, mild-mannered reporter. We are mutants, aliens, walking incognito among the regular humans but with special vision that allows us to see the erotic in things few others can. Kink is our superpower.

CHAPTER 1

LET'S TALK ABOUT SEX, BABY

The Ins and Outs of Erotic Desire

Defining "normal" sexual desire and where eros might come from—strong preferences—the tangled web of sexual compatibility—everyone needs an escape pod— the fallacy of "spicing up a relationship."

FetLife is the Internet's most robust community for kinky folks: as of 2020, it boasted over nine million members. One key feature of the iconic black-and-red site is that it maintains a constantly updated list titled "Most Popular Fetishes," tallied by member interest and activity. On any given day, however, many of these so-called fetishes in the top one hundred aren't fetishes at all, but completely normative sexual behaviors and activities. "Oral sex," for example, was number one on the day I wrote this, with nearly a million FetLife members reporting that they are into it. While certain cultural taboos linger around oral sex, and while it's even technically illegal in some American states, it is hardly a deviant activity. In fact, even the Supreme Court said so, in a 2003 ruling that makes those technical state laws unenforceable: in the majority opinion, Justice Anthony Kennedy wrote that when "two adults . . . with full and mutual consent from one another engage in" oral sex, it's merely a "sexual practice common to a homosexual"—and, let's just say, pretty much every other—"lifestyle." Few people are going to run screaming from the room in horror if a partner brought up the topic the way they might if, say, you mentioned that you were really interested in kinks like anal hook suspension or mummification.

Other "fetishes" on the FetLife top one hundred? Massage. Kissing. *Cuddling.* I'm just gonna go out on a limb here and say that none of those are acts of sexual deviance, either. Maybe we can acknowledge that if the activity is routinely depicted between romantic partners in G-rated family movies—as all of these are—it is probably not kinky.

Which isn't to say that massage and kissing and cuddling are boring or dull! They aren't! They are totally fun and fulfilling and exciting, as evidenced by the fact that even the pervy members of FetLife, many of whom are no strangers to things like anal hook suspension and mummification, consistently rank them among their favored sexual acts. Most people into BDSM—bondage and discipline, dominance and submission, and sadism and masochism—are also into making out and other kinds of perfectly typical physical affection. (In fact, I know an experienced rope rigger and Dominant who thoroughly admits that he's just in it for the old-fashioned penis-in-vagina sexual intercourse that he hopes will result from all the kinky play.) Many kinky folks like—and have—vanilla sex, too.

And there's that word. I said it. *Vanilla.* I want to acknowledge that some non-kinky folks are offended or insulted by the term "vanilla." My response to this is usually something like this: (1) The vanilla bean produces a delicious, rich, and potent flavor enjoyed by many people, and it is an expensive, precious commodity. There is nothing inherently demeaning about the idea of vanilla. Plus, I personally love the flavor of vanilla. Be happy you get the term "vanilla." (2) Since your sexuality is not oppressed or marginalized, you have a privilege in this regard that kinky folks do not. It is the prerogative of those less privileged in this way to make up a (non-demeaning) term for you. You could choose to be magnanimous—and a good ally to the kink community—and simply understand that being "normal" has its perks and that those of us who are not are deserving of compassion. And (3) if the term doesn't feel fun to you, don't use it for yourself.

One thing all sexual beings have in common is a desire for physical sensation and emotional connection. (Asexual people may have a slightly—or radically—different starting point on these desires than sexual—also called allosexual—people. Suffice it to say, this book is aimed at an audience of readers who identify in some way as allosexual.) But no matter how kinky or how vanilla we may be, our sexualities are all complex and varied. So before we talk about *kinky* desire, let's talk about erotic desire in general.

"NORMAL" SEXUAL DESIRE

What is vanilla, or normative, sexual behavior? It's somewhat of an "I know it when I see it" situation, with societal standards and representation determining what we deem acceptable and common. This is because it's also culturally specific: what's normal in one place or era might be completely freaky in another. Consider the great and infamously raunchy civilization of the ancient Greeks, who appreciated sculpture and plays depicting explicit pornographic acts, believed that most people were pansexual, and condoned sex between adult men and teenage boys.

But there is also science behind this idea of "normal" sex. For example, in her essay in a *Clinician's Toolkit for Children's Behavioral Health*, published in 2020, child-protection specialist Amy Russell offers some helpful reminders, such as the fact that from a psychological and developmental perspective, the data shows that it's totally "normative" for preschool-aged children to touch their genitals and look at their peers' genitals; that school-aged children masturbate to self-soothe; that pre-adolescent children often start expressing interest in sex with others; and that teenagers are likely to want to look at nude photographs or other erotica, draw sexually explicit images, and chat online with their peers about sex. Russell also points out that "there is consensus in the field that children under the age of 10 who exhibit inappropriate behaviors should not be pathologized, or labeled 'sex offenders,' 'sexual abusers,' or predators." This stuff should be common knowledge, and yet in our alarmist and sex-negative society, we still need professionals to keep us calm about healthy sexual development.

And because we're almost as squeamish about the sexuality of older adults as we are about the sexuality of children, we likewise need reminders that there, too, a wide range of behaviors are healthy and typical. A 1972 survey showed that as women aged, for example, "being postmenopausal did contribute somewhat to lower sexual interest and frequency, but not to enjoyment." A 2019 article on sex and aging from Harvard Medical School points out that "while it's true that a 19-year-old will have a faster, harder erection and a more forceful ejaculation than his 55-year-old counterpart, it doesn't mean the quality of the experience is necessarily better. On the contrary, the older man has better control of his ejaculations." The article encourages people not to believe the hype about sex ending in middle age: "Because inhibitions often lessen with age, sex at 50 or 60 may include a level of experimentation and playfulness you wouldn't have dreamed of in your younger years," it says. Beware of myths to the contrary, it warns.

Because ultimately, it seems that much of our attitudes about sex are determined by myths, by the very stories we tell about sexuality, and the words we use to tell those stories. What we call "normal," "vanilla," "kinky," or "perverted" *becomes* what is normal, vanilla, kinky, or perverted. A 2016 presentation by then linguistics students Emily Bolam and Samantha Jarvis argued that "language used in the medical community influences and reflects societal perceptions of nonnormative [gender and sexual] identities" and that an overall "lack of cultural representation renders non-normative identities invisible." In other words, normal is what we decide to see, to uphold, and to depict.

WHERE EROS COMES FROM

I use the word "eros" a lot. I like it. It comes from the Greek, and it means desire: it is also the name of the god we usually call Cupid, who wreaked havoc on gods and mortals alike by causing them to lust after and fall in love with one another. Most of the myths around Eros center around the indefatigable power he had, and that lust/ love has, over us. The Greeks recognized that sexual and romantic desire are potent stuff.

Part of why desire is so heady is because it's inherently out of reach: desire implies a search for satisfaction that has yet to be obtained. Another, sunnier way of looking at it is to say that desire is about possibility, about the promise of what is yet to come.

But what is our sexual desire actually *made* of? Where does it come from? Why do we possess it? In an article for *Healthline*, science writer Elijah Wolfson says it's complicated. Although most of us think of desire as a feeling or state of being, he writes that "many scientists and psychologists now believe that desire is, in fact, a bodily urge, more analogous to hunger or the blood's need for oxygen." And of course those urges differ wildly from individual to individual, not to mention over each individual's lifetime.

As we'll see when we begin to discuss kink, the best and most prominent theory psychologists currently have is that all desire—vanilla and kinky—is probably to some extent physiologically and emotionally hardwired, like our "fight or flight" instinct or other evolutionary responses. Sexologists hypothesize that desire is a combination of cues—visual, biochemical, emotional, and otherwise—that spark hormonal activity in our brains and bodies.

I want to avoid an overemphasis on theories that reduce complex human behaviors and responses to mere chemistry, because where would a fetish for silk stockings fit into all of that? But certainly the root of many conventional markers of attractiveness have Darwinian and reproductively centered explanations: big breasts connote successful mothering; thick shiny hair signals good health and longevity.

Our desires also develop over time. Nature and nurture—our innate instincts and what we learn in our environments—combine during our formative years as children and adolescents to shape what we find attractive. A brutal example of this is found in literary and other work about racism in America, such as Toni Morrison's novel *The Bluest Eye*, which describes how Black children are often taught, through dolls and books and other things we give our young, that their own features are inferior to those of white children. There is nothing inherently better or prettier about blue eyes, but long-standing systems of white supremacy uphold this notion in deep and dangerous ways.

Therefore, at the "nurture" level, I also think of our individual desires as salmon swimming upstream: whether we are Asian or queer or androgynous or fat or otherwise marginalized in our own appearance and/or our own attractions, we often have to tune out or unlearn what the culture tells us we *should* want in order to access what we truly seek.

But there is also the undeniable "nature"—biology and chemistry—of desire. The chemical signals we call pheromones might sound like bullshit when used to sell products, but they are real: as Wolfson writes, scientists have found that insects use them to communicate with each other. And though much of our understanding of hormones is incomplete, we do each possess a fancy cocktail of hormones and neurochemicals that work in concert with, and sometimes against, one another to trigger feelings of arousal, passion, comfort, trust, "bonding," and even what we think of as love. Our sexual chemistry is such powerful stuff that triggering it is sometimes the addictive factor in illegal drugs: manufactured substances such as cocaine cause a surge of dopamine, the hormone that causes us to feel pleasure.

Things only get more complex once we're actually getting busy. A 2018 article in *The Cut* by Sarah Barmak reports on the work of sex therapist Rosemary Basson, who, contrary to earlier scholarship by famous sexology pioneers William Masters and Virginia Johnson, argues that when we're engaged in a sexual encounter, our response is changeable, responsive, and nonlinear. (This is a good reminder of why consent works moment by moment, not encounter by encounter: we are all capable of changing our minds at any time about what we do or do not want to be doing.) Basson also says that "sexual satisfaction"—the sating of desire—happens for reasons as complex and individual as desire itself. For example, despite what mainstream porn depicts, achieving orgasm isn't always the end goal of a sexual activity, and climax doesn't necessarily make us feel happy or "finished." That's just another myth of normative sexual culture.

There are many things that desire is *not*. It is not, for example, a Hollywood fantasy of sudden, mad, spontaneous lust at first sight. Studies have shown that the majority of people require a combination of signals and feedback to feel aroused and to want to continue getting down. And the tropes about women in particular "needing foreplay" to get aroused are wrong: people of all genders get most excited when they are gently guided toward an erotic encounter, when they are given undivided attention and told how sexy they are. Even our reasons for wanting sex with someone else are much more diverse than some kind of one-dimensional desire-on-command that is only about pure pleasure: those participating in a 2007 study by researchers Cindy Meston and David Buss at the University of Texas at Austin gave over 235 different motivations behind their desire for sexual intimacy, ranging from getting more physical exercise to wanting to have a baby, from expressing gratitude to preventing their partner from having an affair.

Beyond even these spicy stews of hormonal, emotional, and other motivations and responses, there is much that is still a mystery to us about exactly where and how and why we experience sexual desire. In recent years, scientists have been using technology including MRIs and other ways of scanning the actual brain to see if they can find out more about it all. While the studies have yet to prove conclusive, we do now know that desire lights up certain regions of the brain, including the amygdala, which "orchestrates powerful emotions"; the hippocampus, which "manages our memories"; and the anterior insula, which is "what we use to reflect on the state of our own bodies," according to neuroscience studies published in 2007 and reported by science writer Carl Zimmer in *Discover* in 2009. All of which could indicate that when we sexually long for someone, it is because of a mix of thoughts, feelings, physical sensation, and even nostalgia. Humans are complicated!

CAN WE RECLAIM THE TERM "PREFERENCE"?

"She's just your type," I might say to a friend who's telling me about a new lover. Many of us think of ourselves as "having a type"—or several types. We may find ourselves checking out people with one particular hair color or body shape or kind of smile or style of attire. And because some of these attributes are also politicized—like our skin color or our facial features or our size—talking about "types" can also get sensitive and tricky. Is there something inherently wrong with finding, say, light-skinned Black folks or Asian women or burly men especially attractive? And are such attractions properly defined as kinks, as fetishes?

Because we cannot separate our sexual urges from the cultural context in which we live, these questions are impossible to answer. I'm an Ashkenazi (Eastern European) American Jew raised by Ashkenazi Jewish parents in a largely Ashkenazi Jewish community. I grew up around a lot of shorter people with thick dark hair and plump lips who talked loudly and with plenty of gesticulation. I have known people who have found Jewish girls like me very attractive, and people who do not find us attractive at all. I myself tend to *not* be attracted to Ashkenazi Jewish cis men, but I think the comedian Sarah Silverman (the descendent of Russian Polish ancestors, as am I) and the actors and activists Patricia and Rosanna Arquette (whose mother was also of Russian Polish Jewish descent) are super hot. But if I heard someone outside our community talking about the relative physical merits of Jews, I would probably be pretty uncomfortable, and would start worrying about neo-Nazis and the KKK.

It's all very murky stuff. Let's consider for a minute the notion of a sexual *preference*. We now know full well that sexual orientations around gender are not a choice and therefore should not be referred to dismissively as "preferences." Here's some science on the matter: the sexologist and academic Meredith Chivers found in studies she was conducting in the early 2000s that cis men who identify as gay or straight tend to be "category-specific," which is her way of saying that straight men showed both mental and physical signs of sexual arousal only when shown erotic images involving *women*, and gay men only got turned on when shown erotic images involving *men*. And no matter their orientation, none of the cis men in her study got turned on by images of bonobos, a primate species, having sex. Fascinatingly, the cis *women* in the study, no matter how they identified in terms of sexual orientation and what they said turned them on, showed physical signs of arousal (such as genital swelling) whether they were shown gay porn, straight porn, lesbian porn, or ape porn. This study supports the idea that our sexual orientations go deeper than our intellectual sense of our own desires.

In our broader lives, though, we all have preferences—in the movies we watch, the food we eat, the clothes we wear, the people we're attracted to, and the kinds of sex we have with our lovers. One may prefer wordless sex to chatty sex. One may prefer people with pointy breasts over people with round breasts. One may prefer the feel of silk panties to the feel of lace panties. One may prefer aggressive kisses to gentle kisses. And on and on. While some of these preferences can feel just short of a fetish, something akin to having a "type" or a particular obsession, other preferences may be quite mild and fleeting. I would love to repurpose the term "sexual preference" (and have, throughout this book) to describe the changeable, flexible but still quite adamant tastes and interests of humans in lust.

Most sexual preferences are considered totally normal and vanilla. No one reading this book would be shocked to hear that someone is attracted to a woman wearing a garter belt, for example. Cultural institutions—including Hollywood and the fashion and beauty industries—encourage, enable, and cash in on standard-issue attractions like these, upholding them to the point where it's difficult to separate a personal preference from a commodified shorthand for physical appeal. What gets called "sexy" is a set of culturally specific intersecting norms, and most of us get on board in one way or another, even if these norms defy the urges that gather in our own hearts and minds.

Which means that just because we may be attracted to people who look or act in a way that isn't the dominantly accepted standard in our particular culture at this particular time, it's still not necessarily kinky. For example, if I'm primarily aroused by short, chubby, dark-haired women with full 1970s-style pubic bush (so cute!), that's not what early twenty-first-century America tells me is conventionally sexy, but it doesn't make my preference a kink, or a fetish, per se. In many other cultures and at many other times, such women could easily be considered the most ravishing creatures on earth. And if my preference is relatively mild—meaning I am glad to take a lover who doesn't look like this—and centers around typically sexualized aspects of the human body, like a woman's thighs and hair, then this is me having a *type*.

What distinguishes a vanilla "type" from a full-on kink or fetish is, to my mind, how strong and unusual the preference is. Let's think about spanking (yes, please!) as a way of breaking this down.

Even though it feels rather naughty, spanking is a pretty common sexual activity, and those who partake fall on a spectrum that ranges from vanilla to deviant. (You may be "vanilla" on the spanking spectrum, but "deviant" on the spectrum of another kink—or vice versa!) If you're on the vanilla end of the spanking spectrum, you may get a little thrill and have some fun with an occasional spanking during foreplay, because it feels taboo or yummy, but it's not something you seek out with real passion. If there's spanking in a movie, you might get turned on, but only if it's part of a sex scene you already thought was hot. And although you might think it's fun when you run across a spanking scene by accident, you rarely find yourself fantasizing about spanking, and you don't use it as a search term when you're perusing the Internet for porn or erotica.

Then there are kinky folks who fall into the middle of the spectrum. They might enjoy spanking as part of a larger interest in "rough" penetrative sex, for example. If you're one of these people, you may give or receive spankings harder and more often than vanilla folks do. You might indulge in spanking to the point of bruising, because you like the idea that you've hurt someone or been hurt, that you've marked someone or been marked: the spanking could be a flavor of the power play or role play that you are into. But your spanking usually happens as part of a more involved erotic scene, and it may feel interchangeable with other activities such as face slapping, hair pulling, caning, or humiliation talk. And you feel perfectly happy even if a good session with a lover doesn't involve spanking at all.

But if you're a spanking *fetishist*, an erotic encounter without a spanking just isn't quite *it*. The thing that turns you on most of all is *spanking*. You might require spanking to get wet or hard. You might have very specific instructions about how and where or why you get spanked. (Many spanking fetishists identify as either "stingy" or "thuddy," and covet being spanked with the tools that can deliver that sensation. The tools alone can get a fetishist aroused.) There may be psychological play, or certain toys or textures, or costumes involved. And the spanking may not need to happen during or result in a normative sexual encounter such as penetrative intercourse: the *spanking* is the good part. You might have first realized you had "a spanking thing" long before you were sexually active or mature, when, say, as a child, you saw a nonerotic spanking on a family television show and felt your whole body awaken with desire. Spanking itself might be so central to your fantasy that you might not care about the gender or age or appearance of the person spanking or being spanked. You might not need the scenario to involve *yourself* in order for it to be exciting, or to involve any depiction of sex or nudity or seduction, and you might not even need it to involve *humans*: you might happily masturbate to a children's cartoon image of a dog spanking a cat. You might be able to orgasm just from being spanked. You might be able to orgasm just from hearing the *sound* of spanking. You might be able to orgasm *reading the definition of spanking in a dictionary.*

ON THE UBIQUITY OF SPANKING

I'm curious about the enduring popularity of spanking. Is it popular because it's an easy and accessible activity, a gateway to more hardcore BDSM? Is it because spankos tend to be such dedicated, committed fetishists, unwavering in their predilections? Or is spanking just a really common fetish, perhaps because many of us had early childhood experiences with it that are wrapped up in an emotionally complex ball of shame, discipline, and anticipation? I have no idea, but I think most of us can agree that if you're keyed into it, the spanking kink is *everywhere.*

If that last bit resonates with you, chances are you're a full-on spanking fetishist. Mazel tov! If you can't relate to the spanking aspect but hold similarly magnetic preferences for another activity, that makes you a member of the fetish tribe, too! If what I've just described baffles you, and you are rather someone who may have some preferences, but if you're perfectly okay going without them? If your fantasies and porn tastes don't center around any particular preferences at all? Or if your preferences are the kind of thing you can find in any mainstream magazine or romance novel or R-rated movie? You're probably pretty vanilla. (Which, again, is totally cool! Vanilla is delicious! Mazel tov to you, too!)

THE TANGLED WEB OF SEXUAL COMPATIBILITY

Given all that we know about the fluid nature of desire and preferences, not to mention shame and fear around communicating those desires and preferences, it's kind of incredible that any of us manage to actually *find* other people with whom we can sexually connect. This is certainly true for those of us into BDSM: many kinky people go their whole lives without ever being able to satisfy their perversion with a willing and interested partner. It ain't always easy.

But even if you're completely vanilla, it can still be challenging to find partners who want to do the sexy things you want to do the way you want to do them. Most of us do not carefully curate and customize the kind of sex we have for the particular person we're with that night, nor do we take the time to communicate the details of our likes and dislikes to our partners. As Katherine Angel puts it in her recent book *Tomorrow Sex Will Be Good Again*, in order for us to achieve not just authentic consent but also really satisfying sex, women and others who have been taught to keep silent about their desires "must speak out about what they want. They must, then, also know what it is that they want."

Ideally, we would. Ideally, we'd take the time to tune out the static and tune into our innermost needs and proclivities. Ideally, we could then articulate exactly what we want and search high and low until we found someone who wanted it just as much. But sexual relationships, like all other relationships, necessitate compromise and negotiation. And for most people, it's not easy to have such conversations, even with one's most dearly beloved.

Sexual compatibility isn't as simple as finding someone we think is attractive, or who is our sexual orientation, or who has a libido that is similar to our own, or even who has the same kinks as we do. We often hear about compatibility in terms of libido (usually framed as one person wanting to have sex more often than their partner does). But even *frequency* is not the same as *libido*, and *neither* frequency nor libido are the only factors that make up the overall picture of what someone wants in their sexual relationship. Our sexualities are a complex tapestry of fantasies, preferences, traumas, appetites, and other elements. (Surely these tapestries include unicorns?) And because our sexualities sometimes evolve over time, the discussions are worth having again and again.

For these and other reasons, in order to gauge how and where we sexually match up with our partners, I invite you to answer the following questions, just for starters. (You may think of other questions to add!) You could also give these questions to a partner for them to complete and discuss with you; obviously, if you have multiple partners, you may need to circulate multiple questionnaires! Hurray! The point is that conversations stemming from a questionnaire like this could serve as the start to understanding the mosaic of factors that make up our sexualities.

SEXUAL COMPATIBILITY QUESTIONNAIRE

- *How important is sex to you?*
  Just like some dogs are "food-motivated" and some are "praise-motivated," people (and other creatures) can also be "sex-motivated." How sex-motivated would you say you are? How central is your sexuality to your sense of identity, and how would you define your sexuality? Are you someone who wants to talk about sex a lot, and seek out sexual experiences? Are you asexual, and if so, what does that look like for you?

- *Do you have sexual trauma or baggage that a partner should be aware of?*
  What are your needs around shame, trauma, and/or anxiety? Are there things a partner could do or learn to be more supportive? What might you do if the thing you're into most is something that is upsetting to a partner, such as a rape fantasy or age play?

- *How often do you like to have sex with yourself?*
  How much do you like to masturbate and/or do other things to get yourself off? Would you like a partner to watch you do it? Would you want to tell them about it? Are you someone who gets hurt or offended if your partner jacks off or uses porn or other materials when you're not around?

- *As a general rule, how often would you prefer to have sex with your partner?*
  Do you start getting cranky or depressed if you go too long without physical intimacy with a partner? What do you consider "too long without" within the context of an established

relationship? Would you find it helpful to schedule sex with a partner? Do you prefer to have sex before going to sleep, first thing in the morning, or do you find nooners the most fun? Do you tend to want to have sex with a partner even when you're feeling down/sick/tired/distracted/stressed, or is it better for you to put your sex life on hold in certain situations?

· *What kind of sex are you most into?*
Let's acknowledge that "sex" is not a heterosexual penis-in-vagina monolith. What does "let's have sex" mean to you? What acts would be involved? How much time would be dedicated to it? Are there specific things you need to have happen in order to get aroused? Are those things your current partner knows how to do? Does your partner want to do those things?

· *What tone would you like sex with your partner to have?*
Do you look to sex for comfort? Excitement? Connection? Release? Do you tend to prefer gentle, loving encounters, or do you prefer your sex rough and dirty? Do you want it noisy and wild or tender and quiet? Do you enjoy a lot of talking during sex? What kinds of things might you want to say or hear? What kinds of things would you *not* want to say or hear?

· *How sexually adventurous do you want to be?*
Would you be happy with a comfortable, familiar routine that reliably gets both you and your established partner off, or would you rather take the time and effort to keep trying new things? Does talking about sex, watching/reading sexual content together, or discussing past sexual experiences with a partner feel necessary and fun to you? Or upsetting and painful?

· *While in a particular relationship, do you want to have sex with people other than your partner?*
How often would you like to have sex with other people besides your established partner? In other words, are you or would you like to be ethically nonmonogamous? If so, and assuming your partner is okay with that, what parameters should be established around that? Do you want to be swingers who have sex with other people together? Do you want to be polyamorous

and in multiple ongoing relationships? Do you want to maintain casual "friends with benefits" on the side? Do you want to seek out play partners to quench your thirst for certain desires your partner can't satisfy, but only as a recreational activity? Are you hoping to stay home and feel cuckolded while your partner goes out on the town? How would you handle whatever kind of non-monogamy you agree upon?

· *What are you attracted to in other people?*
Does your partner have the features or attributes you're most attracted to? Are either of you interested in and able to modify your appearances to suit each other's tastes? Might you have to find another outlet for your attraction? Are you okay if your partner finds another outlet? What kinds of other outlets are fine with you, and which kinds are forbidden? Are you and your partner okay with politely and discreetly gawking whenever someone with that appearance walks by?

· *Do you have any kinks your partner should know about?*
Would you like to incorporate a specific kind of dirty talk, sex toy, prop, impact play, dress-up, or role play into your regular sex life? Do you have very particular ideas about how that might go? How important is this kink for your sexual satisfaction, and how often would you need to do it to feel fulfilled? How intense is this kink? Are you able to get aroused without it?

· *Do you have any fetishes—strong and unusual erotic desires—your partner should know about?*
Do your fetishes mesh with your partner's? Does it work for your partner to be on the receiving end of your fetishistic desire? Does it work for you to be on the receiving end of theirs? If one of you has an intense fetish and the other doesn't, are both people going to feel comfortable with that? What if your fetish is something that totally grosses your partner out?

· *What about power dynamics?*
When you and your partner get into an erotic moment, do you want your established relationship dynamic to shift or be

different? Do you want to be—or want your partner to be—stern and scolding? Humiliated? Babied? In charge? Bossed around? Do you want to switch it up? Does your partner want to be in a power dynamic like that?

You can see from this list of questions how easy it can be to believe you are "compatible" with a partner in one way (i.e., "we had sex, and it was hot and/or loving!") but have it turn out that you are not sexually well-matched. An example: you have delightful sex with your partner and you are both wildly attracted to one another. But you'd prefer to have that great sex about once in a fortnight and you don't often masturbate. Also, you detest mainstream porn, especially the "barely legal" kind (i.e., the kind with stars who look, dress, and act as if they're underage but are technically not): it disgusts you. Your partner, however, wants to watch "barely legal" porn on the daily and would be happiest if you fucked every day. No matter how much you love each other, and no matter how good the act of coitus is for you both, these mismatched desires and needs could be a problem. You are unlikely to be able to get over your political distaste for that type of porn, any more than your partner is able to stop getting turned on by it. Problems like this play out as the plot crisis in numerous TV shows and movies.

There are also less common issues. For example, even if you are lucky enough to be in a relationship where you both really want anal on a nightly basis, maybe one person wants to be called a filthy little pig while they are buggered in a dark alley and the other person is looking for soulful, tantric fucking with incense and Gregorian chant. Or maybe you just want to eat pussy all night long and your beloved does not enjoy getting eaten out—or doesn't have a pussy. Or maybe your A-1 turn-on is fucking in front of other people, and even though your lover is so into you and everything you do to them, they could never, ever have sex in public.

I am not championing the idea that we all need to immediately pack our bags and march out of the house if we realize that our partner is not a fantastic sexual match for us. And while I believe that ethical non-monogamy is one possible solution if someone you love is not your ideal sexual playmate, that's another book. Here, I'm encouraging all of us to be understanding and compassionate—first with ourselves, and with our own beautiful tapestry of desires, and then also with our lovers. We can aim for work-arounds. We can compromise or experiment. We can encourage and allow other outlets that feel safe and okay to us. We can remember that our partners have no more ability to quash their specific and complicated desires than we do our own, and we can try to avoid blame, guilt, shame, and resentment and aim instead for curiosity, good humor, generosity, and acceptance.

EVERYONE NEEDS AN ESCAPE POD

I've come to believe that all responsible humans need an escape pod: a way to temporarily jettison ourselves out of our daily tasks and deadlines and into a space that feels new, exciting, and rewarding. If we are paying bills, washing dishes, changing diapers, cleaning out cat boxes, taking care of our elderly relatives, managing our health, and otherwise doing the difficult tasks we all need to do to have a halfway organized life, we need something else, something *fun*.

Lots of things can qualify as *fun*. Playing tennis. Shopping for shoes. Doing puzzles. Reading. Woodworking. Camping.

"Escape pod" fun is a different kind of fun. Escape-pod adventures feel thrilling: a little risky, a little dirty, a little reckless. They get our adrenaline going. They make us feel young. They set us apart from the crowd: not everyone engages in these activities. Escape-pod adventures make us feel proud of ourselves, even a little smug. Our co-workers may have no clue that we do these things on our own time. We might even keep these adventures secret from friends and family.

From what I've seen, there are two ways partnered adults can go about launching their escape pods: as solo adventurers, or in a double capsule. Many couples start their relationship doing escape pod things together: adventurous things like mountain climbing or tango dancing. But then jobs and kids and other tasks interfere, and eventually there is no time or energy for mountains or tangos. In some cases, one person keeps the adventure going without the other. And often, this leads to resentment, estrangement, and long late-night fights.

One very common solo escape pod in our culture is the extramarital affair. Exciting, dangerous, titillating—and completely duplicitous and heartbreaking to everyone involved.

There is another way. The couple can launch a sexy escape pod together. I've spent some time hanging out in the swinger community, and while that world is not without its problems, one thing I'll say about swingers is that because they are choosing to embark on sexual escapades together, as couples, they *share* their dirty little secret, and this can bond them to one another instead of driving them apart. Adventurous sex, of course, is another great escape pod you can share with the person or people with whom you're in love. That sex doesn't have to be kinky, per se: the important thing is that it feels a little out of the ordinary, like an *event*.

CAN YOU (AND SHOULD YOU) USE KINK TO "SPICE UP" YOUR RELATIONSHIP?

If you want to have some adventurous escape-pod sex with your long-term partner because things have been getting stale or dull or otherwise not going so well, should you dabble in some kinky fun? I'm not going to say *no*. But I do want to dispel a myth or two here.

I can't even count the number of times I've seen articles in mainstream media about how to incorporate kink into your love life as a way of combatting the sexual doldrums. These articles inevitably use the phrase *spice up*, for some reason, and they almost always recommend role play and light bondage. (They don't tend to suggest pissing on each other, fire play, or boot licking.)

Most recently I ran across one of these articles in the online parenting-centered site Fatherly under the title "7 Kinky Sex Ideas for Couples Looking to Spice Things Up." Versions of this piece appear countless times: a quick search the day I wrote this yielded almost two million hits, including articles in mainstream outlets such as *Women's Health* ("20 Ways to Spice Up Your Sex Life, According to Sex Experts"), *The Cut* ("How to Spice Up Your Sex Life"), and *Redbook* ("24 Ways You Can Immediately Spice Up Your Sex Life"). I found similar articles across the globe, too, from the British *Gentleman's Journal* ("10 Ways to Spice Up Your Sex Life") to the *India Times* ("This Kinky 30-Day Sex Challenge Will Spice Up Your Sex Life and Keep Your Relationship Fresh") to *Men's Health Australia* ("How You Can Spice Up Your Love Life and Fulfil Your Fantasies"). So *spicy!*

And of course I'm all for people exploring fun sexy games and trying out new things. We all crave variety. If you want to be a bit of a "weekend warrior" around kink, occasionally dipping into some sexual activity for the sake of novelty and exploration, please do! I'm even more thrilled when people in committed relationships have the kind of difficult conversations about desire, arousal, and consent that should—but too often don't—precede such games.

But I also worry about the cumulative impact of these endless articles, and of similar suggestions that come from therapy, self-help books, and the like. Oftentimes, the idea is that people who are unhappy with their lovers could remedy their boredom or disconnection if they would only break out the handcuffs next Tuesday night. I just don't think it works that way.

There are many reasons why the sexual link between two people might weaken or break, and it may have nothing to do with "being in a rut"—which itself might be happening for innumerable complex reasons. It might be because one of you is depressed, or overwhelmed at work, or feeling crappy about your body. It might be because your partner has been doing something that really annoys or upsets you or turns you off. It might be because your relationship has undergone the stress of a major change like a move, an illness, a baby, or a death in the family.

Beyond those circumstantial situations (which can be temporary), we've seen that true and lasting sexual compatibility is complex. No one can transform themselves into an ear fetishist to suit their partner if they simply are not into that.

There's also a bigger cultural problem with viewing kink from this "spicing up" standpoint. As fun as it can be to try some light spanking as a lark, part of my goal in writing this book is to recognize that kink is often a much deeper, more central factor in one's sexual makeup. Kink, and especially fetishism, can be an orientation—it often can't and won't change. If the thing that turns you on to the exclusion of everything else is wearing latex and your partner is allergic to it, the incompatibility is not gonna resolve itself, no matter how much "spicing up" you do.

Another problem: the "spicing up" articles make it sound like trying new things in sex is carefree and simple—that you can experiment for a night, like going out to a restaurant for a cuisine you've never tried before. But sex isn't exactly a take-it-or-leave-it hobby for many of us, and it doesn't exist in a vacuum: our feelings about it run deep, and are tied into the rest of our relationship and all the problems therein. Telling our partner that we don't want to do the sexy thing they want most is so much more fraught than telling them we don't like golf or antiquing, and often leads—unwittingly—to bigger and harder (ha ha) conversations about our innermost hopes and fears. If we can even manage to start the conversation in the first place. Which, if you've been with someone for a long time and have never talked about this stuff, can be really intimidating in and of itself.

Long-term relationships mean long-term dynamics. We develop feelings and narratives and ways of dealing with and responding to one another that become ingrained over time, and it can take a lot of effort on everyone's parts to step out of that pattern and into something else. So if you have believed for years that your partner is not attracted to you, or if you only see your partner as the person who does the dishes and snores, or if you are both angry about money or feel unappreciated, it's unlikely your feelings are going to shift easily, no matter how many silk blindfolds you purchase. Sex can be an amazing way to connect, but connection only happens when there's a general and mutual sense of trust, engagement, curiosity, and respect between the people involved. (This is also, of course, why consent is key to all yummy erotic encounters.)

Our sexual desires are beautiful and complicated and deserve to be treated like more than a fleeting and out-of-the-blue experiment. We need to *talk* about those desires with the people we want to take to bed, so that we both know what to expect and how to get our needs met—without bitterness or unethical behavior—in the very likely case that our primary partner is unable to fulfill every single one of them.

It can be frustrating to recognize that certain things simply aren't possible, including living out every outlandish sexual fantasy we have with a single partner. But talking through our sexual hopes and dreams with one another can sometimes lead to new, unexplored possibilities, from a role play we'd never considered to a re-envisioning of our relationship structure. And the "here are some wild sexual things I've always wanted to try" conversation can be *very* exciting.

CHAPTER 2

TAKE A WALK ON THE WILD SIDE

A Primer on Kink, BDSM, and Fetishes

*Defining kink, fetishes, and other deviant practices — is it
kink if you're not aroused? — the spectrum of fetishistic
desire — consent at the center — some handy acronyms.*

Just the other day, I came across an article in *Vice* about a fetish
I'd never heard of: Fedleg. "Fedleg" is the term being used for
a fetish that grew out of one particular man's childhood fantasy of
painting women's legs bright yellow as a way of humiliating them
for showing off their sexy gams.

Fedleg is like many other fetishes in that it is an attraction com-
prised of both a psychological situation—women being "punished"
and "controlled" for revealing their legs—and the physical mani-
festation of that situation, which in this case is bright-yellow limbs.
The fetish is driven by some pretty common and misogynist urges
around controlling women and their bodies. But in another way,
Fedleg is a singular phenomenon: a fetish someone created online
as a viral lark.

This particular person, known as Jim, was curious to see whether
inventing a fetish from scratch is something one could do. So he took
to Reddit to spread the gospel of Fedleg eroticism. Jim has since
become a successful "influencer," and now has 6,500 members on
his board talking about Fedleg and posting pictures and fan art and
homemade porn. Some (possibly many) of these folks already had

a legs or stockings fetish, so the Fedleg variation provided a wacky twist on something they were already into.

There's an important lesson to be learned here. Maybe your deepest erotic urges have always made you feel isolated and weird. Maybe you are someone who harbors secret sexual desires that seem bizarre and you doubt anyone else has ever had the specific and unusual thoughts you've had. But the Fedleg phenomenon suggests that they probably have.

The age of the Internet has spawned a concept called "Rule 34." Rule 34 states that "if it exists, there's porn for it." In other words, any fleeting and outré sexy scene that has popped into your head has probably already been filmed and posted, turned into homemade drawings on DeviantArt, and played out in stories found on furtive blogs and forums.

My personal theory is that Rule 34 holds true not because of broadband connections but because of the diversity of the human imagination. We now have the ability to digitally share our most private fantasies via sketches, photos, videos, and journals, making our inner erotic lives available for the whole world to discover. But while the means of distribution are new, the urges behind them have been with us all along. What has changed is our ability to connect, as Jim did, with others who might share our freaky fantasies and help us feel a little less alone.

Connection matters. Much—though certainly not all—of sexual expression is about connecting with others. We humans are pack animals—we literally need other people in order to survive, and we need relationships in order to feel happy and fulfilled. And yet even within the world of shameless sexual deviants, many of us worry that what *we* like is so weird or so unusual that we will still be misfits.

This is why I wish that kink wasn't so strongly associated with sadism and masochism, collars and chains—both in mainstream discourse as well as within the kink community itself. I worry that people forget about all the other lovely sexual deviance out there, and that these other kinds of kink get shoved out of the conversation. I believe that the umbrella for nonnormative sexuality should be as wide and inclusive as possible.

How then to define what falls under the kinky umbrella? Let's give it a go.

WHAT IS KINK? AND WHERE DOES SEXUAL DEVIANCE COME FROM, DADDY?

First off, there's confusion around the overlap between terms like "kink," "fetishism," and "BDSM." I use the term "nonnormative sexuality" to encompass all the wonderful diversity of human sexual desire. But that term sounds pretty academic and maybe not so sexy (unless you're into professors?). So instead I use "kink" as the term to describe all manner of preference-based sexual deviance and so-called perversion.

"BDSM" is one of two major subcategories under the kink umbrella. It is itself an umbrella term that, in the words of BDSM researcher Peter Tupper, encompasses and cleverly runs together several "forms of consensual erotic play": bondage and discipline, dominance and submission, and sadism and masochism. Taken together, as Tupper points out, they make up a kind of ritualistic sexual behavior for our time.

Tupper sees BDSM as "playing with the body": using our own or someone else's physical form to "test, modify and experiment" with what brings us erotic energy, excitement, and/or release. Social worker Stefani Goerlich, who specializes in working with people in the kink community, helpfully delineates the different facets of BDSM as three different kinds of exchange: bondage and discipline are about an exchange of *control*, dominance and submission are about an exchange of *authority*, and sadism and masochism are about an exchange of *sensation*. Of course, these facets blur and blend together, the psychological mingling with the physical, but it's still a good way to think about the BDSM acronym and what it connotes.

The second major subcategory under the kink umbrella are fetishes. At the beginning of this book, when describing my own core fetish, I described a fetishist as someone who finds sexual arousal in objects or body parts that aren't normally considered erotic. This is pretty close to the more formal definition offered by psychology researcher Samuel Hughes: the term "fetishist" "describes people with an erotic or intimate interest in specific non-genital body parts, fabrics, smells, fluids, costumes and other non-human objects."

Apart from BDSM and fetishism, what else is kink? Kinky sex is outré sex, bizarre sex, abnormal—or nonnormative—sex. It's sex as extreme sport, sex as consuming hobby.

And it's *sexual theater*, as BDSM historian Stephen K. Stein calls it. I love that definition, because it emphasizes erotic encounters as orchestrated, choreographed entertainment: in other words, anything that goes beyond the expected, sometimes perfunctory ways we have of reaching orgasm or expressing pleasure. As Stein writes in his wonderful work of historical scholarship, *Sadomasochism and the BDSM Community in the United States*, in kinky sex, "appearance and symbolism" are vital: kink "complicates sex," which is one of the reasons we are drawn to it and love it. Kink turns sex into an *event*.

In fact, anything that's not "vanilla" sex could be theoretically called kinky sex. Kink represents the underrepresented, alternative, freaky fringes of sex. Here in America, a quick survey of magazine articles and movie reviews shows that what gets called "kinky" includes sex with props or toys of any kind; sex with slapping or biting or spitting or shoving; sex with costumes and/or role playing; sex with religious or spiritual ritual; sex with punishment, humiliation, or discipline; sex with even mild bondage; sex that is filmed or public; even sex where one person is attracted to another because of age or body size or facial features or what have you. *All* of that gets called kinky.

It's important to remember that kink is a construct. Which is to say that what constitutes kink is relative and subjective, and bound (ha ha) to culture and history. In various eras or locations, "regular" sex could involve kinky staples such as edging or orgasm denial (in the Chinese Han dynasty); scratching and biting (the two thousand–year-old *Kama Sutra* from India has sections on both); or elaborate sex toys (evidenced in ancient Egypt). In nineteenth-century England, the legal age of consent for girls wasn't raised to *thirteen* until 1875—before that, sexual relationships with girls as young as ten had been condoned. Something we currently consider to be extremely problematic and verboten—sex with children—was acceptable just a couple of centuries ago in the Western world.

Japanese culture is notorious for its deep history with deviant sexuality. Artistic rope bondage! Love hotels! Pillow books! Sexually explicit porn and comics available at any convenience store! In many ways, Japanese kink culture is one of the richest in the world, and it has a long lineage—erotic art has been popular and widely distributed in Japan since the 1600s. But, as scholar Mark J. McLelland points out, there is inherent racism in a Western gaze that emphasizes "Japanese libidinal excess, perversity and strangeness." In his 2015 paper "'How to Sex'? The Contested Nature of Sexuality in Japan," McLelland notes that such views "homogenize 'the Japanese' and supposed 'Japanese' attitudes to sexuality which are in fact complex, diverse and highly divisive." He does, however, acknowledge that, at least in twentieth-century Japan, "an interest in the abnormal was not necessarily considered to be constitutive of a specific sexual identity" and that "in the early postwar period . . . the Japanese press was much more open to discussions of 'abnormal' sexualities than were any Anglophone media." In fact, he writes, "non-normative sexual interests were brought together under the rubric ryōki or 'curiosity hunting'" and were widely discussed in mainstream magazines and newspapers.

Back here in our Christian-driven culture, we default to the notion that "sex" means a cis man's penis entering a cis woman's vagina, resulting in male orgasm and ejaculation. (Patriarchal ridiculousness: it's often not considered sex if the man doesn't cum, but it's still considered sex if the women doesn't cum.) Anything that isn't this very specific, heteronormative, penetrative, two-person act has to be described with an add-on in order to differentiate it from, you know, regular ol' "sex": that other thing is *oral* sex and that's *lesbian* sex and that's *group* sex and that's a *female* orgasm and that's *kinky* sex. What's defined as sex in America right now is a prohibitively narrow category that erases much of the fun people have.

The same goes for what we deem "sexy." "Sexy women" are thin and young and conventionally pretty and cis, with hair on their heads and none on their bodies, and they wear tight clothing and perfectly applied lipstick, right? Mustn't the "sexiest man alive" be able-bodied and traditionally masculine presenting, with strong features and defined muscles and possessed of a confident swagger?

In this age of the 'net, a quick search can tell you that we *Homo sapiens* are a lot more varied than these cultural myths. For example, despite the fact that TV shows and Instagram influencers and retails ads almost exclusively portray thinner-than-average women as attractive, a 2011 article in *Discover* magazine by two neuroscientists who studied sexuality search terms showed that straight men go looking for images of "fat" women three times as much as they look for "skinny" women. This vastly higher rate could be because it is much harder to find images of fat women than thin women: the default image is skinny.

Or take monogamy. (Please. Take it far away from me.) Our culture reveres and clings to it: just think of how many movies depict an extramarital affair—or even the potential of an affair—as the biggest crisis imaginable. Movies ranging from *Chicago* to *American Beauty* to *Who Framed Roger Rabbit* hinge on the threat of adultery. But the same 2011 *Discover* article identified cuckolding—a kink where someone is turned on by the idea that they are sitting home alone while their supposedly faithful partner is out having a wild sexual experience with someone else—as the second-most searched-for straight porn category.

If so many people are seeking out these supposedly deviant expressions of sexuality, does a line between kinky and vanilla really exist? Such a line is certainly blurry. And yet I still think it's important to make the distinction. Why? Because kink-shaming is real. Because persecution of sexual minorities is real. Because sexual shame and guilt are very, very real. And because for those of us whose entire sexualities are oriented around something other people don't even consider erotic, the struggle to negotiate relationships is real.

If you do have some pervy tendencies, maybe you are currently thinking *why are some of us kinky?* Or even, *why* me? Is kink a kind of sexual orientation, hardwired in us the way many people feel a hardwired attraction to certain genders? Is something different happening in our brains or our hormonal chemistry, or do our circumstances and experiences shape our desires?

Those are questions I've been asking for a long time. At the moment, there are no definitive answers. Part of the problem is that serious scientific research into sexuality is a pretty recent phenomenon and is not typically well-funded or prioritized within academic settings. (I didn't love the Showtime television show *Masters of Sex*, but it does depict some of the problems faced by human sexuality researchers through the [fictionalized] story of the groundbreaking real-life scientists William Masters and Virginia Johnson.)

Even under the best circumstances, it's really hard to conduct research about human sexuality, because most humans are taught not to talk openly about those kinds of things with strangers . . . or with anyone, really. Rather, we are taught to *avoid* frank discussions of our authentic sexual behaviors at all costs. The collective shame, secrecy, and guilt our culture throws at us means that even the best sexual research is usually conducted with small pools of subjects, which can't adequately reflect the diversity of our communities or of human experience. (That said, the Kinsey Institute at Indiana University is one of the most well-known and respected hubs for academic research on sex in the US, and its ever-evolving resources are definitely worth exploring.)

For these reasons and more, the origins of nonnormative sexuality remain a mystery. In an interview with sex columnist Dan Savage, cognitive scientist Jesse Bering (author of the book *Perv: The Sexual Deviant in All of Us*) said, "Nobody knows why some people are more prone to developing unusual patterns of attraction than others." Or as Savage himself puts it, "The alchemy of kinks isn't fully understood."

That said, researchers do have theories. Here are some of the current leading ones about the whys and wherefores of the kinky human:

Hardwiring. This theory purports that the neurologies of kinksters are different than those of vanilla people, and that our brains are structured toward our preferences before we are born.

When researcher Samuel Hughes conducted a survey of self-described kinky people in 2017, he found that the majority of them first became aware of their kink between the ages of five and ten. According to Bering, "the best available evidence suggests that some people—mostly males—have a genetic predisposition for being 'sexually imprinted' during development," that we are "imprinted" in this way long before puberty, and that these desires are "pretty much fixed" ever after.

This is the dominant (see what I did there?) theory about kink right now in the fields of sexuality science and clinical psychology. (Most experts currently believe this is also why queer people are queer: we're born that way, and nothing can really change our orientations.) It is also the theory to which I subscribe.

Crossed wires. This theory, which is a sort of subset or sister to the "hardwired theory," has been explored by various neuroscientists, including V. S. Ramachandran, whose studies of "phantom limb" phenomena have been applied to the thinking around kink. According to adherents of this theory, kink comes from actual anatomical and chemical differences in brain wiring/mapping and synapses that are either present from birth or that are changed due to acquired experiences. The difference between the "hardwired" theory and the "crossed wires" theory is that the former assumes that the human erotic brain is wired in diverse ways, and all may be considered "normal"; the latter assumes that there is one way our brains are *supposed* to be wired, and that kinky people's wiring has gone astray. One hypothesis within this theory is that people can become kinky when they experience something erotic while simultaneously experiencing another strong sensation—like fear, love, humiliation, or pain—and that their neurons conflate the two so that they are linked ever after. Clinical sexologist Rena McDaniel talks about how fear and arousal cause very similar hormonal reactions in the body, and that our systems may conflate the two.

A slightly different "crossed wires" theory proposes that kinkiness results from the brain remapping something supposedly nonsexual as something sexual due to an impactful situation or encounter. For example, maybe people develop fetishes around silky, frilly panties because our brains associate them so closely with the genitals they cover. Or maybe it's not about where the objects of desire are in space as much as where their associated centers reside in the brain: researchers have found that, in the brain's "body image map," the "genitalia" and "foot" sites are adjacent to one another.

Association/conditioning. This theory holds that kink is something like a learned, Pavlovian response. Example: some Victorians found the sight of ankles arousing because the clothing of the time usually obscured them, and so a glimpse of an ankle felt like a rare and taboo treat. Another example: you achieved your first orgasm while lying on a yellow velvet couch, and ever since, yellow velvet has been very erotic to you. A third example: because a particularly delightful lover had a bristly mustache, you are now really into mustaches and want to feel them rubbed all over you.

Trauma and/or abuse. This is the theory that something bad happened early in your life—you witnessed something horrible or were the victim of sexual, physical, or emotional abuse—and that those experiences gave you your kink. As an example, a past victim of child molestation may later seek out role plays that reenact those experiences, as a way of processing their trauma within (ideally) a controlled, consensual, negotiated space.

This last theory is represented in many television shows, movies, and romance novels. A woman with a cruel father grows up to be an exhibitionist, or a survivor of war grows up to be into bondage. *Fifty Shades of Grey*, much reviled and scorned within the kink community, is perhaps the most famous example: Christian Grey suffered abuse and neglect as the child of an addict, and his trauma is portrayed as the reason why, as an adult, he can't be in "real" relationships and engages only in BDSM instead (as if it's an either/or proposition!). The message is clear: people who are kinky are mentally unstable because of some awful thing they endured, and the kink is a symptom of that problem.

But though media loves to play out this narrative, there isn't any good data behind it. Study after study—including, recently, a thousand-plus-person study from 2020 published in a paper called "The Psychology of Kink: A Survey Study into the Relationships of Trauma and Attachment Style with BDSM Interests" in the journal *Sexuality Research and Social Policy* by scientists in Belgium—have shown no conclusive correlation between childhood trauma and later kinky desire. Such a correlation would be a really hard thing to prove, because how are you defining trauma, and how are you defining kink? Are you equating growing up with a critical parent to be in the same category as growing up in a violent war zone? Are you equating an interest in being blindfolded with an interest in being sucked up by quicksand? Moreover, so many people experience *some* form of trauma, abuse, or neglect—growing up around or with poverty, racism, addiction, death, betrayal, or other kinds of difficulty, loss, and grief—that who among us can really say we came into our mature sexualities free of baggage? Wouldn't it be just as easy (or tricky) to prove that trauma survivors grow up to be vanilla?

It is possible, of course, that kinks develop in multiple ways, and at different phases of life, and through a combination of factors described in the theories above. Someone could have an innate, hardwired fetish as well as other kinks that they came to through conditioning or even trauma. We humans are a diverse bunch.

While researching these theories, I came across more than one sex- and kink-positive source that said, kindly enough, "Who cares why you're kinky? Just enjoy yourself!" And while I appreciate the sentiment, I don't buy into it. This is a book for people who, like me, really *like* to think about sex, and can never get enough of asking why.

I say, let's keep asking why. Let's keep conducting (and participating in) studies about sexual behavior. Let's keep reading articles and books. Let's keep talking to each other. We care enough to question what's deep in the oceans of our planet and what's out there in the stars: doesn't it stand to reason that we also ask about what swims and glitters in our erotic selves as well?

BUT IS IT KINK IF YOU'RE NOT AROUSED?

As kink has started receiving more mainstream attention, an interesting situation has arisen: people are claiming to have kinks but talking about them in ways that aren't particularly related to the *erotic*.

For example, rope bondage has gotten really popular recently in certain BDSM communities. I've seen a huge uptick in the number of rope workshops and activities offered at kink conferences and retreats. For a while, shibari, the Japanese art of binding someone using various intricate knots and patterns, got very trendy. But shibari is a craft for which you must study, buy equipment, and practice. You can't just happen into shibari: it takes time, training, and attention. Shibari expert and educator Midori calls it a "pleasure craft" (which sounds like a cruise I'd like to join). And while for some people it is absolutely arousing to either tie or be tied up, for others it is really more about the *craft* than the erotic pleasure: for those practitioners it's a kind of demanding, kink-derived hobby, artform, or spiritual practice that doesn't have much to do with sex at all.

NOT THAT INTO ROPE, AS IT TURNS OUT

I was once the model for a shibari artist who spent hours winding my body into a stunning corset-like rope creation. Because I'm not really into rope and wasn't attracted to the artist, it was not an erotic experience for me (though I was grateful and felt cute in my little rope outfit at the kink event I was attending!). And when I asked the artist if *he* was aroused, he looked surprised. No, he said, he was just concentrating on how to tie the next knot. So I'd say neither of us qualify as shibari fetishists.

Or let's take flogging. I've gone to kink events where vendors are selling exquisite, artisan-made whips of every possible material, size, and color. People try out the various floggers until they find one they adore and purchase, then play with their new toys for hours. Often, they don't have anyone they are actually flogging yet, but even if they do, they are concentrating more on technique: their expressions are ones of determination and practice, not swoony excitement. They aren't getting turned on.

As someone who cares about language, I wish we could use a term other than "kink" or "fetish"—something like Midori's "pleasure craft," or maybe "pleasure play"—for these kink-adjacent, non-arousing activities. "Kink" and "fetish" have long been defined by their relationship to arousal. They are things that turn a person on. That is categorically different than something that doesn't. And we need to know the difference in order to have better, more consensual encounters.

PARAPHILIAS AND THE SPECTRUM OF FETISHISTIC DESIRE

Let's now dive deeper into fetishes, because to my mind, this is where things get really interesting. (But I'm a fetishist, so I'm biased.)

On the HBO series *Deadwood*, Al Swearengen, the Wild West brothel owner, calls the fetishists who frequent his establishment "specialists": "The thing you gotta know about specialists," he says, "is they pay a premium and they never cause fuckin' trouble." And while of course this isn't universally true, it speaks to the connoisseur-like focus of fetishists, and how deeply satisfied we can be if given the particular, peculiar thing we're after. Fetishes are all about specificity.

The medical and legal term for fetish is "paraphilia," meaning a love that exists alongside (parallel to) other kinds of love and derives sexual interest in an "atypical target." The *para* prefix here can also be translated as a love that is *near* or *resembling* or *abnormal* or *apart from* or—my favorite—*beyond* other kinds of love.

The *Diagnostic and Statistical Manual of Mental Disorders, Fifth Edition (DSM-5)*, describes paraphilia in this way: "any intense and persistent sexual interest other than sexual interest in genital stimulation or preparatory fondling with phenotypically normal, physiologically mature, consenting human partners." (*Intense and persistent*, mm-hmmm. I like that in a lover.) Thankfully, this definition allows for the existence of healthy, consensual paraphiliac behavior. Unlike its previous editions, the *DSM-5* is careful not to pathologize paraphilias: it does not claim that all fetishes are mental health problems requiring treatment. Instead, it differentiates a paraphilia from a "paraphiliac disorder," a situation in which that "love beyond" interferes with a person's ability to live a safe, healthy, productive life.

The word "fetish" was likely first used in the early 1600s by Portuguese sailors who observed people on the Guinea coast of Africa "worshipping" small charm-like objects. Such fetish objects—often pocket-sized carved figures—are found in cultures throughout the world where people believe these figures hold supernatural powers of protection and influence.

In this traditional, nonsexual sense, a fetish could be the lucky pendant that your grandmother gave you, the one you never take off and feel lost without. Or the souvenir football helmet that you must place in a certain spot on the coffee table every time your team plays. Fetish objects command our devotion and obsession; we trust and revere them. In return, they offer us gratification, a sense of security, and pleasure.

This is the perfect way to explain how sexual fetishists feel about the things we fetishize. We revere and worship those things, be they body parts, such as armpits; textiles, such as latex; objects, such as balloons; or acts, such as smoking a cigarette. (These examples, by the way, are all relatively common fetishes. According to a 2020 article from Future Method, a sexuality research site, "armpits" is one of the most heavily searched fetish terms in Indiana and Nevada, for example. Balloon erotica is sought-after in Pennsylvania and Virginia.)

But the armpit or balloon alone is not the fetish. Fetishists tend to have specific parameters for how we want the thing we're into to be presented, interacted with, talked about, and made. So we may swoon over armpits, but only if they are clean and hairy—*or* we might only love shaved and stinky. Those of us into latex may want the material to be bubblegum pink and smelling of talcum powder and stretched over our faces; if someone else is wearing a black latex skirt, we may not care nearly as much. The balloon lovers among us may want to watch comely women lightly stroke large balloons with their fingernails, but get agitated if any of the balloons pop. And those of us who are cigarette fetishists may want an older person to benevolently tap their smoke directly on top of our heads, but only if it's a Lucky Strike; *or* we may want Marlboros put out on our tongues, but only by a stern and sneering cowboy-type.

For the paraphiliac, the devil is in the details. And usually, we can't turn off our attention to those details. A foot fetishist, while walking across a park on their way to work, might be stopped in their tracks at the sight of someone frolicking barefoot in the grass. You know those scenes in movies where the man lays eyes on a beautiful woman for the first time, and everything turns to slow-mo and music starts playing as she whips her hair around her face? That's how a fetishist can feel when suddenly confronted with their obscure object of desire.

As a fetishist, I've always felt that what lights me up feels so powerful, so specific, and so beyond my control or understanding that it is as if a sexuality chip has been implanted in my brain. Experiencing the world through the filter of my fetish has been baffling, sometimes overwhelming—and also fascinating. *Why* do I feel so drawn to this thing that is not arousing to most other people? A curious person by nature, I started researching all this stuff as soon and as best as I could. I kept at it through my teens and twenties, which, luckily for me, coincided with the earliest days of public access to the Internet and an explosion of crowd-sourced information on all manner of obscure topics and interests.

Somewhere along the way I found a handy scale that delineated fetishistic behavior in clear and quantifiable terms. I've thought of this scale ever since, even though I've never successfully located the original source. There are many such tools out there, mostly used to diagnose and determine treatments for criminals or mental health patients. The scale I half remember could have been a version of Rinehart's Sexual Behavior and Desire Questionnaire (1998), the Abel Assessment for Sexual Interest (1995 and onward), the Fetishism Scale (Kurt Freund, Betty W. Steiner, and Samuel Chan, 1982 and other versions), or the terrifically named Total Sexual Outlet Inventory (M. P. Kafka, 1997). (Yes, that last scientist was named Kafka, and one of the Fetishism Scale authors has a name that is one letter away from Freud, both of which delight my literary sensibility.)

Over time, I boiled down whatever scales I read long ago into my own theory of a *spectrum of fetishistic tendency*. It goes like this:

Level 0 Fetishist—You are not a fetishist, as you have no particularly strong erotic preferences.

Level 1 Fetishist—You have some mild and specific erotic preferences, but you can mostly take them or leave them.

Level 2 Fetishist—You have some strong erotic preferences and you are very aware of them, but they need not always be present for you to have a good time.

Level 3 Fetishist—You are strongly drawn to a particular thing, and you probably have specific parameters about what turns you on about that thing. In order to have a fulfilling sexual experience, most often you need to be thinking about or enacting the fetish in some way.

Level 4 Fetishist—Your fetish is so strong and central to your erotic life that it nearly eclipses other sexual interests or needs.

To illustrate the levels on the scale, let's use a combat-boot fetish as an example. Someone without this fetish doesn't think of combat boots as sexual at all. A *mild*—Level 1 or 2—paraphiliac might find themself attracted to people they see in public wearing combat boots and would enjoy it if their partner wore combat boots during sex. A *moderate*—Level 2 or 3—paraphiliac might have strong opinions about which particular brand of combat boots are sexiest and would be delighted to talk about and worshipfully shine the boots of their lover during erotic play. The *serious*—Level 4—paraphiliac might not care who is wearing the boots, or if anyone is wearing them at all: the boots themselves are the focus of the erotic attention, and the fetishist wants to lick and rub them for ages.

It can be intense to navigate the world as a paraphiliac. The experience of getting aroused by things that other people do not think of or intend to be sexual is very disconcerting. I think of the phrase *it colors my view*, or the idea of a "queer lens": I often feel like I'm literally processing the world through a fetishistic filter that turns supposedly wholesome, everyday activities into something lascivious. In my case, that activity is other people overeating. I was recently searching for a fun GIF to send to a friend in thanks for a recipe. But because a certain kind of overeating is erotic to me, when I went looking for a GIF, all the animated images of people and cartoon animals shoveling food into their mouths, or licking their lips, or patting their distended stomachs made me feel like I had just accidentally accessed X-rated material.

The experience of involuntary arousal can feel uncomfortable, confusing, and isolating for fetishists. In a 2016 article by Amanda Mannen for *Cracked* magazine, she interviewed Lee, who is into vore, or the idea of being eaten. Lee told her, "K-Mart did a Halloween commercial where a woman is swallowed and in a bat's stomach. She spends the commercial talking into a camera as stomach walls squeeze on her and drench her in slime. . . . [Watching that commercial around others] was awkward [for me]. It's . . . like watching a movie with your parents and there's a sex scene, but nobody realizes it's a sex scene except you."

I read an interview with a YouTube yoga instructor who acknowledged that many foot fetishists comment—politely and respectfully—on her videos, which made me realize that all of the innocent videos out there of people doing yoga or other typically barefoot family-friendly activities can also serve unintentionally as porn. Perhaps that's not so different than vanilla folks getting turned on by exercise videos of instructors in Spandex leggings, except that people would call the foot fetishist weird for their attraction.

And a reminder about consent: strangers who happen to embody your fetish aren't doing so for your benefit, and you have no right to approach them outside of a mutually romantic context. If you're in an enthusiastically consensual sexual relationship, great, have at it and worship at your lover's bare feet if they're good with that. But that yoga instructor you don't know is not posting her video in order to turn on foot fetishists: she is doing her nonsexual job. If you happen to be turned on by that stuff, keep your arousal to yourself. To make it known is to violate someone's privacy and consent: it's like being a flasher, which is a gross and illegal thing to be. We should never wave our sexual desires in someone else's face—literally or figuratively—unless they have said that they want us to do so.

BECAUSE CONSENT IS AT THE CENTER OF IT ALL

One outcome of kink finding its way into mainstream cultural discourse is that confusion has arisen about the difference between negotiated, mutually consensual kink and the kind of predatory behavior that is all too common in our society.

If you hear that spanking is a fun way to liven things up, should you surprise your partner with it the next time you're having sex? Should you spontaneously and playfully call your lover a bad little slut in bed? Can you unilaterally decide to tie your new friend to a bedpost because it looked cool in a movie? Should you DM that stranger on Instagram to tell them how hot you think their shiny nylon shorts are?

No. Nope. Absolutely not. In kink—really, in all sex of any kind—consent is *everything*.

Before you try a particular sexual activity with a partner, you must have an open and honest conversation about it first, and the person you're talking to must respond, enthusiastically, that they are interested. Tell your darling exactly what you are interested in, make it clear that you are eager to hear their genuine response, and then *listen* to and *respect* that response, rather than forging ahead with whatever was already in your dirty little mind.

As scholar Peter Tupper points out, "BDSM is a form of human *play*"—italics mine—and is "optional, not obligatory." There is no circumstance under which participating in a kinky activity is mandatory or required. One *always* has the right to opt out, leave, or say no. And in fact, Tupper rightly says, if consent isn't present, what you're doing isn't kink: it's "brutality and victimization."

I want to acknowledge that most of us have very little practice and few role models for talking openly about sexual desire. We may hold fear and self-loathing about our preferences. It takes trust, time, and experience to have good conversations about sex. But it is also the only way forward. Anything else is unethical, potentially dangerous—and, in its most extreme forms, criminal.

The good news is that people who are active members of healthy kink communities tend to have experience in this arena. Unlike most Americans, experienced kinky people are often quite comfortable asking someone they just met what they're into, how hard they like to be whipped, or if they want to be petted when in doggie mode.

The bad news is that there are still jerks in those communities, just like there are everywhere else. Just because someone acts like Sir Domly Dom (as this prevalent, arrogant type is often called) does not mean they have any clue what they're doing—or how to give one particular submissive what they want. So don't equate a seasoned BDSMer with an ethical one. When considering a new play partner, spend plenty of time talking about what you hope will and will not happen, ask around to find out what that person's reputation is, and have a solid escape plan in case things go awry.

Kinky people aren't superior to vanilla people—we can suffer the same communication breakdowns around sex. True, that breakdown might be about needle play or a gang bang that didn't go off as planned rather than a ruined anniversary dinner, but the same truth holds: we have to tell each other what we want, continuously, because it can change from minute to minute, night to night, year to year. Someone who loves being called a filthy pig might not enjoy that after a particularly bad day at work—or they might want it even more that night. We have to tell each other what we desire, and we have to ask. So no matter whether we're scheduling some "pick-up play" (spontaneous kinky "scenes" between strangers or casual acquaintances at a sex event) or approaching our spouse, each individual encounter and partner must be treated with caution and care.

I get angry when a fetishist presumes that because they saw someone else doing or having the weird thing they adore, it means that they have the right to approach that stranger or talk to them about it. Take the shiny-nylon-shorts example from earlier. I've worn 1980s-style nylon track shorts in summer, because I think they are fun and comfy. I didn't even know there was a fetish around this item until I posted vacation pictures on social media and started getting comments and DMs from strangers: men (always men) who posted at length about how great these shorts are, asked for more pictures of the shorts, told me to wear the shorts more often, or generally wanted to get to know me because I wore the shorts. In many cases, they were sort of sneaky about it, trying not to let on that they had a sexual fetish. But since I'm a fetishist, I could tell right away what was going on.

And listen: I'm delighted to know that shiny nylon shorts are a fetish. Cool! Everyone's thoughts are their own, and we are all free to have them. But in this situation, I wasn't wearing nylon shorts for a fetishist's pleasure: I was posting what I viewed as a nonsexual outfit, and was doing so on social media, not on a dating site or sex forum. If I did happen to post on a sex- or dating-specific site, thus indicating that I'm open to receiving such contact, even then *one should respectfully ask* if one can wax rhapsodic about the shorts before broaching the subject.

What does it look like to respectfully approach someone about your kinky interest in them? If I'm in a sexy space—be it a swingers' club or dating app—I like to indicate my interest as unassumingly and unthreateningly as possible. If in person, I approach the person I think is cute or who seems to be into my kink and say, from a few feet away and in a friendly tone, "Hi! I just wanted to let you know that I think you're attractive and I have a hunch that our interests might align. If you might be interested, we can talk about it and maybe do some stuff! If not, I hope you have a great day!" Online, I might send a private message saying much the same. In either case, unless they immediately respond in the affirmative, I dial down my interest.

One key to negotiating kink (or any kind of sex) in a healthy, consensual way is to back off quickly if a lack of interest or pleasure is indicated. Sometimes that lack of interest is very obvious: the person says no, or looks horrified, or they step away, or they end the conversation, or they tell you to fuck off. All of these are clear signs that you should swiftly and briefly apologize and never bother them again. Sometimes, however, it's not so clear. Sometimes people are shy, or caught off guard, or overly polite, or ambivalent. They may go along with a situation past the point of actually enjoying it. If someone seems uncomfortable or unresponsive, it is a sign that they are not fully accessing their pleasure. And we all deserve to fully access our own pleasure when and how and with whom we choose.

In a wonderful piece by philosopher Becca Rothfeld for the *Boston Review*, she writes that consent without enthusiasm—"hollow consent, unaccompanied by inner aching"—is rampant and an issue we don't talk about enough. "Sex that is merely consensual is about as rousing as food that is merely edible, as drab as a cake without icing," she says. "Heterosexual women are forever licensing liaisons that don't excite them—perhaps because they have despaired of discovering anything as exotic as an exciting man, or because it no longer even occurs to them to insist on their own excitement, or because capitulation to unexciting men is so exhaustingly expected of them and so universally glorified in popular depictions of romance." The formidable Oxford philosopher Amia Srinivasan writes in her debut essay collection, *The Right to Sex*, that her female students regularly report that they regard their erotic lives as "at once inevitable and insufficient."

So let's try, when we're able, to move beyond sex that is, in Rothfeld's words, "consensual but underwhelming." Many people use the term "enthusiastic consent" to describe what we're aiming for, and while, in an ideal world, everyone would engage only in things about which we're enthusiastic, we know that's not reality. Professional intimacy coordinator Mia Schachter, who calls themself the "Consent Wizard," points to the work of sexological bodyworker and intimacy coach Betty Martin, who created a framework called "The Wheel of Consent" and who "talks about the difference between *wanting* and being *willing* to do something. Wanting to do something means it's your own desire; being willing to do something means it's someone else's desire." That is, many of us are sometimes willing to try to or engage in sexual activities, and that willingness is on the continuum of consent, even though the consent may not be wildly—or even mildly—enthusiastic.

Another problem with the focus on enthusiastic consent is that it requires everyone involved to feel *exactly the same way at the same time*. It's nearly impossible to gauge whether this is the case, and even then, the levels of enthusiasm can shift from second to second and minute to minute. These realities are part of what make enthusiastic consent an unhelpful, binary framework. Instead, we can work to create a space for our partners and ourselves where we feel able to express our boundaries, and as much enthusiasm as is realistic and authentic. We convey these things through what we say, but also through what we do: our body language, our responsiveness, and our ability to be present. Schachter describes the mutually consensual space we should aim for as a realm of "care, desire, joy and satisfaction."

All of this can be hard enough for vanilla people in a sex-negative culture, as Rothfeld implies above. Add in the complicating factors of kink, and it can get tricky. I'm not just talking about the importance of establishing consent with new partners during pick-up play at an event. It can be hard to tell our *long-term* partners what we want, especially since what we want—and what they want—is always evolving, and also we love them, so we don't want to hurt their feelings. Sometimes we've been doing the same thing with our partners for years, and we don't know how to say that we have stopped wanting to do that thing we once loved. Sometimes we are scared of what might happen if we admit to our beloved that we're craving something new and unusual.

A lot of kinks revolve around power exchange (pXe), role play, and pain or impact play of one kind or another. (See the chapters ahead.) And that's where things get really interesting regarding consent. Say you like to be poked with needles. Great! But in order to enthusiastically consent to being poked with needles, you require a partner who knows what they're doing, and can do it safely, and will respect your boundaries. Maybe you want to be poked by needles, but you do not want that person to touch your ass. Or you do not want that person to whisper sweet nothings to you while they do it. Or you only want to be poked by needles while flute music is playing. You have to talk these things through first: they aren't just going to magically happen the first (or one hundredth) time you get together with another willing needle fetishist.

A common misperception (even among many experienced pervs!) is that if you're submissive (a "sub," or s-type), you're generally glad to be told what to do, even in your nonsexual life, or by all your sexual partners. But kink is about our *erotic* life and identity, not who we are in the rest of our lives. Most submissives only want to be told what to do in certain situations, within certain limits, by someone we trust or even love. Submissive folks, like everyone else, pursue the erotic life, identity, partners, and activities of our choosing; our submission doesn't mean that we surrender our preferences.

ACRONYMS

Kink communities use acronyms to talk about consent and guidelines: the most common are SSC, RACK, and PRICK. Many events and venues use these acronyms on signs, handouts, and registration materials as shorthand to indicate that anything that does not fall under these general rules is banned, and those who violate these guidelines can get kicked out. You will see language like "at our events, we practice RACK" or "this organization supports SSC play, and if you see something that seems to violate these guidelines, please notify a staff member immediately."

Here's a brief guide to the acronyms, though they all imply similar things:

SSC stands for "safe, sane and consensual." Self-explanatory but still a useful—if reductive—guideline for those pulled toward kinky play. According to BDSM scholar Stephen K. Stein, it's the most popular term, used both by people just getting started as well as veterans within the BDSM scene.

RACK goes beyond SSC and stands for "risk-aware, consensual kink." The term was developed by BDSM community member Gary Switch in 1999 to acknowledge that some of the things we perverts do, no matter how hard we try to do them safely, involve a certain level of risk, and that the notion of safety—whether physical or emotional—is subjective: while it may be the goal, it can never be guaranteed. Kinky activities that involve things like needles, fire, or choking are potentially dangerous no matter how much you've practiced (and not everyone who does them *has* practiced). Physically demanding activities like erotic wrestling or even a basic game of "I'm chasing you around the living room" can result in injury, the same as in any sport. RACK also leaves out the "sane" part of SSC because some kinky play is purposefully designed to edge away from what we think of as "sane" and toward something more fanciful, imaginative, involved, or wild. Finally, RACK implies that part of the negotiation around consent should include a conversation about the risks involved, much like the talk your doctor is supposed to have with you before a medical procedure. You should know exactly what you're signing up for before you choose whether or not you want to do it.

PRICK takes RACK one step further, standing for "personal responsibility, informed consensual kink." This means that once you've done your negotiation, you are expected to advocate for yourself and let someone (your partner, a dungeon monitor, the event host, someone standing nearby) know that you need assistance.

These acronyms have emerged over time, and no doubt there will be more to come, if there aren't already.

The kink community is also well-known for its use of "safe words." Safe words are kind of a cliché and get made fun of, but they can be genuinely useful. A safe word can be a word, phrase, gesture, or other cue that you establish with your play partner(s) ahead of time, as part of your overall negotiation, to use in an emergency if you suddenly want to stop a scene or otherwise revoke consent. To make it clear that it's a safe word, the phrase or gesture should not be something you'd typically or accidentally do or say: it could be shouting out "wombat" or tapping your elbow three times. Many kink events have default safe words and cards—usually "yellow" for *slow down* and "red" for *stop*—that you can use if you haven't negotiated your own. Kinky (and other) people use safe words instead of "no" or "stop" because many of us say words like "no" or "stop" when we are in fact experiencing deep, consensual pleasure. If we are playing a role play game or are involved in a D/s (dominance and submission) scenario, we may even shout out things like "You're hurting me!" or "Get away from me!" when we mean quite the opposite. Safe words can be used to distinguish play-acting from the real deal.

All of these tools only work, of course, if everyone involved takes them seriously and understands how to put them into practice: in the kink world, knowledge, skill, experience, and the ability to communicate and listen are very important. Not all kinky people know what they're doing, or follow these protocols, but at least a standard vocabulary of consent *exists*, which is more than you can say for much of the vanilla-sex universe.

One final thought on consent for now: I recently heard about a relatively new job in the movie industry, an "intimacy coordinator." (This is the field in which Mia Schachter, of Consent Wizardry, works!) Trained in movement, choreography, and other skills, the intimacy coordinator is responsible for talking through what's about to happen with all participants in a sex scene. According to a 2020 article by Adrienne Westenfeld in *Esquire*, "This challenging and necessary work is so much more than choreography—it's . . . a constant negotiation of consent and communication, with intimacy coordinators balancing the safety of performers alongside the vision of writers and directors." Westenfeld interviews intimacy coordinator Ita O'Brien, who says of her job, "What's so important with a scene is what the positions will be. Once we know the shape, we agree on touch. Where can we touch? Where's your yes? Most importantly, where's no? Once you know what body parts are in play, we walk through the scene, getting agreement and consent."

Tasking a professional with this work is long overdue in Hollywood. But it also strikes me that we could all use an intimacy coordinator in our lives. My primary partner pointed out that I played this role for him once, when I organized an edging scene for him at a sex event with a bunch of our kinky friends. (For the unfamiliar, edging is where you arouse a person while holding off orgasmic release as long as possible.) In order to pull the scene off, I'd talked to him weeks beforehand about his boundaries, hopes, expectations, and concerns. And then I contacted each of our participating friends separately to ask what they would be comfortable doing and not doing, when would work to schedule it, and how long they should expect it would go. This kind of advance planning is not the kind of thing most of us associate with naughty sexual adventures, but by obtaining clear and ideally enthusiastic consent from everyone beforehand—and assuring them that it was 100 percent okay if any of them changed their minds at any point—we were able to set the stage for what turned out to be a supremely hot and fun time.

On a smaller scale, my primary partner and I often chat with each other over the course of the day about what we might do later in our bedroom that night. *I have an idea for a game*, one of us will text the other. *Would you be up for some neighbor kid/MILF role play tonight?* And the other will text back, *Maybe, but my back is a little achy, so can we work around that?* Checking in with each other in this way is exciting—and a good reminder of how attracted we are to each other—but it's also pragmatic and considerate prep.

It's not easy—or possible—to achieve enthusiastic consent 24-7. Most of us end up occasionally doing things, sexually or otherwise, that we later regret, and we can learn valuable things from those experiences that can inform our future actions. But enthusiastic consent is an ideal we can strive toward, with vigilance and joy. As Becca Rothfeld puts it, let's "demand electrification" from our sex lives. (I'll leave it up to you to decide if you want to be literal about that "electrification" and grab your violet wand or e-stim set.)

Finally, I cannot state this strongly enough: consent is not a footnote to kink. It is not an ancillary topic. *It is the necessary foundation to every single partnered act described in this book.* So please read on with that in mind. I invite you to bookmark this section and return to it often as you go forward.

CHAPTER 3

HEAVEN HELP ME FOR THE WAY I AM

Taboos as the Heart of Kink

The four P's (categories of taboo)—kinks you can't try in real life—objects that are closer than they appear—some controversial thoughts on pedophilia.

KINK, TABOO, AND THE FOUR P'S

Let's say I'm turned on by watching someone smoke a cigar. We all know tobacco is bad for us, and smoking is no longer universally glamorized in our culture the way it once was. So there is something about being into cigars that is considered a little naughty. Naughty enough, though, to call it a kink? I'd argue that since, as evidenced in movies and so on, it's still generally accepted that smoking can look cool and sexy, a simple attraction to cigar smoking isn't a kink. No one would think I'm a freak just because I get a little swoony when someone lights up a stogie.

What gets a little more complicated—and thus what wanders into the realm of kink—is when I want the person smoking the cigar to put it out on my head or tongue, or when I want to spit-polish the black leather boots of that person while they smugly puff away.

So where's the boundary between a socially acceptable vanilla turn-on and kink? Perhaps the line is drawn when our attraction goes beyond what's society-approved sexy and toward things that are cultural taboos: attractions that are driven by a nonnormative relationship to *power*, *psychological dynamics*, the *putrid*, and *pain*.

Let's call these taboo factors the four P's. These are the things that, if we did them outside of an erotic and enthusiastically consensual context, would be morally and ethically wrong and could get us in serious trouble.

What is taboo and even "wrong," of course, is also somewhat culturally specific, but the four P's are categories I think most of us can agree upon. Here are some brief thoughts on them, since we'll continue to explore them all in depth in future chapters.

Power. Although we don't tend to think about it much, every one of us is locked into non-negotiated power dynamics every day. When we feel resentful of something our boss tells us to do at work, when we reprimand our kids, when we slow down to avoid being pulled over by the cops, we are operating within—and tacitly participating in—a system of power. Sometimes we hold the power; sometimes others do. Many of our interactions are largely determined by how we understand a particular power dynamic to work. We don't text our professors in the middle of the night, we don't curse at the bank clerk, and we don't beg our assistants to perform their assigned tasks. At least, we understand that this is how society is *supposed* to work, and that there could be trouble otherwise.

Kinky power play happens when we take those unnegotiated power dynamics and turn them into sexy fun by either exploiting, exaggerating, or undermining the way it usually works. If we pretend to humiliate the partner we adore and "force" them to do menial tasks, that's playing with power. If our lover role plays the part of a teacher or prison guard or bratty teen, that's allowing us to explore the limits and possibilities of power in a way we don't usually allow ourselves to do.

And power exchange is hot because it feels wrong. In healthy relationships, we don't dominate, plead, coerce, or control our partners: that would be abusive. We aim to treat each other with respect and care. All of which is why an enthusiastically consensual game that lets us fool around with power can be so exciting. (If you are in a relationship where you are fearful for your safety because you are being actually dominated, coerced, or controlled, please seek help and call the National Domestic Violence Hotline at 1-800-799-7233 or TTY 1-800-787-3224. You can also text START to 88788.)

Psychology. In our daily, nonerotic dealings with the ones we love, we are not supposed to fuck with their heads. For example, we shouldn't lie to them: we all know that good relationships are built on trust and honesty. Nor are we supposed to taunt, humiliate, or threaten our partners: those acts are signs of an abusive relationship. (Again, if you are in a relationship where you are being taunted, humiliated, or threatened in ways that feel bad to you, I urge you to seek help and call the National Domestic Violence Hotline at the number above.)

But one thing I find really sexy is when, as part of a role play game, I tell my partner that I'm too sleepy/sick/innocent for him to fuck me, he promises that he won't, and then he does. I freaking *love* that game. "Lie to me," I'll beg him. "Swear you won't do it." In that particular moment, within the safe confines of our intimate time together, I *want* to pretend that my trust is being broken into little pieces. If my partner lied to me in any other context, though—about gambling away our money or neglecting an important responsibility or some other genuine breach of trust—I would not put up with it for one minute. There would be fury, disappointment, hurt, and possibly a divorce.

And if one of my lovers called me a filthy slob while we were naked and making out, I'd be devastated, even if they were just being playful. I'm not personally into humiliation—it's not a kink I enjoy. But that's just me. There are boatloads of folks out there who want nothing more than for their otherwise loving and caring partners to call them dirty little pigs, or who want to be threatened with discipline. Again: not as *actual* ridicule and never in anger. It's only kink if those words are being said from a place of affection and playfulness, and to someone who is thrilled to hear them.

Psychological games often intersect with various kinds of power play. Personally, I think this psychological stuff is some of the most potent and exciting kink around—and also the most underrated and underexplored. As we know, the brain is the largest sexual organ we have, and there is so much that we perverts can do to utilize its powers to the fullest extent.

The putrid. Most people in the twenty-first century have been socialized to be averse to rank smells, bodily fluids, feces, and other things we consider literally "dirty." We are generally germophobes who believe that cleanliness is next to godliness. And we still hold Puritanical beliefs about the ickiness of our own bodies and bodily functions. For example, while I don't consider myself particularly squeamish and I wiped poop from children's butts for many years without complaint, I still can't bear to watch the scene in John Waters's *Pink Flamingos* where (spoiler alert!) Divine eats dog shit off the street.

I'm not alone in that. Shit, piss, blood, and sweat tend to evoke some measure of shock and repulsion in most humans, at least in the context of sexual activity. Hell, even the *sexual* fluids that ooze out of our bodies can gross us out—and they're *supposed* to be there when we are getting hot and heavy! So people who are wildly aroused by licking up menstrual fluid, drinking urine, or burying their face in someone's stinky armpits are considered outré, even though their numbers are legion.

We also tend to get grossed out by dirt, foul odors, and other evidence of mess and decay. Some psychologically minded theorists would say that this is because such sensory experiences remind us of our lack of control over nature, of death, and of our own mortality, all of which are generally not sexy to the average *Homo sapiens*. Here again, kinky folks beg to differ, which is why there are huge fetishes around sploshing (basically, wet and messy food fights), boot licking, mud, farting, and more.

Speaking of culturally normative fears around mortality, there are also kinks about grandmas and other embodiments of aging. These are also deeply taboo, because it's so ingrained in us that we are supposed to be repulsed by the bodies and sexual desires of elderly women. To a lesser extent, our culture is disgusted by sexuality in elderly people of other genders, too, but misogyny definitely plays an intersecting role in this fear. We covet and sexualize the figure of the "maiden," the comely young woman, star of all mainstream romantic and sexual material. Meanwhile, "crones"—old women—are the complete *opposite* of sexy. So pervasive is this myth that it's the plot of many horror and fantasy narratives: the beautiful young woman, the object of desire, turns out to secretly be an old witch with wrinkled skin! Terrifying! Disgusting!

So of course kinky people are all over this taboo: gerentophilia (attraction to the elderly) is a fetish, and as we know from Rule 34, there's porn for it. Plenty of porn. Yet it remains one of the least studied and scientifically documented of the common fetishes, with no mention made in Kinsey's major works, for example.

Pain. Humans aren't supposed to like pain. Painful sensation is an evolutionary warning system that is there to tell us when to get out of harm's way, to keep us safe and alive. If our physiological wiring doesn't know to resist pain, we are likely to endanger ourselves. And we're not supposed to enjoy inflicting pain, either: people who do are seen as mean, bullies, criminals, insane. Finding pleasure in receiving or giving pain is a big no-no that sets off all sorts of alarm bells in the average vanilla human. (And for good reason, so here again: if you are in a relationship in which you are being physically harmed against your will, I hope you will call the National Domestic Violence Hotline listed in the earlier section on *power.*)

And yet, despite all that evolutionary biology and logical resistance to harm, deriving pleasure from pain—either giving or receiving—is probably one of the most common kinks out there. Sadists. Masochists. (Together, they are known as *S/m*—the capital *S* dominating the lowercase *m.*) Anyone into spanking or slapping or whipping. Anyone into more esoteric forms of impact play such as violet wands (electric shock/stimulation), cupping (placing glass cups on the body that vacuum up the skin underneath them), or needle play. All these kinks reward their participants with endorphin- and/or adrenaline-releasing experiences.

My guess is that this is because most of us have experienced pain and pleasure as a continuum. It feels good—and bad—to press on a bruise or clean our ears with cotton swabs. It feels bad—and good—to lift heavy weights or get tackled in a football game. And it feels good and bad to make out for so long that our lips swell, or to have someone give us a hickey, or to get fucked really hard up the ass. I'd posit that we experience a kind of pain right before orgasm . . . and then we feel *really* nice. I have a theory that even the most elaborate impact play is actually a stand-in, or a replication/simulation, of the pain-pleasure we often experience during normative acts of passion.

Most people, even most vanilla people, know this. We know that it's utterly delightful to be consensually shoved up against a wall or to pull someone's ponytail during sex. We know that it's hot to chase our partner, wrestle them, and pin them down until we are both panting from the exertion. We know it's a badge of honor to be fucked until we're sore. The pain-pleasure continuum plays out in almost every kind of sexual encounter we can think of. What's wild is that S/m and other pain-based kink practices are still so taboo and titillating. It seems to me that S/m is perhaps one of the most common kinds of kink because it's so closely linked to mainstream sexuality, and that it isn't really that out there after all.

KINKS YOU CAN'T TRY IN REAL LIFE

As far as mutually consensual activity between adults goes, this book is a pretty judgment-free zone. And even for those of you whose kinks are really fraught and problematic, I still see you as my compatriots. Nonetheless, there are lines that should not and cannot be crossed, and I want to be clear about those. And of course, these lines all have to do with consent.

Here's the thing: anything—everything—is okay to explore *in your mind*. Within the cozy confines of your own imagination, you can delve as deep into whatever perverted fantasies you are capable of creating. Go for it.

PROCEED WITH CAUTION WHEN GOING PUBLIC

CAVEAT: Think twice before you tell anyone about these darkest, weirdest fantasies. It's probably wise not to tell anyone at work. You might not even want to tell your lover unless they've specifically asked you to—and even then, be careful. Especially if kinky porn of any kind is involved—even if you only watch or read or otherwise consume it and are not the maker of it—the implications can be severe. People are fired, imprisoned, and otherwise prosecuted for their fantasies in this way: although it's hard to gauge the scale of this persecution due to human resources departments' confidentiality policies, some people have reported losing their jobs after being outed as members of the kink community, since it is not inherently protected in one of the federally protected categories (race, color, creed, sexual orientation, gender identity, age, national origin, disability, genetic information). The threat of such retaliation is even more common. A kinky air force veteran reported to the National Coalition for Sexual Freedom in 2014, "This constant threat of loss of career and livelihood has impacted me in countless negative ways."

In terms of *acting* on those fantasies: as long as a kink is played out as a clearly understood and negotiated game of pretend between enthusiastically consenting adults, you can really do anything you want—keeping safety, risk, and responsibility in mind, of course.

But the bottom (and top, and middle) line is this: only two or more adults, in their right minds and of their own free will, can enthusiastically consent to sex. No being, creature, or object over which we wield non-erotic power has the ability to give consent. Such power differences inevitably, indisputably, insurmountably *block the possibility of enthusiastic consent.* And the only kind of sexual activity that is ever okay is the consensual kind.

If you are reading this book because you are someone with an intense kink that is impossible to practice ethically or legally, please know that I have deep empathy for you. I understand what it's like to have one's erotic urges feel like a microchip implanted in the brain. However, I'm also here to tell you that no matter how deeply wired you seem to be toward attractions in these arenas, you *cannot* and *must not* act, in the real world, on fantasies involving animals, children, students of yours (of any age), employees of yours (ditto), sleeping or drugged or otherwise impaired people, or any other beings who are not in a position to truly consent.

Let's take death—or, for our purposes, sexual attraction to corpses—as an extreme example. Necrophilia is a fetish, but since the dead cannot consent, there is no way to act upon this fetish other than in your fantasies. (A slight digression: can someone explain to me why William Faulkner's classic short story about necrophilia, "A Rose for Emily," is assigned to schoolchildren? I read it in eighth grade, I think, and yes, it's literary, and yes, it's spooky, and yes, the kink is only subtly hinted at, but nonetheless, how is this considered appropriate material for kids while perfectly vanilla depictions of sex are routinely banned?!) Nor is there any safe or ethical way to put into practice fetishes like vore (eating or being eaten by someone) or anything else that normally results in serious injury or death.

In terms of animals, you can certainly *pretend* that your partner is a loyal and submissive puppy and you are their strict but loving master. And for mutually consenting adults, there's nothing wrong with you and your partner *pretending* that one of you is a cute little kid—even an infant!—and the other is their nefarious (or adoring but twisted) guardian. Have at it!

It is *not* okay, however, to do actual sex things with actual animals or children. In any way. Ever.

As a member of the kink community, I believe we need to be honest with ourselves that some of our kinky brethren are fetishists who find themselves involuntarily, inexplicably attracted to animals and children. For folks sexually oriented in these ways, it may not be possible for them to alter these attractions, any more than it's possible for us to alter our desires for spanking or power exchange or shoes. And we can understand that just because someone has a really disturbing fantasy, it does not mean they are going to act on it. Because while we can't always control our desires, we *can* control our actions.

This stuff is difficult to talk about. But I want to make the following statements.

First, in the case of animals: no matter how close we are to them, and no matter how much we project our human experiences onto them, we do not have a clue about the inner lives of other species, and we cannot ever assume that our sexual desires are shared by them. Moreover, as humans, the literal kings of the jungle and every other ecosystem on earth, we are in a constant nonconsensual dynamic with other animal life in which we wield (often deadly) control, whether we are swatting a fly, luring a hummingbird to our feeder, hunting deer, petting a house cat, or dumping plastic into the habitats of marine life.

(This is only tangentially related, but I also harbor harsh opinions about people who call their pets "fur babies" or refer to themselves as the "parents" of these animals. Maybe that's because calling your animal your "child" ignores truths about power—truths that also underlie our understanding of consent. Attributing human agency to nonhuman creatures can lead to well-intentioned but poor decisions.)

Second, in the case of human children: this is a big one, and an obvious one. It is 100 percent clear that children can never consent to sexual behavior with adults. Adults have power over children. Power precludes consent. No adult should ever act on any sexual impulse with any child. It is wrong, bad, and illegal. End of story. (I do have further thoughts about how we tend to think and talk about pedophilia in this culture; see below).

Far more common than actual acts of bestiality or pedophilia are everyday violations of consent around power and impairment. Tragically, the news is full of harrowing stories about sexual assaults in which one person is in a position of authority over another, as a teacher, employer, or celebrity. There are terrible cases where intellectually disabled or senile adults are sexually victimized. And many people have been traumatized because of a sexual encounter that happened when they were extremely drunk or high, passed out, asleep, or otherwise impaired. These are all examples of people who are not in a position to consent. We can all contribute to ending the rape culture by being aware of these factors and stepping in—by alerting a staff member or dungeon monitor, or calmly and casually trying to steer a potential victim away from predatory behavior—if we encounter someone in such a position of sexual danger.

OBJECTS THAT ARE CLOSER THAN THEY APPEAR

All of that is very clear-cut. But here is a more complicated and interesting moral question: it's obviously fine to masturbate to a fantasy that you are in a long-term romantic relationship with a vacuum cleaner whose every setting is more arousing to you than the last, but what about acting on *that* fantasy, or any fantasy that involves an inanimate object?

It could be argued that a vacuum cleaner couldn't care less about what sexual games you play with it, because, having no sentience, no brain, and no emotions, a vacuum cleaner literally cannot care. It's actually pretty common to do "sex things" with inanimate objects, be they a vibrator, a pillow, a showerhead, a magazine, or a cherry pie. I'm not suggesting here that people never masturbate into a sock or on top of a leather jacket. Let's be reasonable.

I'm talking about something far less common. Objectophiles or objectum-sexuals are people who are deeply, romantically, and sexually attracted to objects. Stories about objectum-sexuals tend to become notorious: many of you have probably heard of Erika Eiffel, the woman who held a commitment ceremony between herself and the Eiffel Tower, whom she views as the love of her life. While definitely on the kookier end of the kink spectrum, Erika points out in a 2015 article in *Vice* that her fetishistic relationship with the monument is not unlike the animist religions of Japan, where she lived for a time. Those who follow animist spiritualities believe that all objects have their own spirits, and that it's possible to communicate with those spirits. In Japan, as Erika says, "if you have a headache, you'll rub the Buddha [statue]'s head and then rub your own; it's an exchange of energy." And anyone who has ever cherished and carried on a long-term relationship with a guitar or a car knows humans place immense value on inanimate objects, often naming them and pampering them and mourning their eventual loss. In Erika's words, "It cannot be disputed that we all possess relationships with objects in our daily lives, from heirlooms to devices that enhance our quality of living."

In a 2010 study on the subject, the clinical sexologist Amy Marsh wrote that the objectophiles she surveyed are similar to any other kind of higher-scale fetishist, only in this case the "range of emotional, romantic and/or sexual attractions" they experience are to objects, not people, and are intense enough that objectophiles often forgo or dispense "with human romantic or sexual intimacy." Although these people often "serve as a kind of ready-made sexual sideshow" to the public, Marsh writes, objectum-sexuality is a "genuine—though rare—sexual orientation." It is part of the overall "continuum" of relationships humans have with their objects.

And, I'd say, it is part of the even larger overall continuum of fetishists of all kinds. Being attracted to a tower is not such a far cry from being attracted to a more typically kinky object, such as a pair of silk stockings. Beyond the intensity of attraction, a key difference, perhaps, lies in the amount of reciprocity the human believes exists between them and their literal love object. Some objectum-sexuals believe that their beloved object loves them back, and some do not. Some of the respondents to Marsh's survey wrote that they harbor no sense that their object returns their affection. "I do not feel that my objects have any thoughts about me," wrote one. Another stated, "Although there can be a little amount of mental role play, I am fully aware that objects are inanimate and that this mostly is a one-sided relation." Another said, with more doubt, "I'm not quite sure whether my beloved object can feel attraction or whether this can be defined in the same way like it is for human beings." And still another wrote, poignantly, "I would like to know what my object finds attractive about me."

And therein lies the rub. (Ahem.) Because I want to argue that even if there is no harm done (that we can fathom) from being sexually involved with an airplane or an armchair, it may still be problematic to view these as relationships, because a relationship implies that an airplane or an armchair can consent. Most people (other than objectum-sexuals) agree that a vacuum cleaner isn't sentient, but what about a tree? Or, as *Blade Runner, Her* (great movie;

highly recommend!), and other such sci-fi texts predict, what about AI or a robot?

To my mind, convincing oneself that inanimate objects can consent to sexual and/or romantic relationships is dangerously parallel to convincing oneself that a child can want an adult to fondle them, or that a sheep is agreeing to be sexually active with a human. While it can be hard for us to imagine sex with objects as violation, I think it is wise for humans to remember that our humanness limits us. It limits our understanding as well: we do not know all there is to know about this universe. So as a way of practicing humility in the world, it seems that, within reason, we humans ought to limit our sexual relationships to our own realm.

SOME CONTROVERSIAL THOUGHTS ON PEDOPHILIA

While we're talking about things one must never do in real life, I want to discuss one of the most infamous kinks of all: pedophilia.

My argument is this: actual pedophiles—who may go through life without acting on their urges—need to be considered separately from the far more common sexual abusers of children who do terrible things not because of a kink or a fetish, but out of a desire to control or hurt. There's an important divide between the *kink* of pedophilia and the widespread fears related to pedophilia in our culture, some of which actually lead us to neglecting the very children we're supposed to be protecting.

There's also a real difference between people who might see a teen and think, "Hot!" and people with a fetish for adolescents. If your adult friend enjoys discreetly and respectfully checking out lithe young women in bikinis on the beach, that does not make them a pedophile; it merely means they admire the appearance our culture deems attractive in women. Such attractions are the most vanilla kind of sexual desire I can think of, and as long as adults keep their sexual distance from those much younger than them, there's no harm in noticing (or fantasizing)—and assuming they pursue sexual activities only with people their own age, it's not accurate to call them pedophiles.

These conflations of non-fetishistic behavior with an actual fetish create real problems. As scholar James Kincaid argues, by focusing our attention on the idea of pedophiliac activity, we ignore the more mundane and common issues we need to address when it comes to child welfare. In a 2000 piece for *Salon* he wrote, "In the whole range of [child] abuse problems that come to the attention of social service agencies, sexual child abuse is the most rare. It ranks far below neglect, emotional abuse and physical abuse [of children]. . . . Yet sexual child abuse attracts almost all our attention and most of the money spent on child abuse." Diverting resources and attention away from the far more common dangers that kids face does children a disservice.

Likewise, while it's sadly true that many children are sexually molested, most of that abuse is coming from family members and others who are damaged people enacting criminal behavior as a way of wielding power over someone they know. These abusers may have other psychological problems—impulse-control disorders, violent tendencies, substance addiction—but, according to studies such as the ones done by David Finkelhor, professor of sociology and the director of the Crimes Against Children Research Center at the University of New Hampshire, they're not acting upon a kink. Finkelhor told *Vice* in 2016 that "it is very important for the public to understand that most child molesters are not pedophiles."

Saying that a child molester is a pedophile implies that this abuser is attracted to children. But like rape, child molestation is not about sexual attraction or desire: rape and molestation are about predatory, abusive behavior. Child molesters aren't seeking out sexual experiences with children as much as they are taking out their anger and frustration on whomever happens to be defenseless and available.

It's important to be clear about that difference. I'm grateful for thoughts by philosopher Brian D. Erp, which he shared online in 2017: he writes that "pedophilia and child sexual abuse are two different things, and confusing them is harmful to children." Pedophilia, as a fetish, is an "involuntary sexual attraction," and "so long as it remains disconnected from behavior, is probably not wrong in and of itself." Because, as I put it a few pages back, you can do anything you want *in your mind*.

We don't know exactly how many people have the pedophilia fetish, but recent studies estimate that it's 1 percent or less of the population, and almost all known pedophiles are cis men, the majority of whom have other psychiatric disorders. (There have been no recorded cases of pedophilia among cis women.) Like other fetishists, these people tend to have very specific and narrow attractions: a pedophile (someone who is involuntarily attracted to children before they reach puberty) or hebephile (attracted to pubescent children of middle-school age) probably has powerful responses to certain kinds of children or aspects of children; such fetishists are unlikely to also have a normative sexual response to someone who is sexually mature. Thus, pedophilia is justifiably categorized as a psychological disorder. Having a true pedophilia fetish is a serious impairment: there is no moral, consensual outlet for this attraction, even in the realm of erotica.

As Erp and others point out, the majority of pedophiles limit themselves to fantasies, feel horrible about their desires, and do not act on them. But sadly, pedophiles rarely seek treatment, because the fetish is so intensely stigmatized. Erp argues that "if the goal is to protect children from harm, as it should be, then we should stop stigmatizing [the fetish of] pedophilia *per se*" and instead start and then keep "stigmatizing those who actually sexually abuse children for whatever reason." I'd extend this argument and say that rather than expending resources busting people who watch child porn, we prioritize going after the people who make it, because that's where we'll find actual children in danger from predators.

Finally, I want to make the point that a culture that is unhelpfully paranoid about pedophilia is bound to run into problems when defining who is and who is not a child, because when we start talking about teenagers, things get more complicated. I was seventeen and in high school when I had penetrative sex for the first time, with another seventeen-year-old. I believed then, and believe now, that many of us are ready to engage in consensual sexual activity at that age. But in 2015, when a sixteen-year-old in North Carolina took nude photos of himself to text to his sixteen-year-old girlfriend and she sent some back, both were charged with possession of child pornography, and the young man was further charged with sexual exploitation of a minor—that minor being himself. That's ridiculous. Teenagers in romantic relationships with people in their own age range are not pedophiles, and consenting teens should be able to express their desires to one another.

CHAPTER 4

CHAINS AND WHIPS EXCITE ME

On Sadomasochism

*Pain as a conduit of pleasure—sadism and masochism and
the perverts who gave those terms their names—BDSM
contracts, an origin story—what do we do when we do S/m—
the controversy around "topping from the bottom."*

I f one were to play a word-association game around BDSM, the most
likely terms to arise would probably be ones like "paddles," "rope,"
"riding crops," and "handcuffs," all of which are connected to pain,
all of which further connect with the whole range of the BDSM acronym: one can use these props to restrain someone, employ them as
discipline, and administer them as part of power and/or sadistic play.

The brilliant Susan Sontag called pleasure derived from giving
or receiving pain "the furthest reach of the sexual experience." And
more than perhaps any other single kink, the idea of getting off
from getting hurt looms large in our collective imagination. Is this
because the activities associated with sadism and masochism are
some of the most visually compelling kinks, especially as depicted
in movies or books? Is it because they're more common than other
kinds of sexual deviance? I imagine both the aesthetics and the sheer
number of people who have dabbled in sadistic and masochistic sex
have something to do with their prevalence, but I have another theory as well. Maybe sadomasochism—also known as S&M, or SM, or
S/m, or S&m, with or without the capitals, and broadly defined as

impact play and other pain-driven predilections—is popular because it is to kink as running is to physical fitness: the most accessible type available, with relatively safe and easy entry points.

Hear me out on this analogy. Running is a pretty easy form of exercise to try. You don't have to pay for a gym membership or online subscription or even hunt down a video to follow, the way you do for Zumba or yoga. You don't need to learn a bunch of complicated skills, the way you do for mountain climbing or deep-sea diving or wrestling. You don't need to invest in equipment, the way you do for biking or skiing. You just strap on some shoes (or not! barefoot running is a huge thing!) and head out your front door. You *can* get more fancy about it if you want to, but you don't *have* to. You could run for years without taking a lesson, buying a single thing, or going anywhere special to do it.

Same with the impact play part of sadomasochism. Although there are workshops on the safest spots to slap or kick your lover and there are custom-made whips for sale, you don't *need* any of this stuff to deliver or receive the kind of sensation that gets all your juices flowing. You can simply (and consensually!) haul off and smack someone on their ass or twist their nipples or grab their balls—or ask a trusted partner to do these to you—and you're good to go.

So maybe S/m is the go-to kink because anyone can give it a try. And because it's just on the other side of rough sex, which many vanilla people incorporate into their bedroom fun. And because, as is the case with a "runner's high," our biology is primed to deliver a jolt of delight along with the pain when we are on the receiving end of some negotiated physical duress.

Or maybe it's because humans are accustomed to sacrificing our comfort for a greater gain. As Tupper points out in his book *A Lover's Pinch: A Cultural History of Sadomasochism*, throughout our history, humans have chosen to push our physical and psychological limits in an effort to reach spiritual—and maybe sexual—bliss: we have fasted, taken hallucinogens, agreed to undergo scarification or cutting, participated in grueling pilgrimages or hikes, sat in sweat lodges, and so on. These primal experiences connect us to our animal natures and often lead to moments of insight or higher consciousness. S/m is another path to this kind of experience.

PAIN AS A CONDUIT FOR PLEASURE

Research has revealed scientific reasons as to why so many humans associate pleasure with pain or experience the two on a single continuum. In a 2015 article for the BBC, science writer Zaria Gorvett points out that although we humans think of ourselves as evolutionarily programmed to avoid pain, that's a vastly reductive view of ourselves, one that neglects to take into account the many physically grueling activities so many of us choose and enjoy. Such pleasurably painful activities include eating spicy food, getting tattooed, running marathons—and receiving consensual beatings from our sweethearts.

As Gorvett writes, "The link between pleasure and pain is deeply rooted in our biology." Pain causes endorphins to be released by our nervous system, a reaction that works on the same principle—and often with the same level of intensity—as taking opiates. (Gorvett calls endorphins "the body's own narcotics.") Endorphins are powerful and stimulate, as Gorvett puts it, "the brain's limbic and prefrontal regions—the same areas activated by passionate love affairs and music." Intense exertion can also cause our "bliss chemical," anandamide, to bind to the same receptors in our brain that bring on the "warm, fuzzy pleasure" we get from cannabis. In other words, pain is probably our original "natural high," and in fact, something similar to our current idea of a runner's high may have helped our early primal selves survive on long hunts and depleting journeys on foot. Just like opiates and other drugs, the hormones that flood our systems as we deal with pain can end up producing an elusive and addictive hormonal-physical response we learn to crave.

And there's a reason why the French call orgasm *la petite morte*, or "the little death" (a term also used for a brief faint or blackout): when we are overwhelmed by sensation, we go to a place that can feel like euphoria, an out-of-body experience, or a numbed-out pure state we liken to death itself. Personally, I experience orgasm as a particular and delicious moment of tension-and-release, akin to jumping off a diving board or scratching an itch, and apparently I'm not alone: a 2011 study that mapped the brains of women while they masturbated found that getting close to climax lit up over thirty different areas of the brain, including those linked to pain. Sexology researcher Barry Komisaruk, who studies "the neural pathways by which genital stimulation gains access to the brain," in other words, the science of orgasm, points out that facial expressions during climax "are often indistinguishable" from the faces we make when we're exerting ourselves in ways that cause intense physical discomfort.

Obviously, though, there are many types of pain. For example, there's the kind football players get from dodging tacklers while dashing for a touchdown and then there's the kind they get from tearing their ACL, and these types of pain aren't the same thing, as evidenced by the fact that every year, hundreds of NFL players relish the former and dread the latter. Not all pain is created equal, and not all pain leads to pleasure. Paul Rozin, a psychology researcher, coined a term for the human urge to seek certain kinds of *non-damaging* (safe, sane, and consensual) pain and suffering: "benign masochism." Rozin says that this category of "hedonic reversals"—a term I love, because it sounds like a tarot card reading—includes not just the kind of physical and erotic masochism associated with BDSM, but also asexual sensory activities such as watching horror movies, staying up all night, hearing a disgusting joke, getting nauseous on a roller coaster, jumping into a cold ocean, listening to sad music, or eating hot peppers.

SMARTER OR WEIRDER THAN A CHINESE TREE SHREW?

I find it fascinating that it is speculated that humans are among one of a few animal species who seek out such hedonic reversals. "Generally, when an animal experiences something negative, it avoids it," Rozin says. The one other species that seemed to enjoy chile peppers, for example, is a small primate called the Chinese tree shrew that turns out not to feel the burn of them because of a genetic mutation. To this data, I respond: first, never fully trust human speculation about other species, because what do we know about the inner lives of our animal brethren; and second, while one could say that our "safe-risk-seeking" ways make us smarter and more innovative than other animals, those habits could also show us to be a bit more stupid and ridiculous than other animals. Or just weirder, more complicated, and more successfully predatory.

Our responses to pain and pleasure aren't just physical, of course. A 2019 article by science writer Maria Cohut for *Medical News Today* talks about the complex psychology wrapped up in the pleasure-pain continuum, pointing out that our experience of pain can be "highly dependent on the context" in which we're experiencing it. A 2020 *Journal of Sex Research* study entitled "Physical Pain as Pleasure: A Theoretical Perspective" hypothesized that "a multitude of interconnected factors . . . alter the experience of BDSM pain, including: neural networks, neurotransmitters, endogenous opioids and endocannabinoids, visual stimuli, environmental context, emotional state, volition and control, interpersonal connection, sexual arousal, and memories." In other words, slicing our fingers open accidentally while cooking is rarely fun, but we might get totally turned on by a romantic, erotic cutting scene in a candlelit room, and this emotional element can actually decrease the sensation of the pain. Moreover, Cohut points to studies that have found that "voluntarily-experienced pain during . . . erotic play" can trigger intense "interpersonal bonding" and an "increase in trust." (Note the emphasis on consent here: it's the *voluntary* nature of this play that sparks the positive emotional context required.) And that trust goes both ways: experienced BDSMers will not be surprised to learn that even though a sub may be the one with the bruises following a fun play session, both participants report parallel emotional states—including a feeling of closeness and security—after a scene.

Another reason we seek intense physical sensation is to escape our daily routines and roles. As that 2020 *Journal of Sex Research* study concludes, "Pain can focus attention on the present moment and away from abstract, high-level thought," therefore providing "a temporary reprieve . . . from the burdensome responsibilities of adulthood." As a type A, hyper-responsible intellectual who analyzes almost everything I come into contact with, I can personally testify that getting deeply connected to my body through intense physical sensation—whether that be through a walking meditation, wild dancing, a vigorous hike, or rough play during sex—is one of the surest and best ways I know to stop thinking for a moment and just *be*.

The pain delivered through S/m can be a shortcut to the mind-body connection. Other forms of BDSM can be enormously satisfying, but even when engaged in through stand-alone scenes, they take forethought and effort. Let's take power exchange, or pXe, as an example. To engage in the cerebral cat-and-mouse game of D/s involved in power exchange, which goes beyond pure physical sensation to get at feelings of authority and surrender, one needs to commit to a more psychological level of play. Many folks who enjoy pXe play with it as an ongoing lifestyle that involves carefully designed high protocol and domestic discipline guidelines performed regularly. This stuff might be appealing to Virgos and other planners, but less so for folks who prefer their kink spontaneous and serendipitous.

Which is not to say that S/m is always freewheeling or cavalier. Many practitioners of these kinks are extremely serious about them, and for some, being a sadist or masochist is as core to their identity as a fetish: an intense and hardwired sexual orientation. Some of us only experience our full and fully satisfying sexual selfhood through the receiving, or giving, of pain.

In any case, as Gorvett, the BBC science writer, beautifully phrases it, our choice to engage in the hedonic reversal that is non-damaging or fun pain is "a uniquely human indulgence." To prove this point, she cites a study that showed how a certain painkiller seems to dull both pain and pleasure for its users—"an indicator," she writes, that pain and pleasure operate "on shared biological pathways," and have therefore probably "always been intertwined" in our biological experience.

SADISM AND MASOCHISM, AND THE PERVERTS WHO GAVE THOSE CONCEPTS THEIR NAMES

A couple of things to note right up front as we discuss S/m. As a term, it comes from the early days of psychology in the late 1800s. (The more inclusive term "BDSM," which "ropes" in bondage, discipline, and dominance and submission, only dates back to the early days of the Internet in the 1990s.) One can write or speak the term S/m any way one wants. Some people have very strong feelings about capitalization and combination (or lack thereof) within the term "S/m," as those elements imply certain things about the parity (or lack thereof) of those engaging in this kind of play. In any configuration, however, the acronym stands for sadism and masochism, and the two always go together: in order for a sadist to be sexually fulfilled, they need a masochist, and vice versa, which is why the conjoined term "sadomasochism" exists. (It was introduced by none other than Freud in 1889.) A sadist is someone who enjoys delivering (and witnessing) pain, and a masochist is someone who enjoys receiving pain.

Sadists are often conflated with "tops": both sadists and tops are in the physical position of delivering pain, and they're also in the psychological position of wielding the power associated with delivering that pain. Masochists, meanwhile, are often conflated with "bottoms"—the receiving or passive participants. (These terms can be confusing since in the gay male community, the terms "top" and "bottom" refer to whose orifices are being penetrated during sex, not whether someone enjoys giving or receiving pain or if they're involved in BDSM at all.)

There's also some muddy overlap with notions of dominance and submission. Commonly, Dominant, D-types, Doms, or Dommes (those Dominating capitalizations are optional)—the ones who exert power and control—are thought of as sadists and tops. Submissives, subs, or s-types—the ones who relinquish power and control—are thought of as masochists and bottoms. But these parallels aren't always true: there are D-types without a sadistic bone in their bodies, and there are s-types who don't like pain. There are also s-types who prefer to play only as tops, in the role of a "service top": for example, acting as a good butler or handmaiden by providing a relaxing whipping or spanking to their D-type. And one can certainly find sadists who love to be on the receiving end of a gentle massage from time to time, making them, in that moment, a sadistic Dominant bottom.

Some people use all these terms interchangeably, and others think of them as distinct and are very particular about how they use them as identifying markers. Proceed into this heated and ongoing debate at your own risk! One common (although, again, highly debated) distinction is that sadism and masochism are about *arousal through giving or getting pain*; topping and bottoming are often more centered around *any type of physical sensation*, pain-related or otherwise, and simply refer to who is giving and who is receiving; and dominance and submission are about a *psychological power dynamic*. (More on this later in this chapter.)

To complicate matters even further, while the terms "sadism" and "masochism" came into usage specifically to describe the desires of sexual deviants, at this point in our culture both are thrown around rather freely to describe criminal behavior and acts of cruelty that have nothing to do with erotic arousal or joyful activities between consenting adults. For example, a child who tortures animals, a guard who attacks prisoners, and a soldier who abuses civilians are all likely to be called "sadistic," but these are not consensual acts and usually there's no eroticism involved.

Likewise, people call themselves "masochists" for working long hours at the office or eating food they don't enjoy or doing other activities that are about neither pain nor sex. I found a wholly un-helpful article by Lissa Rankin, a physician and author of self-help best-sellers who, after briefly acknowledging that a "sexual masochist is someone who likes pain as part of sexual activity, which can be a healthy and empowering kink," goes on to say that there are "also less healthy types of [psychological] masochism that manifest in people's personal and professional lives." She then gives as examples berating oneself for gaining weight or spending too much time trying to save the planet(!). Dr. Rankin, let's not call those things sadism, then. Let's not use the term "sadist" for environmental activists or people who are occasionally hard on themselves. Let's come up with other, more accurate terms!

With influential voices like Rankin's using these kinky terms so loosely, it can be tricky to differentiate when people are using them to talk about true and consensual S/m and when they're exagger-ating, being metaphorical—or referring to problematic issues such as domestic abuse or sociopathy. Ugh. So let me be exceedingly clear: in this book, I'm talking solely about *kinky, erotic* sadism and *kinky, erotic* masochism, as performed by responsible and self-aware perverts committed to consensual play.

An example: I had a sadist friend who once told me, "There's just nothing I love more than beating the shit out of my partner." In the context of a vanilla conversation, this would be alarming: one should obviously never harm their partner in any way. But my friend is a person who is morally opposed to inflicting violence on someone else without their consent; he is also an anti-racist activist, a feminist, a trans man, a former sex worker, and generally a really woke dude. The kind of "beating up" he was talking about was exclusively the fun, raunchy kind where the other person is happily pleading for more.

The terms "sadist" and "masochist" were both coined by the German psychiatrist Richard von Kraft-Ebbing in 1888 to describe sexual desires and behaviors—i.e., kink, or, as he put it, sexual "psychopathologies." As an early pioneer in the field of psychology and sexology, Kraft-Ebbing was working to demystify human sexuality in all its forms and advocate for better and more productive treatments for people who had been diagnosed as insane. Kraft-Ebbing was a colleague of Freud's and an influence on Jung, his scholarly work was respected in its day, and among other relatively progressive (for the time) views, he opposed the German criminalization of homosexuality.

But his naming of sadism and masochism is fraught. Kraft-Ebbing derived these terms from the names of real, historic figures whose sexual escapades are very hard for us to gauge as far as the level of consent involved. Far from clearing things up, the lives and works of these figures only further complicate what we think we know about sadism and masochism.

"Sadism" is a reference to the eighteenth-century French politician, aristocrat, philosopher, and writer Marquis de Sade. Because of the time and circumstances in which he lived—and the fact that his libertine, obscene works of erotic literary fiction were lost and/or banned for a good century after they were written—it is nearly impossible to judge whether the marquis was a bold hero of sexual deviancy or a violent criminal suffering from severe mental illness. It's all further muddled by the fact that Sade was a nobleman who lived through the tumult of the French Revolution, so it's unclear as to whether the imprisonment that he endured was for sexual misconduct or more political reasons. Either way, he spent the last three decades of his life in and out of prisons and insane asylums during years of enormous political upheaval, and may or may not have still been in prison when the Bastille was stormed in 1789. (Some aspects of his life in prison were far from grueling, though: he dined on gourmet foods and kept an extensive library of his favorite books.) Many of the details of his story are lost to time, his incarceration, and the revolution. Even his notorious S/m dungeon was looted.

While Sade has been revered by artists and rebels for the past century or so, his legacy is problematic. In his notorious novels, some of which were written while he was imprisoned, the scenes he describes are hard to stomach—much less justify—even for a seasoned BDSMer. He describes repeated acts of torture, abduction, coercion, and violence. Among the brutalities depicted are the rape of seven-year-old children and grisly ritualized murder—and because of the context of his era and his questionable sanity, it is impossible to know if his aim was to shock and arouse his readers or justify his own turn-ons and actions. The very outré quality of his works, though, has cemented their cult status. But although Sade's writings were enormously influential on literary figures who came after him, they are not exactly a good read: they sound like the florid, obsessive work of someone who is mentally delusional, which they most likely were.

While his extant works—including the novels *120 Days of Sodom* and *Justine*—are works of fiction, by all accounts Sade may have been criminally abusive in real life: he was involved in scandal after scandal, some of which involved harassing or beating sex workers. While some of his fans argue that Sade was merely trying to be shocking in his writing as a bid for celebrity or as a philosophical act, it's pretty clear that he did some atrocious—and definitely nonconsensual—things. In one of the most disturbing biographical stories that's been passed down through history, in 1774, Sade moved to a chateau with his family, taking along five teenaged servant girls whom he then locked in the dungeons and forced to act out elaborate sexual rituals and orgies that he designed and directed. (By some accounts, Sade's wife helped him evade subsequent prosecution by bribing the girls' families.)

But Sade continues to loom large as a symbol of hedonism and artistry. At least one line of his descendants has unearthed (literally, from a bricked-in wall) personal letters that allow them to think of their infamous ancestor as "a decent human being" who wrote sweet-natured missives to his wife and children, according to an interview with one of those descendants, Hugues de Sade, in a 2015 article for *Smithsonian Magazine* by Tony Perrottet.

Was Sade a "literary genius" and "martyr for freedom," as Perrottet puts it, or a disturbed and toxic man who wielded his power and privilege over others to satisfy his own twisted whims? Or both? And perhaps more to the point, why do modern-day sexual libertines continue to view him as a folk hero?

That's a discussion for another time, but I will give Sade this: almost everything you read about here in this book—watersports, incest role plays, whippings, total power exchange—were described in detail in his works over two hundred years ago. This could either mean he was ahead of his time, perversion-wise, or that this stuff has always been part of the underground culture of human society. Either way, when he chose to write about it, Sade left no kinky stone unturned, and his sexual imagination was seemingly limitless.

While Kraft-Ebbing alluded to a historic figure for the term "sadism," he chose to honor—or condemn—one of his contemporaries, Leopold von Sacher-Masoch, with the term "masochism." (Confession: when I was younger, the name "Sacher-Masoch" sounded so much like the term "sadomasochism" to my ears that I thought both terms came from Herr Leopold's name and didn't know the marquis had anything to do with it.) In 1870, at the same time that Kraft-Ebbing was beginning to publish (and continually revise and expand) his groundbreaking scholarly work *Psychopathia Sexualis*, Sacher-Masoch—who, like Sade, enjoyed a privileged background—published a novella called *Venus in Furs*, which was, like Sade's novels, at once innovative, philosophical, and extremely filthy. This short work describes a D/s heterosexual relationship in which the protagonist, Severin, has a distinct fur coat fetish and a desire to be brutally beaten and humiliated by his lover Wanda, whom he trains (see the section on "topping from the bottom" later in this chapter!) to treat him in this way. Through satisfying this desire, he is able to heal from childhood trauma and feel whole.

As in Sade's novels, the porn of *Venus in Furs* is theoretically in service (ha ha) of larger political arguments. In a 2010 essay, academic Sean K. Kelly writes, "The sex of [Sacher-Masoch's] plots is one that the author himself understood as serving the dual function of exploring the possibilities of human freedom and critiquing the political imagination of his own age." But in other ways, the novels by these two writers are quite different: *Venus in Furs* is a far more measured, thoughtful, and literary work than *100 Days of Sodom*. One scholar calls Sacher-Masoch's novel a "page-turner," whereas most agree that it's hard to get through even one page of Sade. The renowned literary theorist Gilles Deleuze compared the talents of the two thusly: "Of Masoch it can be said, as it cannot be of Sade, that no one has ever been so far with so little offense to decency. This leads us to another aspect of Masoch's art: he is a master of the atmospheric novel and the art of suggestion." Bonus: Sacher-Masoch's work is also more likely to be a truly arousing read. But as with Sade, Sacher-Masoch's literary output was probably more autobiographical than not: after this death, his private secretary wrote a biography in which he outed his former employer as a real-life submissive with a fur fetish, and his ex wrote a tell-all complaining of what she endured in their marriage.

In 2021, a graphic—as in comic book–style—biography of Sacher-Masoch was published called *Man in Furs*, written by literary biographer Catherine Sauvat, illustrated by Anne Simon, and translated from the French. I can't speak to the accuracy of the research behind it, but it makes interesting claims. It portrays the kinky relationship between Sacher-Masoch and his first wife, Angelika Aurora Rumelin, who had pursued him with the express purpose of fulfilling the fantasy he'd written about in *Venus in Furs*, but later claimed that she'd been forced into acting as his Domme. *Man in Furs* also depicts Sacher-Masoch as miserable about having his legacy reduced to Kraft-Ebbing's medical term, and also makes the case that Sacher-Masoch's second marriage was vanilla and therefore, you know, *better*, and shows him as mostly renouncing the fetishistic mind that fueled his early and most notable works. (The author also hints that after *Psychopathia Sexualis* became popular, Kraft-Ebbing was flooded with letters by fetishists desperate for someone to listen to their own deviant obsessions, which I imagine did happen, and I wish I could see those letters!)

Like many of us fetishists, Sacher-Masoch seemed to bend toward his predilection at a very early age. He wrote about a youthful infatuation with a cruel fur-wearing aunt, as well as a scene he witnessed at age twelve: his cousin wearing a fur-trimmed coat and carrying pistols on her belt to protect the family from the rebellions breaking out in their home city, Prague. (It does sound like a stylish look!) He also noted that a few years later, in Vienna, he saw a Rubens painting of the artist's pretty young wife, naked except for a fur robe that covers only her hips and vulva. (The painting is unofficially and slyly called "The Little Fur.") The image would stay with him for the rest of his life.

Sacher-Masoch got to act out his kinky desires with real-life partners, including his mistress, Baroness Fanny Pistor Bogdanoff, and Rumelin, his first wife, whom he met three years later. A photograph I found online of Fanny and Leopold shows her holding a whip while reclining on a chaise in a fur-trimmed cloak, with Leopold gazing adoringly at her from his position at her feet. It's fantastic. The baroness became the inspiration for Wanda in *Venus in Furs*, which is why it's very odd that she's completely left out of *Man in Furs*.

SACHER-MASOCH AND THE ORIGINS OF THE BDSM CONTRACT

Not only did Sacher-Masoch (involuntarily) lend his name for the term "masochist"; he also may have single-handedly invented the concept of a BDSM contract. In 1869, he and his lover Fanny wrote up and signed a kinky Dominant/submissive agreement. The text of the contract is available online through the website Humanities Underground; although I couldn't trace the text back to an original source and therefore can't totally vouch for its veracity, its language is cited in numerous biographical works. The contract states that Sacher-Masoch would act as Fanny's 24-7 servant throughout their planned trip to Italy, sitting behind her on the train and otherwise enacting servitude to her. She, meanwhile, agreed to wear furs as much as possible—especially while actively Domming him.

The contract is admirable: an early template of the good negotiation and enthusiastic consent that kink educators recommend using today. It laid out terms and parameters and made sure that everything described was feasible and realistic for functional daily life and a healthy relationship. The "slave," for instance, was given six hours a day to do his tasks; his "Mistress" was not allowed to pry into his correspondence or works in progress. Within that container, which allowed Sacher-Masoch to maintain his career and personal freedoms, he was to treat his sweetheart and Domme "as a precious gift," and Pistor was allowed to discipline him for missteps in any manner she chose.

Even more impressively, the contract holds that Leopold could not "lay claim" to Fanny's "love" or "any right to be her lover": in other words, she owed him no sexual favors or devotion during this time and was encouraged to fuck other people. (Admittedly, it's likely that this was mostly due to another fetish Leopold had: being cuckolded. He begged other women he was with to "betray" him by sleeping around, often demanding and personally arranging more action than the women wanted to take on.) Perhaps my favorite part of their contract is that the terms were for six months only: when the contract ended, the two agreed to return to their prior egalitarian relationship (described in the contract as "loving"). In fact, it's theorized that the couple mutually decided to end the contract even earlier, after what seems like a fabulous and sexy AF trip, and amicably went on their separate pervy ways.

To my mind, this contract is everything a good D/s contract should be: it's short and easy to follow, it limits its terms to a set time period, it allows for regular vanilla life to continue, and it includes elements that satisfy the proclivities of both parties. I love that it also accounts for protocol around the dissolution of the relationship dynamic. Recently, friends of mine in a 24-7 D/s relationship decided to split up, and the (multi-page!) part of their contract that outlined how they should go about this transition has been hugely comforting to them both during a very difficult and unsettling time. So, a word to the wise: as heartbreaking as it may be to contemplate, as you're thinking through the fun details of a kinky power exchange contract, make sure to also include plans for its end, just in case.

I'm so impressed and moved by Leopold and Fanny's contract that I propose in its honor an International Power Exchange Day for December 8, the day of its signing, and invite the whole BDSM community to use this holiday to discuss, renegotiate, or recommit to the D/s protocols in their own relationships.

WHAT WE DO WHEN WE DO S/M

But enough about the historical roots of the terms, fascinating as they are. What do sadists and masochists *do* to scratch their perverted itches?

As in all kink, the answer depends entirely on the individual sadist and individual masochist, as well as on their mood, health, and feelings on any given day. Some sadists want to gleefully inflict as much actual (but non-damaging) pain as possible (often known as "heavy play"); others are interested in lighter activities such as face-slapping. Some get their sexual kicks entirely from the S/m itself and couldn't care less about intercourse or other vanilla staples; others want impact play as part of or alongside penetrative sex. Some masochists are happiest covered in bruises so they can have evidence of just how much they can take; others don't want anyone to leave a mark. Some sadists might want to kick their masochist—boldly but carefully, having studied exactly which fleshy parts of the anatomy it's safest to kick—with steel-toed boots on one evening, then cuddle with them on the couch while watching a Disney movie the next evening. Some masochists might want to be called a disgusting worm one day, then praised as a faithful little doggie the next. Some revel in disciplinary actions such as spankings or chastity belts; still others might enjoy more psychological forms of power exchange such as being ignored or made to wait for one's supper, which is eaten off the floor. Some S/m folks want blood to be drawn, or for things to be otherwise extreme and brutal; others want to wade delicately into the adrenaline rush with some light spanking or hair-pulling.

Often, the kinky pleasures of S/m and power dynamics get entangled with fetish objects, physical sensation, and other delights. For example, one could really enjoy getting spanked as "funishment" in part of a long-term D/s dynamic or stand-alone S/m scene, but still not be a true spanko. While a non-fetishist who likes a good spanking will often want to be spanked in a specific way (bare-bottomed vs. clothed, with a hairbrush vs. a riding crop), they don't organize their whole fantasy life around those details. A spanko, on the other hand, is likely to have a set formula in mind for exactly how their ideal spanking session would go, and while they may be happy to have a less-than-perfect play session if that's all that's available, that little freak's internal heat-seeking fetish missile will not deviate from its course.

And while some masochists and sadists are similarly committed to their one core desire, others switch back and forth, enjoying both roles. I know quite a few masochists and submissives who spent years being on the receiving end of the whip or paddle or rope-rig, only to later decide they wanted to taste what their tops had been doing all that time. Some of those rope bottoms I know have gone on to be in-demand rope tops, dealing out as much pain and restriction as they once received with the wisdom that comes from being on the other side of the rigging.

Much like bi- or pansexuals, "switches," as they're sometimes known, are too often ignorantly dismissed as people who haven't made up their minds yet, or whose masochism or sadism aren't "real" because they like both. But that's absurd: just as many of us are attracted to more than one gender, many of us encompass more than one kink, and want to explore various facets of ourselves and our sexualities. And in any case, kinky folks ought to know better than to try to lock one another in boxes (I mean, unless that's what we're into). We of all people should celebrate switching and all manner of sexual adventuring; we ought to recognize that the path to erotic self-actualization can take many interesting twists and turns.

Just as with other kinds of BDSM, there is no right or wrong way to do sadomasochism, as long as all parties are practicing safe, consensual, risk-aware kink. If it feels like it edges up against the pain end of the pleasure-pain continuum and transports both giver and receiver to a trance-like state of bliss, arousal, or release, it counts as S/m. Follow your heart and your instincts and seek out inspiration and guidance from within the actual kink community, rather than trying to make your scene look like a porno or R-rated thriller: few movies (even "amateur" porn flicks!) offer realistic, safe, or particularly creative approaches.

With those caveats provided, here are some important aspects of sadism and masochism to know about:

> *Impact play.* Much of what gets called S/m can be grouped under the label of impact play, also known as rough body play. This simply means any kind of practice in which a person enacts some kind of sensory force—such as kicking, spanking, flogging, or punching—on someone else. Impact play can lead to sexual arousal—and often other kinds of more standard-issue sexual play such as making out or penetration—but people also find it satisfying in and of itself. Like a deep-tissue massage or time in a hot tub, impact play can be a gratifying sensual experience that provides relaxation, comfort, or release, reaching a place that one masochist beautifully calls "a primal victory."
>
> The stereotypical S/m scene features iconic impact play gear such as whips and restraints, but you can use whatever tools are readily accessible—including spoons, hairbrushes, belts, shoes, and your own fists and feet.
>
> If you want to engage in impact play and need a primer on safety and skills, there are plenty of good resources out there. (Some are listed in chapter 10 of this book.) In general, it's wise to focus impact on the better-cushioned parts of the body, such as the thighs and ass, and to avoid delicate areas such as the head and feet, as well as the major organs located in the torso.
>
> *Intense stimulation.* In their important 1993 book *Different Loving*, pioneering kink scholars Gloria and William Brame use the term "intense stimulation" to catalog the "countless forms of extreme sensory experimentation" and "pleasurable discomfort" explored by sadists and masochists. Under this heading they include a whole host of pervy delights, including hot wax and ashing, clamps and clothespins, piercing, electrical stimulation, and cock-and-ball torture (CBT) and other kinds of body

stretching and compression, which often use specialized weights, pulls, and rings. One might also include forced orgasm, in which the "victim" is ordered to masturbate, or held under a vibrator or other such device, until they beg for mercy.

Psychological torture. Sadism isn't limited to the realm of physical torment. Consensually fucking with someone's mind can be just as terrifying, and adding psychological play to your scene can really ramp up the response for all involved. Kidnapping scenes, role play, threats, humiliation, or even just a simple game of hunter-and-prey are often super juicy fun for sadists and masochists. Games and scenes have the added benefit of amplifying physical sensations, which are necessarily limited by safety rules and good sense. For example, a bout of knife play that is going to result in one tiny cut on the finger can be prolonged into a deliciously scary hour-long session by making it part of an elaborate, talked-out scene. Alternatively, such scenes can be entirely imagination-based, making them imminently portable and adaptable: you can say "I'm running after you, and you have no place to hide!" while lying snuggled up with your lover in bed.

Rough sex. Full disclosure: although I have decent pain tolerance (evidenced by three natural childbirths I thoroughly enjoyed), I'm not into pain sexually. I am, however, into dauntingly intense physical experience, which means, as I've mentioned elsewhere, I like it when sex feels like an *event*. Sometimes the "event" can come through role play or psychological games, but most often it's delivered via a big thick cock or cock simulator and some good hard pounding. I love feeling cleaned out, barely able to take how hard I'm getting fucked. Bonus points if there's hair-pulling or being tossed around like a rag doll: I love being forcibly flipped over to my lover's preferred next position mid-intercourse. And I have a real thing for being shoved up against a wall . . . though I've only rarely experienced it, because it's frankly often difficult to find a nice clear wall and someone of the right height and weight.

I don't think I'm alone in these desires. As Jean, a smart cookie interviewed in *Different Loving*, puts it, the trope that many women (and others) have rape fantasies is probably less accurate than their having "ravishment fantasies." (The notion of rape fantasies is discussed further in chapter 5.) My guess is it's pretty common to crave that feeling of being fully and wantonly possessed: my D-type partner says that one of the things he loves most is when the s-type person he's playing with grabs him frantically and rolls around with him like they can't get enough.

THE CONTROVERSY AROUND "TOPPING FROM THE BOTTOM"

It's common for people in the BDSM community to look down on what is deemed "topping from the bottom." This is when a bottom, masochist, or submissive dictates what their top, sadist top, or Dominant does to them—"micromanaging the experience," in the words of sex educator Kenneth Play—and therefore does not really acquiesce control the way one expects the subjugated partner to do. A headline from a 2021 *Men's Health* article by Zachary Zane baldly states, "If you're topping from the bottom, you're doing BDSM wrong."

While these S/m gatekeepers are quick to qualify that bottoms should definitely speak up where their own safety is involved, they nevertheless insist that masochists and submissives are supposed to be the passive recipients of their experience. They see "topping from the bottom" as a sign that the masochist doesn't trust the sadist, or that the s-type isn't a "good sub."

But I think this is a supremely simplistic view. First of all, while power is certainly the gasoline that fuels much of kink, not all bottoms are into giving up their power: some are purely into the sensory experience, and they want to dictate the exact parameters of their own pain, which is understandable and ought to be respected.

And just as some might critique a type-A bottom for trying to take charge, one could also critique a top who is so insecure or unimaginative in their role that they can't collaborate with a bottom who is trying to redirect a scene for their own pleasure. It's a broad generalization to say that all masochists want absolutely no say in what happens to them: in fact, some might be much more able to enjoy themselves if they are at least somewhat in charge of what happens next.

And then there are those situations in which the bottom *has* to top: they may be in a relationship with a partner who does not share or fully grasp the kink, and directing the action is the only way that the bottom is going to find the experience they seek. In *Different Loving*, the authors interview a hetero couple in which a lifelong masochist with a penchant for cock-and-ball torture is married to a vanilla woman who says "the idea of hurting someone is not appealing, even when they want to be hurt." Nonetheless, the couple arrives at a place where the wife has become "willing to experiment," but points out that although she might be the one wielding the tweezers or whip, it's her husband who is the "leader." "He's the one who has taken us to this," she says, "and he knows far more about it than I do." In such relationships, "topping from the bottom" is appropriate, compassionate, and vital.

In the end, all kink is—or should be—a yummy game of pretend, and as we know from childhood, pretend games are only fun when everyone involved is willing to adapt and isn't taking things too seriously. The only things that ought to be taken seriously in S/m are safety and consent. The rest should be a wild, engaging ride.

Let's let some actual masochists and sadists have the final word here. In a 2019 article in the online queer culture magazine *Them*, author Alexander Cheves interviews a few different folks who identify as kinky, asking them to share what they are into and why. One sadist, Ava Adore, boasts of having gone from rough body play to increasingly "taboo and crazy" activities such as needle play and drowning, saying that "all have been elating, cathartic, and just downright fun. Having the space and relationships to explore my masochism is something I appreciate in spades." Another interviewee, John, says, "I'll never forget my first experience as a sadist," which took place at a gay dungeon. A stranger complimented his flogger and begged John to beat him, which, John says, "made his cock jump." Their flogging session was euphoric, with John paying close attention to his bottom's whimpering: as John put it, "It's beautiful to get lost in the experience, so I'm not sure how long it lasted." Afterward, John held his play partner's "shaking body" and says, "Knowing that I got to put someone into that headspace, into that level of submission—I was honored. [And] he told me during aftercare that he was honored, too. That's what it boils down to—mutual respect. You want to feel honored with the person you share that experience with, especially when you're the one who is hurting them."

CHAPTER 5

LET'S PLAY MASTER
AND SERVANT

On Dominance and Submission

The fantasy of the rape fantasy—power exchange
(and the importance of consent in sexual non-consent)—
a fetish for stability?—what it means to be
leather—"queer 1950s household."

As we've seen, much of kink revolves around notions of power. Who's in charge? Who is submitting to a beating or humiliation? Who is giving themself over to another for their enjoyment? And no matter how temporary, consensual, and playful these games are, the very idea that anyone might "play" with the very loaded thing that is power is highly fraught, as is the BDSM use of terms like "Master" and "slave."

And no wonder: we live in a culture that is both marked by current abuses of power and also still reeling from our history of enslavement, land seizing, and colonialism. People have been dealing with this stuff throughout human history: every enslaving culture, every pillaging of a village, every genocide or ethnic cleansing is an abuse of power writ massively large and horrific. On a more personal scale but just as common throughout our history—and very much with us in the present day—are instances of authority figures forging or demanding inappropriate relationships with their subordinates: parents cruelly punishing their children, professors sleeping with their students, police officers beating the people they arrest, bosses harassing their employees, prison wardens demanding favors from the inmates under their watch. Every #metoo story is about an abuse of power. I daresay everybody reading this book has been on one end or the other of the kind of nonconsensual abuses of power that we encounter in family dynamics, intimate relationships, and workplaces.

So why would anyone want to take that horrible reality and purposefully reenact it in their sex lives? My theory is that it's exactly *because* so many of us deal with abusive behavior in our regular lives that we choose to reinvent it within our erotic lives: there we can control the duration and outcome, and playing with power can be attached to pleasure and release. Kink lets us bend these toxic encounters into something healthy, cathartic—and even fantastic. Essayist Larissa Pham came to similar findings when she interviewed people about the appeal that reinventing our relationships around power holds in a 2016 piece for the culture magazine *Complex*. One person interviewed, Xan West, points out that "BDSM give us a framework for thinking about power." Another interviewee, identified as Lauren, says that kinky play "happens through a filter of careful consideration, respect, and agency that removes most of the poison of patriarchy."

THE FANTASY OF THE RAPE FANTASY

Let's jump right in with one of the most discomforting kinds of power play of all: that which centers around the idea of rape, commonly called a "rape fantasy." Note that here, and throughout this chapter and book, we are not talking about actual rape. Actual rape in any form—be it within the boundaries of an established relationship or by a stranger—is horrible, violating, and criminal. We are talking here about playing with the *idea* of rape—specifically, ideas around force, sex, and non-consent—within an enthusiastically consensual relationship.

This is, of course, inherently perplexing. How can one play a fully consensual game about an activity defined by lack of consent? Why would anyone want to play such a game?

And yet study after study has shown that somewhere between 31 percent and 57 percent of cis women harbor rape fantasies. The real numbers are probably higher, since many people are embarrassed to admit this, even in an anonymous scientific study. (It's important to note that almost all research into rape fantasies focuses on cis women. Also important to note is that, according to statistics from the National Sexual Violence Resource Center, one in five female-identified people report having been raped, compared to one in seventy-one men. So for the purposes of this discussion, we are talking about rape in the erotic fantasy lives of women, who are also the most likely to be actual victims of rape in this culture.)

In 2008, Joseph W. Critelli, a professor of psychology, and Jenny M. Bivona, a clinical social worker, published an article in the *Journal of Sex Research* in which they reviewed over thirty years of (mostly American) research to discuss the rape-fantasy question. In the introduction to the article they write, "erotic rape fantasies are paradoxical: they do not appear to make sense. Why would a person have an erotic and pleasurable fantasy about an event that, in real life, would be abhorrent and traumatic?" They list various theories that have been put forth over the years: that rape fantasies are a kind of masochist kink stemming from a desire for degradation or suffering; that rape fantasies stem from a biological impulse in which females (of various mammalian species) have to "surrender" to males as part of mating rituals; or that rape fantasies are a work-around response to a sex-negative culture, a way for women to indirectly express a desire for sex without being deemed a "slut." They also discuss Susan Brownmiller's Second Wave feminist theory that rape fantasies are a byproduct of a culture of toxic masculinity: that women default to this self-harming fantasy because of patriarchal conditioning. Critelli and Bivona dismiss all these theories in turn as "unlikely" or "deficient" in their capacity to fully explain the prevalence of rape fantasies. They found, rather, that rape fantasies most likely stem from an overall "openness to sexual experience" and fantasizing of all kinds, which they found goes hand in hand with high self-esteem and a generally sex-positive outlook.

I have long held my own amateur theory about rape fantasies, which is that they are not as much a fantasy about rape as they are a fantasy about being desired. And scientists agree: as Critelli and Bivona state in their paper, "The essential idea . . . is that the rape fantasy portrays the woman as so attractive, seductive, and desirable that the man loses control, breaking core expectations of civil decency in order to have her." I think of this as the *Gone with the Wind* theory: Rhett Butler's rape of Scarlett O'Hara is a romanticized expression of his passion and his "bad boy" persona, which is exactly what Scarlett finds attractive about him. (I will admit that, as a fourteen-year-old reader, I found that scene in that problematic novel *very* hot.) It may be more accurate to call such scenarios "masculine-assertiveness fantasies" or "overcome-by-lust fantasies" or, as the woman interviewed in *Different Loving* whom I quoted earlier put it, "ravishment fantasies."

I'm reminded of the viral 2008 Craigslist post entitled "just fucking fuck me already." The anonymous poster, who identified herself as a heterosexual cis woman, proposed that once a couple has established mutual attraction and interest—i.e., *consent*—the man should "please take charge." The post repeatedly instructs men to check in with women during a sexual encounter to gauge whether or not they are okay with what's happening and notes that the idea of wanting the man to take charge "applies to the bedroom only, and does not mean that she wants you to . . . treat her like less of a person." At the same time, the woman who posted the message—a self-proclaimed powerful "raging feminist bitch" in her everyday life—champions the idea that many women like to get fucked hard and rough, with hair pulling, spanking, and other exciting add-ons.

What this Craigslist poster was describing is not a rape fantasy, but it is a bold request for consensual, healthy expressions of assertive sexuality. As one homemaker put it on a call-on radio show about the novel *Fifty Shades of Grey*, "Moms"—and, we can assume, other people who spend their days invisibly mired in responsibility and mundane tasks—"want to be adored and ravaged," ideally in equal measure. Even in that notorious book, roundly despised within the BDSM community but superficially depicting a powerful man deep into his role as a Dominant, Christian Grey washes his lover's hair, pays her bills, and brings her meals.

But for a host of very good reasons, most of us don't feel comfortable fully expressing our adoration for others. We live in a culture where people of all genders worry about how much or little our desire is welcomed. And of all men, it is often those who are most sexually ethical—who would never rape anyone—who, when confronted with a request to act out such a fantasy, are the most afraid of doing anything that could be seen as inappropriate. So it makes sense to me that one end result of this necessary and wise cautiousness is the desire to *pretend* to throw all sexual restraint to the wind, to *role play* without propriety or decorum.

The crucial differentiator, of course, between the victim of an actual rape and the receiver of a rape role play is *agency*. Writer Noah Berlatsky talks about this in a 2013 article for *The Atlantic* about rape fantasies: he cites a woman identified as Johanna, who had been interviewed for Nancy Friday's groundbreaking 1973 book on women's sexual imaginations, *My Secret Garden*. Johanna, who had been raped, speaks in Friday's book about how her sexual fantasy life after her assault revolved around a recasting of that attack with her own pleasure at the center. As disconcerting as this is, Berlatsky points out that for rape-victim survivors like Johanna, their actual rape was outside of their control, but their fantasy life is entirely *in* their control. Even if that sense of agency sometimes comes with more guilt and ambivalence than empowerment or healing, being in control of the script changes the experience and can even provide a powerful corrective to the past trauma.

Perhaps most importantly and obviously, Critelli and Bovina point out that "erotic rape fantasies are not realistic depictions of actual rape." Psychologist Paul Joannides writes that many so-called rape fantasies involve being overtaken by someone the fantasizer finds attractive, and that moreover many rape fantasies do not involve fear, violence, disgust, rage, or active resistance (though some do, and that's okay, too!).

In any case, the main conclusion of the Critelli and Bovina study is that there ought to be more research about the whys and wherefores of rape fantasies, that this future research should explore the topic "across demographic characteristics such as age, ethnicity, and sexual orientation," and that it should also use "samples from cultures that are . . . more egalitarian than that of the United States." Hear hear. (There is a book published in 2018 by psychologist Justin Lehmiller called *Tell Me What You Want: The Science of Sexual Desire and How It Can Help You Improve Your Sex Life* for which he conducted a large survey of sexual fantasies, but that's still work by a cis white American man, so clearly there is more that could be done.)

No matter *why* some people want to play kinky games that involve pretend rape, the fact is they do. As long as everything is enthusiastically consensual and thoughtfully negotiated, playing out rape fantasies is healthy and normal. A woman interviewed for a 2018 *Vice* article on the subject told writer Jennifer Billock that she is a rape survivor who also chooses to role play rape with her partners, but that it's been a hard road to get there. She says, "I used BDSM and the playing-out of rape scenes as a way to try to take back my power. I hoped that willingly giving up control would help me feel liberated." She says the approach did not work for her and has caused further trauma. However, because it's important to her to be able to incorporate her deepest-held fantasies into a fulfilling and even healing sex life, she sees it as a process and has not given up.

Obviously, this can be intense stuff. A kink gathering that I attended offered "kidnappings." Before the event, registered attendees could fill out a form requesting their own kidnapping. They were asked to indicate the tone, timing, individuals involved, and other elements they did or did not want as part of their requested scene. These requests were then coordinated by an experienced attendee who hand-selected a team of community members to help carry out the plan. The kidnappings had become a well-known and beloved feature of the gathering. You might be waiting in line for lunch, talking to your friend, when you'd see a group of people dashing past in hot pursuit of their "victim," who would often be screaming in a mix of genuine fear and surprise and delight.

There's a term for this flavor of role play in kinky-land: consensual non-consent, also known as *CNC*. CNC includes rape role play, but it's broader than that: any time you devise a game in which you are *pretending* to not want something to happen that you and your partner(s) both know that you *do* want to have happen, it's CNC.

If I say, "Not tonight, honey, I have a headache," and then wink knowingly at my partner and wriggle up against them and whisper *Take me anyway!*, it's consensual non-consent.

Of course, CNC scenes are not always this cute and benign. I might fight my lover off with my fists while cursing a blue streak as they try to "take me." I might want them to tie me down and insult me while they "force" themself on me. In such role played scenes of consensual non-consent, the *idea* of rape is about more than just desire. It's also often about an air of entitlement, an element of brutality, and a sense of surprise. And even though rape fantasies are often more about seduction than violence, we should not dismiss the kinky folks among us who *do* crave fear, disgust, or active resistance.

CNC may work best as advanced-level kink, ideally executed by experienced practitioners or long-term partners who are experienced at the art of communication and negotiation. For obvious reasons (such as consent and past trauma), CNC can get complicated fast, and there are many ways it can go wrong. But when it goes right—aided by strong communication—it can be really exciting and powerful.

PXE (OTHERWISE KNOWN AS POWER EXCHANGE)

In chapter 3, I delineated what I called the four P's: four factors of kink that, if taken outside of a sexy consensual context, would be genuinely wrong or unhealthy. Let's discuss the fourth, *power*, in further depth.

As I've already mentioned, although lots of BDSMers playfully upend norms around authority and surrender, the psychology of power is serious stuff, and it's important to know where the boundaries are, because they are so easy to overstep. And overstepping can be very upsetting, especially for individuals who have to deal with *disempowering* situations on a daily basis. We are all impacted by real abuses of power small and large, and the more marginalized identities we hold, the more likely we are to be on the receiving end of these abuses. Black folks are more likely to experience it than white folks. Women more than men. People with disabilities more than nondisabled people. Children and the elderly more than working-age adults.

The poor more than the wealthy. But no matter who we are, we will likely be told to do something we don't want to do by someone who holds authority over us—a police officer, a medical professional, a supervisor, a landlord—over the course of any normal week.

It makes sense then that politically astute, ethical, justice-minded people can be uncomfortable mixing overt shows of power (and powerlessness) with sexual pleasure. We know first-hand the damage abuses of power can cause, and so we understand that we should treat our lovers and partners as equals, and that healthy relationships are built on mutual respect.

It is unthinkable, for example, in a vanilla context, to chain your partner to a bedpost and deny them their dinner because they didn't mop the floor just right. In real life, that's an abusive relationship, one that would warrant legal intervention and an order of protection. ("A pattern of behaviors used by one partner to maintain power and control over another partner in an intimate relationship" is the actual definition of domestic violence and should never be tolerated. Contact the National Domestic Violence Hotline at 1-800-799-7233 or TTY 1-800-787-3224, or text START to 88788 if you are seeking support in planning for your safety.)

But one way some of us kinky people cope with the misery-inducing abuses of power we encounter in our everyday lives is to reclaim it within the confines of a consensual sexual scenario. To people in a thoughtfully negotiated and playful D/s pXe (Dominant-submissive power exchange) dynamic—people who do this stuff only in the realm of the erotic, who make time for it in between walking the dog together and talking about their workdays—playing a game in which one of you is chained to the bedpost could be a super fun date night.

Power exchange relationships can look any way you want them to look, from TPE (total power exchange, aka 24-7), in which the dynamic provides an ongoing framework to your entire relationship, to more casual and episodic play sessions. The D-type can be a Mommy or Lord or a Master or a top or whatever pretend role they choose with their partner. And the submissive (or sub or s-type) can be a babygirl or a boi or a slave or a bottom when they choose to give over their control. What defines all good power exchange is not the labels or the roles you give yourself, or even what you do within those roles: good pXe happens when all players involved have thoroughly communicated their needs and fully consent to relinquishing or taking power. As Alesandra, the author of the blog *Dom Sub Living* puts it, in any power exchange relationship, "The goal should be for both partners to feel more fulfilled and taken care of" through the dynamic.

Both sides of the power exchange bear responsibility for the game, and both have to put in effort to make it succeed. It might seem to outsiders that it's all easy livin' for the D-type, having their grapes peeled for them while they luxuriate on a chaise lounge, but there is real work involved with being a good Dominant. You have to pay attention to what kind of experience your s-type wants, both physically and mentally; come up with (at least some of) the creative ideas for role plays, scenes, and toys; take action; and help hold boundaries. You have to access your ingenuity, as subs sometimes enjoy being pushed to their limits, and it's up to the D-type to figure out when enough is enough, or when a protocol is impractical or detrimental. You may get tennis elbow from administering repeated spankings. You may be asked to provide serious aftercare—holding and listening to your partner as they come down from a particularly intense submissive experience. The kind of psychological domination required for power exchange can be just as draining and demanding as submission. As one professional dominatrix put it, "It's easy to just fuck somebody. But to fuck with somebody's *head*, you really have to understand where they're coming from, and you have to build your own character, too. I worked for ten years to establish this persona."

And while erotic power exchange can be sexy, it doesn't necessarily revolve only around sex. Power exchange relationships are often forged through rules and protocols about who cooks meals and opens car doors (as well as who gives hot-oil massages and gets penetrated on demand). Lest you think that it must be the s-type who does such things, you'd be wrong: it can be just as appropriate for a D-type to insist on opening doors and cooking meals out of a sense of authority or protection as it is for an s-type to do so out of a sense of obedience or devotion. A D-type can assert authority by doing all the manual labor or demanding that they get pegged.

Any and all kinds of service can be ways of showing another person you care about them and are paying attention to their needs, and with just a little imagination, can be encoded as either dominance *or* submission. My Daddy Dom, for example, is not into S/m: in fact, he loves cuddling, and I "spoil" him with gentle, loving physical affection as an act of my submissive service.

Likewise, there are "service Doms" and subs who "top from the bottom," as well as many other folks who perform styles of power exchange that defy stereotypes. There are people who try an occasional pXe protocol with a casual play partner just for fun. There are couples who dabble in power exchange on special occasions, and others who aim to maintain a hardcore "24-7 Master/slave TPE high protocol relationship"—though even the most ardent practitioners of this lifestyle will admit that they can't and don't keep it up all the time. As sex writer and submissive Kayla Lords points out, "power exchange is about giving up or receiving control and power. If that happens for five minutes once every six months, it's just as valid as [living] a micromanaged M/s dynamic [where you] can't go to the bathroom without permission. Even 24-7 power exchange isn't always 24-7. Try telling your vanilla boss you can't go to that afternoon meeting without your Dominant's permission. That's not how real life works, and we all know it."

And despite what some kinky gatekeepers might say, no kind of pXe is "bad" unless *the people in the relationship* feel that it's not going the way they want it to go. That said, as the mainstream culture has been growing more aware of systemic injustice, so too has the kink community. While individuals and organizations within BDSM still use historically loaded, problematic terms like "Master" and "slave" within pXe contexts, the community is also seeing more discourse around the ethics and impact of such usage when employed outside the confines of a private relationship.

My dear friend Sinclair Sexsmith, a white BDSM educator and writer who used to describe their relationship with their primary partner and spouse as Master/slave (M/s) but later described themself as "living in a 24-7 authority exchange dynamic that is rooted in the lineage of leather queers," has done a lot of thinking about this issue. This thinking was necessitated in part because in 2020 they and their partner, rife (Sinclair's s-type), won the International Master/slave title, a prestigious award in the leather community that has been around since 1990. Back in 2016, Sexsmith had written a piece for *Autostraddle* in which they'd delineated their thinking at the time on the philosophical difference between D/s and M/s dynamics. "The key difference, I came to understand through reading [the M/s memoir and guidebook] *Slavecraft*," Sexsmith wrote, "is that the erotics played with between Dominants and submissives are because the Dominant's and the submissive's desires align," whereas a "slave's" core desire is to be told what to do, and to obey. Sexsmith went on to note that while they "hesitate to use the words master and slave, since the history of slavery in the US is predominantly specific to Black folks," they recognize that the word "master" can also denote an earned accolade, as through the *mastery* of a craft.

Fast-forward four years to 2020: When Sexsmith and rife won the Master/slave title, they used that platform to foster important conversations about the terms—and declared that they would no longer use them in public settings. Their past usage of those terms, Sexsmith wrote on their blog *Sugarbutch Chronicles*, had been a kind of "deluded bliss" that ignored the material reality of the oppression that many people in the kink scene experience. As Sexsmith puts it, by doing away with the public usage of "Master" and "slave" as terms, "no one is asking that the practices of our life-long love in power exchange change." Rather, it is simply that "members of our Community . . . are telling us that the use of A WORD is harming them." It should be a no-brainer to be caring enough to cease that use within community settings: doing so is our "duty," says Sexsmith.

After all, at its root, power exchange is a collaboration, a kink that works best when everyone involved is highly attuned to one another and their needs. In fact, you could say that the whole point of pXe is to get in better synch, whether that be with the entire community or with your own lovers.

Power exchange can also bring a sly, exciting tint to tasks that might otherwise feel not so fun. If I make a fancy dinner for my partner and it turns out she has to stay late at work, that might really piss me off. But if she's my D-type and she texts me that I better keep dinner ready for her and dress up in something flimsy to greet her at the door when she gets home, the whole disappointing night has suddenly turned into charged, flirty fun for both of us. Deciding that you are "serving" your partner—as either a D- or s-type—can transform ironing, trips to the market, workouts, home repairs, and other duties into pleasurable, titillating events. Other positive side effects of power exchange can include stress relief, a way of quieting the mind, spiritual or psychological insights into one's past trauma or baggage, the release of endorphins from an intense pleasure/ pain experience, a sense of validation and purpose, and reducing relationship static through clearer roles and boundaries.

Collars—and chastity belts, and other worn markers of D/s—may look cool and signal our relationship status to others in the know, but first and foremost they are validating for the wearer, serving as a physical reminder of the benefits of being an s-type. The removal or giving back of a collar can likewise denote a relationship's end. One of the most recognizable symbols of BDSM, collars come in "play" and "day" varieties, and within the power exchange community, they have long-standing and real meaning. "Play" collars can be more showy, and might even be used functionally if they have an O- or D-ring that can be attached to a leash or grabbed by one's Dominant. "Day" collars tend to be more subtle, and are often held in the same regard as a wedding ring: a symbol of commitment to one's D-type. Because many of us don't want to ever remove our collars, a day collar could be a dainty, office-appropriate necklace with a padlock or key motif (most jewelry brands carry such designs, even Tiffany!) or a handcuff-like bracelet that locks on, à la the iconic Cartier LOVE design, which comes with a tiny screwdriver. Others get a tattoo somewhere on their body that denotes their "owned" status. No matter what kind of collar it is or how or where it's worn, it is a potent talisman. Every time I look down at my sterling brace- let with the padlock charm, I am reminded that someone I love has promised to take care of me, and that I have promised to take care of him in return, in ways that are both vanilla and kinky.

But a collar is, in the end, just a symbol. The D/s relationship is forged through consistent behaviors, rituals, and attitudes, not a piece of jewelry.

One of the more complex kinds of pXe can be found around money, that most fraught topic. In domestic violence situations, money can be used as a form of control, and even in a non-abusive context, money is one of the most common sources of tension within relationships. All of which is probably also why some power exchange players include negotiated financial rules in their relationship protocols as a way of edging right up to that most discomforting subject. For example, a D/s relationship might involve an old-fashioned allowance, given to the s-type as a sign of pampering and taken away if their duties have not been fulfilled. Or the D-type might turn household bookkeeping duties over to the s-type as a sign of trust and a bestowing of responsibility.

Others go even further. Hayley Jade, the author of a 2017 article on the kink financial domination for *Vice* Canada, writes that "the whole basis of financial domination is power exchange. It's not about [the Dominant, usually a woman] 'being superior,' it's about [the sub, usually a man] choosing to give up their power to [someone] they see fit to hold it." Or as Pro Domme (paid Dominant or dominatrix) Cherry Torn says, "Financial domination is the ultimate exchange of power. It's what men are raised to do in their lives: to work really hard and make money. So men fetishize their wallets in a way that is incomparable" to anything else.

To indulge a kink for financial domination, or findom, some people hire a professional. In this consensual client-professional relationship, which plays with taboos around capitalism, wealth, indulgence, and psychological control, the client (sometimes called a "cash slave") is not being swindled. He—because he is almost always a he—is intentionally seeking out a person who will put real effort, time, and skill into fulfilling a sexual fantasy that involves taking his money, and thereby his power. (Mistress Marley, a Black sex worker, educator, and entrepreneur who started the Black Domme Sorority, sees her findom work with white subs as an act of reparation.) In findom, as in other kinds of pXe, "the relinquishment of power itself triggers a sexual release," as a *Vice* video on cash slaves puts it—although the release need not always be sexual, and the *seizing* of that power by the D-type often can trigger release as well. The cash slave is *choosing* to be in this dynamic and still has a say in how much money and power he's giving over; the D-type has a responsibility to pay attention and heed those boundaries.

Which brings us to a crucial point. One way to tell whether you're in an abusive, unsafe relationship or a consensual, kinky relationship is to consider an oft-cited adage about dominance and submission: in order to surrender your power, you have to *have* some to begin with, and you have to be able to *take it back* at any moment and for any reason. Otherwise there is no actual "exchange": there is just power being wielded in the all-too-common toxic ways.

I came across some insightful reflections on total power exchange and its real-life parallel, actual slavery, by Russell J. Stamburgh, a sex therapist who has studied kink—and consent—for over forty years. Stamburgh writes on his blog, "Modern kink has come to recognize that the desire for submission and dominance is a kind of figure/ground illusion. The political requirements of consent, stemming as they do from inherent democratic equality, mean that even in 24-7 sexual slavery, Master and slave begin negotiation from a position of equivalent agency." An individual forced into actual slavery, by contrast, has "no power, no personhood, and no essential value whatsoever." Actual enslaving, he writes, was "mundane, not exotic; utilitarian, not romantic." An enthusiastically consensual and negotiated "Master/slave" relationship, no matter how 24-7 or hardcore, is foundationally and diametrically opposed to real-world enslavement.

We can find ways to be mindful about this as part of our pXe games. When I enact a submissive role with a partner, I am doing so to upend the agency I enjoy every day. At various points and with various partners, I have taken on s-type roles of different flavors. I'm sure this would confuse many of my vanilla friends and family, since in my normal, nonerotic life, I'm known for having a take-no-shit, highly opinionated, and strong personality. This, of course, is exactly why I've chosen to step into the sub role in my erotic life: because it's *so damn different* than how I otherwise enact my identity. As an extreme cash slave named Stevo put it in that *Vice* findom video, "I was in management my whole career. I told other people what to do all day. I'm not submissive at all in the outside world"—and, for him, that's why it's so hot to have a stripper or Domme take his money. Your mileage may vary: some people prefer to be intimidating both

LET'S PLAY MASTER AND SERVANT | 111

on the jobsite and in the bedroom, and some folks who are obsequious people-pleasers out in the world stay so with their lovers.

I, however, am most happy when I'm a particular kind of submissive in a long-term relationship with someone who is choosing to be the flavor of D-type that works for me. I like to be of service, do special tasks, and make myself sexually available to my Dom; currently, this is my husband (although this man was my Dom for a few years when I was previously married to someone else, too). I like to fix his cocktails. I like him to praise me and call me a good girl. I like him to make decisions about what I should wear or where we should eat out. I like him to hold me down and toss me around during sex. In all these cases, he is doing these things because I want him to, and because he wants to, and because we've discussed and processed it all together ahead of time.

People unfamiliar with the concept of power exchange might hold preconceived notions of how my D/s relationship looks in action—notions that would quickly evaporate if you saw us together on a typical day. Because here are some things my Dom does: Folds my laundry. Makes sure I get to my professional engagements on time. Chops the veggies for dinner. Attends my lectures on feminist theory and discusses them with me afterward. Packs my toiletries for my work trip. Boxes up the things I need to mail out. Yesterday he called himself my "valet." He "serves" me as much as I "serve" him, in ways that work for both of us and the relationship we've established.

Like many other s-types I've talked to, I enjoy the break from "decision fatigue" that comes when this person I love and trust tells me what to order for dinner or how long to suck his cock. I make decisions, large and small, all day long. It can be a huge relief to consensually and temporarily surrender to someone else's will. And when we play it out as D/s power exchange, it feels subversive and sexy, a fun game, rather than a defaulting to traditional gender norms or typical marriage dynamics.

"A FETISH FOR STABILITY"

At a kink workshop I once attended with my D-type, taught by the inimitable Sinclair Sexsmith and their s-type, the attendees were talking about power exchange and what draws us to it. One person in the circle said, "I grew up with a lot of disruption in my life, so I think the reason I'm into the D/s dynamic is because I have a stability fetish."

Minds *blown*. Nearly everyone in the circle gasped and nodded. Yes! Us too!

My partner and I talked about it afterward. I grew up with a perpetually angry mother; my parents fought a lot, loudly; there was stress about money and job security; it always felt, to us kids, like we were walking on eggshells. My D-type lost one parent to suicide; the other was an alcoholic. We are both the oldest sibling in our families, and we both stepped into adult responsibilities while still kids. We both grew up yearning for a kind of stability we had seldom experienced. In other words, we have lived our lives feeling anxious, vigilant. No wonder we are drawn to a power exchange dynamic that defines when we can expect to have duties—and when we can relax and be taken care of. Nothing gives us more pleasure than being able to count on simple pXe protocols that help us both feel pampered and secure.

The "stability fetish" that leads to a desire for a D/s relationship can come from other sources, too. The romantic relationships most of us see modeled in our families and communities often involve a lot of unhealthy patterns, such as expecting that your partner can read your mind and know exactly what you want, or that taking out life stress on your partner is something you're entitled to do. We also see nonconsensual game playing and testing: *if you really loved me, you would stop watching your favorite TV show right now*. Or *if you think I'm attractive, then why don't you buy me things?* Or *you seem to be in a bad mood, so rather than ask you what kind of support you most need right now, I'm just going to avoid you for a while*. In the face of such counterproductive relationship expectations and assumptions, it can be a huge relief to have decided, together, ahead of time, how you want to be praised, criticized, "disciplined" for spending too long gaming, or "rewarded" after a big presentation at work.

Let's face it: even outside our intimate relationships, we live in a world full of uncertainty and instability. Climate change. Viruses. The shrinking middle class. Conspiracy theories. Cancer. The rapid-fire pace and constant onslaught of social media. Decision fatigue. Who *wouldn't* want to escape from all of that into a temporary world where all the rules of engagement are perfectly and mutually laid out?

LEATHER: BEYOND THE TEXTILE

One of the most fascinating ways kinky people have satisfied their power kinks and stability fetishes is through leather. And when I say leather, I don't mean folks who just like putting on a pair of chaps or caressing a worn-in sofa. I mean leather as in leather culture and also leather families, the intricately and resolutely hierarchical subculture within a subculture.

Leather is a vital part of kink history and a full-fledged culture of its own, involving regimented groups (called families), rituals, uniforms, contests, venues, art, and more: in historian Stephen K. Stein's words, leather is a "distinct subcultural identity" that, like all subcultures, has codified powerful identity markers such as ways of dressing, cruising for partners, and other ways of being that "create a tribal identity."

As Stein says, the term "leather" is a "multivalent symbol," "both overly broad and too limited," encompassing gay and lesbian sadists and masochists, fetishists who crave the textile, people who find security and pleasure within a specific leather tribe, and those who choose to dress in the iconic leather style: a blend of military, motorcyclist, and cowboy. While many of its members do like wearing motorcycle jackets, biker hats, chaps, combat boots, and other leatherwear, that's only one small part of what makes someone leather, and some leatherfolk do not engage in BDSM sex.

I'm not leather myself, so I once again turned to leather titleholder Sinclair Sexsmith to share their own understandings. Sexsmith told me, "People in a leather family might be involved sexually, romantically, or in a power dynamic, or they might not—just depends on the structures that have been set up. The term 'leather household' indicates a literal place, a house that is run with leather values, by a leather family, often with hierarchy and roles within the family. So the leather house might be a leather family that lives all in the same house, and a leather family might live in multiple houses." Either way, leather families and houses usually have a very intentional hierarchy laid out, so that "people know who they are in charge of and who is in charge of them, who they report to."

Leather culture dates back to at least WWII. It stands to reason that when large numbers of men are drafted, military ranks will inevitably include large numbers of *gay* men. One can imagine that some gay men of the 1940s found appeal in certain aspects of military life, including the homoerotic camaraderie, the handsome uniforms, and—for those into that sort of thing—the strict protocols and rituals defined by clear understandings around authority and obedience. Men's-only spaces also might have made acting on one's desires a bit more possible.

At least, this is how it worked for the visual artist Touko Laaksonen, who became known as Tom of Finland. As Valentine Hooven's official biography on the Tom of Finland Foundation website puts it, "When Stalin attacked Finland and Tom was wearing a lieutenant's uniform, he found nirvana in the blackouts of World War II. At last, in the streets of the pitch-black city, he began to have the sex he had dreamed of with the uniformed men he lusted after, especially once the German soldiers had arrived in their irresistible jackboots." As Tom of Finland, he created the sexy illustrations that celebrated what has become the iconic leather Daddy look: a heavily-muscled, strong-jawed, broad-shouldered, mustachioed, leather-clad, and well-hung macho man in Aviator sunglasses. These illustrations set into motion the iconic look and body type that exist to this day. Durk Dehner, director of the Tom of Finland Foundation, states that "Tom's leatherman image has manifested itself as a style of clothes, build, attitude and lifestyle," a look that is familiar to most Americans via mainstream and mustachioed rock stars such as Freddie Mercury from Queen, "the sailor guy" (Paul Rutherford) from Frankie Goes to Hollywood, and "the leather guy" (Glenn Hughes) from the Village People.

These post-war years were also when the aesthetics and badassery of military life gave rise to the working-class biker and greaser subcultures, which emerged as edgy embodiments of all things hyper-masculine. Predominantly from Italian American, Chicano, or Latino working-class backgrounds, bikers and greasers preserved the adherence to protocol and ritual, as well as the close-knit tribal nature of military service, but added an anti-authority attitude in response to being marginalized. The cinematic James Dean/Marlon Brando version—a uniform of tight jeans and leather jackets—lit up the world's sexual imagination in the 1950s, and in the early 1960s, Kenneth Anger began making his experimental film fetish master-pieces, such as *Scorpio Rising*, which celebrated queer love, occult ritual, and biker boys.

This is around the same time when Tom of Finland's explicit versions of those hunks began appearing in international "physique" magazines. According to queer culture historians such as activist Jesse Monteagudo, physique magazines were obstensibly an outlet for the burgeoning midcentury bodybuilding community, but found their true audience with closeted gay men starved for porn. As Steve Hogan and Lee Hudson's 1998 book *Completely Queer: The Gay and Lesbian Encyclopedia* states, "By the end of the 1950s, physique mag-azines were arguably the most openly—and self-affirmingly—gay male publications available to a wide American audience." Tom of Finland biographer Hooven writes, "For much of the fifties, those little physique magazines were not just an aspect of gay culture; they virtually *were* gay culture." And according to Stephen K. Stein, that's also when gay motorcycle clubs began to spring up around the US and other countries, many remaining robust well into the 1970s: the California Motor Club's Carnival gathering in 1977 brought together ten thousand leather-clad men. Jack Fritscher wrote of the Carnival, "The mix of men and drugs and open-mindedness was so rich that a man's life could be changed, revolutionized and transmorphed in a moment."

These underground leather bars catered to gay men and other sexual outliers: Satyrs, a gay motorcycle club, opened in LA in 1954, and similar spots were breaking ground in all the usual-suspect locales: New York, San Francisco, Sydney, Amsterdam. In 1964, *Life* magazine did an unsurprisingly narrow-minded article on the burgeoning leather bar culture. The article's focus on the perfectly named Tool Box bar in San Francisco had the unintentional effect of pulling a nation of starry-eyed gay boys to the city. In 2010, an ABC news piece on the historic article reported, "Many gays across the country saw the photo [of the leather bar] as an invitation to move to San Francisco." Artist Mike Cafee, who was featured in the *Life* photos taken at the Tool Box, noted that the piece also made the important point that "not all gays are effeminate" and that "in San Francisco, they'll pretty much let you be yourself."

In Leatherpedia, the nonprofit crowd-sourced wiki for the global leather community, an article on leather culture makes a similar point. It talks about how leather "also reflected some men's disaffection" with other kinds of gay male culture focused on things like opera, musical theater, and campiness. The macho approach and style of leather is probably why, the article says, the gay male leather community "became the practical and symbolic location for gay men's open exploration of kink and S&M" (as it was known back then, before the burgeoning Internet made "BDSM" the preferred term in the 1990s). As Sexsmith told me, "Leather is less of a club and more of a subculture, which has many differences, many aspects of community, education, volunteering, organizing, fundraising, play, celebrations, and more."

What it meant to "be leather" got codified in 1972, when gay activist (and former air force sergeant) Larry Townsend self-published *The Leatherman's Handbook*, which became an instant classic in the underground scene. Though it is mostly made up of deliciously smarmy first-person accounts of the early leather bar scene, queer historian and writer Jack Fritscher calls Townsend's work a "combination etiquette book and *Boy Scout Handbook*" for the gay S&M crowd. (Fritscher himself was Robert Mapplethorpe's lover, a follower of Satanism, and worked for the early gay publication *Drummer* before creating his own, raunchier zine, *Man2Man*—both of which, in his own words, were meant to "be read with one hand"; he also taught college.)

Sexsmith notes that while the leather subculture is most heavily associated with "authority exchange of various types," it also crosses over into "discipline, sadomasochism practices, and spiritual practices." The appeal of those kinks, of course, transcends gender and sexual orientation. I like how gay S/m activist and writer David Stein put it in a 2011 interview for kink lifestyle blog *Leatherati*: "A very large part of what passes for 'Leather culture' stems from gay leathermen, and much of the rest from leather dykes. . . . We didn't invent sadomasochism, of course, nor bondage, slavery, fetishes, dominance, or submission. But it's our spin on these things that has shaped kink discourse—and practice!—in the English-speaking world for at least the past 40 years." Leather culture helps sustain the symbols, gear, and rituals that give BDSM much of its distinctive cachet, from motorcycle caps to handcuffs to kneeling at a D-type's feet.

One of the pleasures of participating in leather culture goes right back to the whole "stability fetish" concept. Leather is a highly regimented scene: it's a place where honorifics like "Sir" and "Daddy" are common. The Phoenix Boys of Leather group, for example, which has since 2002 organized mentoring, fundraisers, events, and weekly meetings, maintains bylaws including meticulous descriptions of membership criteria, voting rules, and the group's seal.

Leather has also literally saved lives. Sexsmith told me that throughout the AIDS crisis of the 1980s, leather families channeled their ability to organize and delegate into a "mind-blowing, massive community effort" in "fundraising, caring for the sick and dying, tending to the living, advocating for resources and activism, and continuing to find ways to have intimate play safely." These changes had to happen rapidly and often through underground channels, yet managed to make an enormous impact. Sexsmith says, "Almost all of the safer sex practices that are fairly mainstream now" in both queer and straight culture—including the use of condoms for anal and oral sex—"are due to leather community efforts in the 1980s and 90s." In a 2017 article on the leather scene for *Rolling Stone*, Matt Baume reports that during the AIDS crisis, a leather family trained one of its members to provide hospice care for others living in the communal house. In many ways, leather households are actually seeking to access the advantages of traditional nuclear families—just in an alternative way, one that works for them, and with "chosen family" rather than blood relations. Plus with more interesting daily routines—and much cooler outfits.

Leather culture also preserves legacies and lore that might otherwise have been erased from history, helping queer-centered spaces to proliferate. For example, Avatar, the oldest gay men's leather club in

LA, gave rise to a sister club, Leather & Lace; both launched in 1983. According to Leatherpedia, Leather & Lace "learned the 'old guard' traditions from the men of Avatar" and brought them to California dykes. (The clubs met at a bar called Cuffs, and I love the description of that space given by the folks behind Dirty Looks, an org that plans queer events: "Cuffs was one of dozens of long-lost spaces in the neighborhood that fostered a rebellious, leathery attitude. Opened in 1981 at [the] height of the Silverlake leather scene, . . . the small beer bar had a reputation for being dark and crowded in a manner that fostered a certain degree of camaraderie among its patrons. . . . It [was] reportedly so dark that whoever entered from outside was blind for a moment before their eyes could adjust.")

Today, leather culture is not limited to gay men and is arguably most actively practiced by nonbinary and trans folks, who find life-saving shelter and community in leather families and houses. In those communities, they often apprentice in the storied arts of the culture, including bootblacking (shoe polishing, but with a kinky twist) and bondage. And while some aspects of the culture remain the territory of gay men, even the annual International Mr. Leather conference and contest—begun in 1979 and still going strong—now has caucuses for BIPOC, women, people in recovery, and others to discuss the issues they face within the leather community. Other leather events have likewise evolved into inclusive spaces for people of all genders and sexualities: one of the most well-known and long-running, San Francisco's Folsom Street Fair—a veritable public playground of leather-related kink that began as an outgrowth of a neighborhood beginning to fill with BDSM boutiques in the early 1990s—declares its mission to be anti-racist, anti-gentrification, and decolonizing.

RESPECTABILITY POLITICS AT PRIDE

In the past few years, a debate has been raging about whether or not kink has a place at Pride parades—events that have become increasingly mainstream, corporate, and family-oriented. As many of us BDSMers point out, though, the annual pervy spectacular that is the Folsom Street Fair has been NSFW, kinky as fuck, and proud of it since its inception in 1984, so it is at least as old and as popular as many major Pride events. According to BDSM historian Stephen K. Stein, in 1993 a group of more than five thousand black-clad people participated in a major LGBTQ+ march on Washington carrying a "S/M Leather Fetish" banner and the new black-and-blue stripe leather Pride flag with a heart in the corner. I believe the queer community should honor the kinky trailblazers in our midst and preserve spaces where nonnormative sexualities of all kinds are visible and celebrated.

"QUEER 1950S HOUSEHOLD"

I wanted to close this chapter with a mention of "queer 1950s household," which has to be one of the most delightful and useful terms I have discovered as part of my own kink journey.

According to a group on FetLife with this name, the term refers to "re-creating" the idea of the 1950s "any way we'd like." "Who says that 1950s households can't be queer or even (dare I say it) feminist?" asks the group's "About" page.

We know that we tend to fetishize the things that are most taboo, so we can see why twenty-first-century woke babes might be titillated by playing out the rigid and outmoded power play we associate with *Leave It to Beaver, Mad Men*, and other representations of heteronormative, suburban midcentury married life. For those of us who enjoy bending power around to suit our kinky fancies, it makes sense that there is real appeal in the idea of doing one's household chores while wearing a fluffy crinoline and stiletto pumps, or instructing your lover to sit at your knee while you drink your after-work cocktail. There is something soothing—and also naughty—in indulging in these anachronistic roles, especially if our own politics, lifestyle, and/ or identity are the furthest thing from traditional.

Those interested in queer 1950s household may yearn to bring old-fashioned etiquette—polite *pleases* and *thank yous, sirs* and *ma'ams*—back into their lives. Or they may be interested in wearing back-seamed nylons and a garter belt, or a proper fedora, even when just going to the Laundromat. They may want to sit down to a formal, home-cooked dinner every night. Or they may want strict bedtimes and other elaborate domestic protocols, complete with disciplinary action when breeched. Still others might want to lean hard into play-acting a conservative and clearly defined role of "stern but protective husband" or "good little wife," especially when this involves fucking with the typical genders assigned to those roles.

Why? Well, while too much structure can certainly be oppressive—and is often wielded most over those with the least agency—most humans feel happiest when we have at least *some* parameters about what to do and how to do it, especially at a time when our culture doesn't provide much in the way of meaningful tradition or protocol. In our casual age of flip-flops, sweatpants, and looking at our phones at the dinner table, it's no wonder why some of us long for a more formal and fancy tone, not to mention more romantic rituals in our relationships.

Personally, I love the phrase as a shorthand for how any otherwise normative action can take on a kinky twist. One member of the queer 1950s household FetLife group described how, to the outside world, she appears to be a traditional housewife to a man who works a very masculine nine-to-five job, but within the privacy of their own home, he becomes the submissive and she is utterly in charge, which is the way they both like it. Another group member proposed a lavish and kitschy scenario for a queer 1950s porn film featuring an all-female car shop, complete with car chases and cat fights. Another described themselves as a strong, educated, genderfluid person who also is an owned and collared slave living in a 1950s household with their master. Still others find the queer 1950s household a safe space in which to be their old-school butch or high-femme selves. Even within the realm of this very niche kink, there are so many different ways one can play it.

In my own life, I identify as queer (femme and pansexual, to be specific), and I'm a feminist, 100 percent. I make my own decisions and have never let a partner of any gender determine my path in life. I have a successful career. I split domestic labor, including childcare, with my male partners. (They actually do far more of the housecleaning than I do.) All of which is why, when a male partner carries my luggage or opens the door for me, or when I put on an apron and bake cookies, it feels unusual and amusing—even downright subversive. In these moments, I like to whisper *queer 1950s household*, as a reminder to myself that every choice is valid and every choice can be sexy and outré—as long as it's actually a *choice*. (If I was married to a cis man who *demanded* that I bake cookies or refused to let me carry my own bags, that would be another thing entirely. But I'd never be with someone like that.)

Is "queer 1950s household" a term you can bandy about and trust that others will know what you're talking about? Not really. You can find a few related blogs and indie pornos out there about it, and some organizers in the BDSM community hold queer-1950s-household-style events such as high protocol dinners and training in domestic discipline. But there are many people deep in the kink scene who will have never heard this term before. Unless we all start using it more often!

CHAPTER 6

SHE'S GOT LEGS

On Fetishes

The spectrum of fetishistic desire—partialism, including but not limited to feet and shoes—sensory paraphilias—smoking, spanking, and other obsessed-over activities—when your thing is "atypical situations"—the love of bodily fluids.

We've looked at the major BDSM components of kink: sadism and masochism, dominance and submission. But what about the kinky stuff not covered in that acronym? What about the other most notoriously deviant urges, sexual fetishes?

What about fetishes indeed. As a fetishist, I struggle with how fetishistic desire is marginalized even within the kink community. As I noted back in chapter 1, although the premier website for all things kink calls itself FetLife, when you click on "Fetishes" and toggle over to "Most Popular," only three of the top fifty listed could be accurately called a fetish: high heels, pantyhose/stockings, and leather. The rest are either non-fetishistic kinks, such as discipline or gang bangs, or slightly-risqué-but-still-rather-vanilla stuff like mutual masturbation or talking dirty. And even though high heels, stockings, and leather are actual (and prevalent) fetishes, lots of people are attracted to these items in ways that aren't fetishistic.

For someone who has wrestled since childhood with unusual, potent, and inexplicable desires and who goes to sites like FetLife seeking community and reassurance, the lack of material about actual fetishes can be disappointing.

While conflations between fetishes and other kinds of kink are frustrating to me, this is mostly a problem of semantics. Like all terms associated with kink, the word "fetish" is used in wildly inconsistent ways. I acknowledge that I'm being a stickler by trying to nail down these definitions, but the words we use to talk about this stuff matter: we need words to communicate with one another, make ourselves understood, and even find willing and enthusiastic partners. In a world where so much of my sexuality feels strange and impossible to relay, I need the word "fetish" to mean something solid.

What could be considered a fetish? I offered some explanations in chapter 2, but let's talk about it a bit more here. One dictionary definition of a sexual fetish is "an object or bodily part whose real or fantasized presence is psychologically necessary for sexual gratification." The various components of this definition—the real *or* fantasized presence; the *psychological* necessity; the idea of *gratification*—are key to fetishism and are what make it a subcategory distinct within the broader notion of kink.

Whereas other kinds of kink center on general types of behaviors or actions (such as pain or power exchange), as stated earlier, a fetish is usually incredibly specific, and, for the fetishist who craves it, almost supernatural in the hold it has on them. Unlike other kinds of perverts, the fetishist's obsession with their object of desire is so total that the fetishistic reaction is often triggered even in nonerotic contexts. So while a kinky-but-not-fetishy rope bunny (as they're known) might adore being tied up and suspended by their partner in a dungeon scene because they are into the psychological and physical fun of bondage, or submission, or a combination thereof, a rope *fetishist* could go into a state of deep, transcendent bliss simply by happening upon the sight and smell of some hemp cord on a routine trip to the hardware store. Both fetishists and other kinds of kinksters enjoy *doing* stuff with or to the items, textiles, or appendages they adore, but fetishists can get a powerful kick from the mere existence, proximity, or mention of that object. In this way, we are a slightly different breed of deviant than other kinky folks.

The fetishized object or body part, beyond providing an almost involuntary sexual jolt, is also usually deeply comforting to the fetishist. In a 1988 essay on folk fetishes, the nonerotic talismans found in cultures around the world, anthropologist Roy Ellen detailed four facets of the talisman's hold on its user: a) embodying a cultural principle, b) being seen as a living entity, c) operating as a direct connection to the principle it represents, and d) an attribution of power. One could argue that a leather fetishist, for example, does the same with the pair of combat boots they swoon over: they see the boots as embodying toughness and offering a conduit to that sense of authority; they treat the boots with the kind of respect usually reserved for actual people; and they feel soothed or blissed out when shining, licking, or otherwise hanging out with the boots.

Just because a person finds something sexy does not mean they have a fetish for it, especially if that object is also considered sexy in the vanilla world. Let's take high heels as an example: most people would agree that these have some erotic edge to them. But how far does your attraction to heels go? Would you find a gorgeous chick in stilettos just as sexy when she takes them off and curls up on your sofa? Would you turn your gaze to the woman instead of the shoes she has just discarded? If so, you're probably not a high heel fetishist. You're just someone who, like many others, finds the look of high heels attractive when someone is wearing them.

THE SPECTRUM OF FETISHISTIC DESIRE

In chapter 2, I discussed the spectrum of fetishistic desire, a theory I've derived based on research I've read combined with personal and anecdotal experience. The basic idea is that all of us have sexual preferences: looks, behaviors, smells, and activities we find more attractive than others. For some of us, those preferences are mild. Others may have preferences that are pretty strong but are still more of a general attraction than a fetish: for example, I am initially drawn to dark-eyed people more than blue-eyed people, but beyond that initial attraction, I don't fixate on my lovers' eyes or eye color, and it doesn't get in the way of finding someone appealing. For those who have preferences that veer into fetish territory, however, what we are sexually drawn to can feel like a supercharged magnet that we can't pull ourselves away from.

In chapter 2, I also presented a scale to explain the spectrum of mild-to-fetishistic preferences, from Level 0 (no fetishistic preferences) to Level 4 (hardcore fetishism). To recap here with another example, a Level 0 fetishist with urophilia, or an interest in pee play, would have no particular interest in incorporating urine into their sex life, and is likely a little weirded out by the thought of trying it. A mild pee fetishist might feel some excitement thinking about piss as part of a sexual encounter: maybe they'd like to watch someone urgently pee before sex, or get aroused by porn that has some piss play in it. An example of this level of urolagnia could be Tim, an interviewee in a 2019 *Out* magazine watersports article who said, "It's a bit casual for me. It's not my main kink. I'm more into bondage, but I like the humiliation factor of getting pissed on." A more serious fetishist would actively seek out erotic materials featuring urine and enjoy the smell, taste, and/or feeling of piss, but wants these things as part of play that leads to other sexual activity. By the time we get to a Level 3, or true, fetishist, we're talking about someone for whom the very thought or image of urine-related stuff turns them on, and sex just isn't at its height for them unless there's some engagement in the specific piss play of their fantasies. And whatever that particular predilection is, it's probably been thought about (and gotten off to) a thousand times, obsessively and formulaically. Level 4, or hardcore, fetishist is primarily sexually interested in the urine itself: urine feels magical, intoxicating to this person, like a drug. Other kinds of sexual play pale in comparison, and almost all fantasies center around pee.

True fetishes tend to feel hardwired within us, and many of us have early childhood memories of getting aroused by this seemingly noneerotic thing, be it a pair of nylons, a pregnant belly, or a boxing match. Lots of people enjoy spanking, but when I listen to interviews with real spankos, they talk about being kids who masturbated while reading the definition of spanking in a dictionary. In the short documentary *The Spanko*, by filmmaker Charlotte Tyran, fetishist Steve describes how, as a kid, he knew that the things he was attracted to were "weird, messed up and not what other people were thinking about." He was lucky enough, though, to find girlfriends during his high school years who were happy for him to lightly spank them. As a millennial teen, he was also able to find "a visual feast" of spanking porn online, but he still wrestled with shame about his obsession. He didn't find true happiness until adulthood: after experiencing the breakup of a relationship and a near-fatal accident, he found his way into the New York City kink scene. (He describes a spanking club that was almost wholesome—a potluck with snacks and cookies, attended mostly by older folks, "akin to a suburban barbecue.") He also talks about how his love of spanking tends to trump all other sexual preferences, including age and gender. This, too, is what separates a spanking fetishist from someone who merely likes to get spanked as part of another, non-fetishy kink such as sadomasochism: the fetishist is so besotted by their talismanic object of desire that they don't get too hung up about the person who comes with it.

Chris Hawke, who has organized piss-centered gay events such as Golden Boys USA, was interviewed for the article on watersports in *Out* by Mikelle Street, points out that a fetish can be a "path" that one is on, and one's interest can deepen (or wane) over time. That's why a scale like the one above only measures how someone feels on a particular given day or phase of life. That said, such scales like this can help us understand how the intensity of a particular sexual desire or preference can vary from person to person—and how kink itself is a spectrum that encompasses everything from a mild curiosity to an all-consuming passion.

Even at their most intense, fetishes are only a problem—a pathology—if they interfere with one's ability to participate in healthy relationships or conduct the day-to-day necessities of one's life. While it can be admittedly difficult for hardcore fetishists to find a partner who meshes with their particular predilections, one can also find some satisfaction through fantasizing, online forums, and, yes, porn. In fact, "porn" for many common fetishes is rampant on YouTube and even Instagram and other social mainstream media: after all, if your fetish has nothing to do with genitals but instead features, for example, fully clothed people sitting around brushing their hair, or smoking cigarettes, or popping balloons, the content is not categorized as erotic and so channels don't ban it. As we saw in the introduction, fetish porn can even—especially!—be culled from children's cartoons, anime, comic books, and other "wholesome" media.

But that doesn't mean I think that the hardcore fetishists reading this should give up on finding the perfect mate. You'd be surprised at how many freaks are out there who might share the thing you think is so weird about yourself. Go on FetLife or browse around the Internet and see what you can uncover. (Just remember to clear your history!) My own fetish—people who act proud of their big, full bellies, preferably while they're also drunk—is uncommon and specific, and yet I have pulled up page after page of such videos on YouTube, posted by users with names like SecretBellyStuffer and Gaining Gamer. One I especially loved was a sort of role play in which a gay "Business Daddy" in suit and tie eats and drinks an enormous amount on camera while explaining how enticing his belly is to the partners he hooks up with. This particular video has over one hundred thousand views and a thousand likes, with comments (by people other than me!) such as "this might be the sexiest thing I've ever seen in my life."

Browsing around on YouTube or Instagram can also reassure you that others hold your interests, even if you don't meet your next playmate there. Steve, the subject of *The Spanko*, goes from lonely and depressed to full of joy by seeking out play parties, kink community, and well-matched partners. He says, "I don't even want to think about what it would have been like if I had not figured out a way to indulge what I thought was the worst part of me, something I had always been ashamed of and wanted to change."

I often wonder if various, seemingly unconnected fetishes spring from the same neurological or psychological well. Though theories abound, there is no one answer. In an essay published on the blog of Sofia Gray, an eBay-like commerce site for used underwear, sex writer Jaimee Bell posits some hypotheses about the origin of stuffed-animal fetishes, drawing a parallel between those who are into used panties and those who are into plush dolls. "You're attached to them," she writes. "Maybe even attracted to them. They make you feel safe. . . . You've attached meaning to these things . . . [and] they are things that you feel connected to even though they are just things." (This is also an excellent way to define fetishes in general.) Bell goes on to theorize that sexualizing stuffed toys could come from an association with the carefree days of youth, and the release and relief of being able to let go of adult responsibility—which strikes me as similar to what's experienced through submission, masochism, and a host of other surrender-type kinks.

Just as certain fetishes relate to certain other aspects of kink, fetishes themselves can be grouped into various—and sometimes overlapping—categories. I've delineated some such categories here, some of which are formally designated by psychologists (such as partialism) and some of which are more informal groupings (such as those attracted to activities). This might help people who feel alone in their unusual desires see a connection between themselves and others with kindred interests.

PARTIALISM: THE MOST INFAMOUS FETISH

If we were to play a word-association game and I said the word "fetish" to you, you might respond "foot." Foot fetishes are probably one of the most well-known and common fetishes, appearing in everything from Dostoyevsky's novels to Quentin Tarantino movies. (A 2020 article in *Volta* charts the trajectory of sexualized feet in Tarantino's films to prove how much bolder and more noticeable his inclusion of bare feet has gotten over his career.) Like all types of fetishists, people who are into feet have specific attractions and desires. One person might be into beautifully well-groomed, clean, shapely feet slipped into a satin ballet shoe, while another might be into a natural bare foot skipping through a grassy meadow. Some people might want to lick the sensitive sole; others might want a toe job. A fetish is often a full-sensory kink, involving not just how something looks but also the textures, smells, tastes, and/or sounds associated with it.

Foot fetishes are also a perfect example of partialism, which psychologists consider as any fetish that involves an attraction to an isolated part of the human body. I don't count attractions to booties, cocks, pussies, and other typically eroticized bits as partialist fetishes. But when we get into parts that most humans either sexually ignore, dismiss, or find themselves repulsed by—such as feet—that's when we're in partialism territory. According to a 2007 study from Italy, partialism might account for up to a third of all fetishes. Fetishized body parts include armpits, eyeballs, navels, and noses; in a 2021 article for *Men's Health* on odontophilia, or tooth fetishes, reporter Emily Leibert describes how she once met a stranger at a party who immediately began asking her in-depth questions about her canine teeth, to the point where he seemed "distracted by the very presence" of her cuspids.

Akin to partialist fetishes—and, according to that same Italian study, probably comprising another third of all fetishes—is an attraction to objects *closely associated* with specific parts of the body, such as shoes and underwear.

Amputee fetishists also probably fall in this general partialism category: they, too, desire a detail of the body not typically sexualized or even accepted. However, if the fetishist is more into the *cause* of the amputation than the amputation itself, that might fall under a different category. I read an interesting essay by Aleks Kang, who lost a leg after being hit by a car in her early twenties. At first, Kang saw her stump as shameful and unattractive, but then started to find sexual partners who lusted after this exact attribute. As she wrote in *Vice* in 2016, she discovered that "having people want me with that sort of desperate hunger was an intoxicating force I could use to my advantage." Eventually, though, after years of wooing women with amputee fetishes, she says, "I realized my social and sexual life post-amputation was empty. I thought being a fetish gave me power—that it was some great trick to get women in bed—but instead, it surrounded me with lovers who saw me as a peg leg, not a person."

When it comes to long-term relationships, none of us want to be desired only for how we look or smell or what clothes we wear: we want to be loved as our full selves. That said, I personally believe that as long as the relationship is in all other ways healthy and egalitarian, it can't *hurt* to have a wild and consuming attraction to an attribute that our beloved just happens to naturally possess, can it?! If you are crazy about hairy armpits and you shack up with a swarthy someone who never liked shaving anyway, isn't that a win-win?

SENSORY FETISHES: BALLOONS, PLUSHIES, LATEX, AND MORE

Just as there are many types of sensory experiences that BDSMers pursue through S/m impact play (do you like it thuddy or stingy?), there are also many types of tactile sensations fetishists seek out: silky or sticky, squishy or stiff. All five senses may be involved: some fetishists prioritize the smell of sweat or the taste of suede, while others go mad for the sound of clogs clattering on the floor or the soft feel of an earlobe. Certain sensory fetishes are also partialist: a hair fetishist, for example, might want to rub their face in their partner's coiled curls; a denim-jeans fetishist might want to inhale the scent of a pair of 501 Levis worn for a month straight.

The community of "'looners," or balloon fetishists, is a prime example of what it means to be sensory-oriented. Balloons engage through sight, smell, touch, taste, *and* sound. In a 2019 *Allure* article on 'looners, Sophie Saint Thomas writes that within that community, there are "poppers" who love the experience of a balloon popping and "non-poppers" whose love of balloons means *not* wanting to see, feel, or hear them popped. As Saint Thomas points out, whatever extremely niche desire one might have for balloons, there's fetish porn for that (again, often involving fully clothed people and seemingly nonsexual to a vanilla viewer). One of Saint Thomas's interviewees, Brandon, said, "I am in the middle ground, a semi-popper: . . . I love seeing members of the opposite sex interact with balloons, including popping them, but I find it difficult to pop balloons myself." (Which brings up another salient point about fetishists: some of us want to directly possess—wear, consume, pop—our beloved texture or body part, while others of us prefer to worship the fetish on someone else.)

Satisfying a lifelong erotic balloon fantasy could be as simple as picking up a pack of balloons at a party store for a few bucks, or as involved as sourcing specialty balloons made for pervy purposes. Likewise, fetishists known as plushies sometimes stick with the loyal companions of their youth and sometimes save up for life-sized faux-fur friends, complete with handy orifices.

I also put textile fetishes—such as those for latex, rubber, and leather—in the category of sensory-driven paraphilias. Just like the other sensory fetishes described here, textiles can involve not just texture but also scent, flavor, and auditory input. In a personal essay I found on the latex commerce site LaidTex, company co-owner Alex praised the material's resemblance to taut skin, its ability to provide a "slick slide," its air of superhero protection and mystery, its distinctive scent and squeak, and the intensified temperatures experienced while wearing it.

ACTIVITY FETISHES: SMOKING AND WHISPERING AND TICKLING, OH MY!

This "activity" category of fetishistic desire is also driven by sensory experience. It is centered not on body parts, clothes, textiles, or inanimate objects but on physical activities that are distinct from the impact play/sadistic realm. Common activity fetishes include smoking, whispering, tickling, and wrestling.

Attitude can play a big role in these fetishes. For receivers and givers of tickling—'lees and 'lers—enjoyment is determined as much by whether the scene involves humiliation or glee as it is by the implement used to tickle (from fingernails to a feather duster). And no matter what else tickling may mean to a specific person, at its core it's about losing control. In a 2019 article for *Paper*, journalist Sandra Song interviews a professional Dom called MiscAlleneous, who explains how the fun of tickling comes from it being a kind of playful torture but without any actual hurt. Although MiscAlleneous says some of their clients enjoy softer, sweeter tickling sessions, others want "mind games," interrogation, and other forms of torment that the Dom themself takes pleasure in.

In other words, the *psychology* fueling the activity fetish is key. Smoking fetishist Andrew, interviewed by Tierney Finster for *MEL Magazine* in 2016, talks about lusting after a badass woman who "enjoys smoking and doesn't care who objects." Andrew actually gets turned off if the smoker seems to feel guilty about their bad habit: for him, "smoking is a demonstration of [a woman's] authority and freedom to be who she wants to be." That attitude—combined with "specific . . . mannerisms" such as "dangling a cigarette from her mouth while fishing through her purse for a lighter" or "when a woman is smoking while she's driving her car" and an attraction to "all-white cigarettes"—is what floats Andrew's nicotine-stained boat.

In the early days of the Internet, when I was first researching my own fetishes online, I came across a post written by a smoking fetishist who described how, when out in public, their head swiveled and their jaw dropped whenever they saw a stranger throw their cigarette down onto the street and grind it out with their shoe. At the time I lived in a big city, and after reading that I remember going out into the world and noticing, for the first time, just how common this sight was. I'm not myself a smoking fetishist, so I had never even noticed the action before, but once primed to pay attention to it, I realized that this potentially erotic act was happening all the time. It could transform waiting at an urban bus stop into a titillating experience.

ASMR: A BOON FOR WHISPER FETISHISTS?

The whisper fetish community is experiencing a similar windfall due to the surging popularity of ASMR—it must feel as if the whole world has suddenly become their personal porn stash! Whisper fetishists find nothing more arousing than listening to someone speak in low, sighing tones, and for those unfamiliar, "ASMR" is a nonclinical term that stands for "autonomous sensory meridian response": people affected by it report feeling a (nonerotic) visceral head tingling and a deep sense of relaxation in response to sounds like hushed voices. Over the last decade or so, there has been an explosion of mainstream interest in ASMR as a sleep aid, prompting a proliferation of whisper-oriented YouTube channels. But of course, for whisper fetishists, such sounds rev them up instead of soothing them to sleep. Your mileage with ASMR videos may, of course, vary: the same sounds that drive one person wild with desire and lull another into a deep state of relaxation can be horribly grating to a third.

As nonsexual material that, for some, is very sexual indeed, ASMR videos must be a huge boon. If whispering is your fetish, you can easily access a veritable plethora of ASMR YouTube videos, podcasts, and other media for free in the privacy of your own home, where you can then masturbate to them to your heart's content.

I've had my own such fetishy experiences, though they are a bit more about the sensory than an activity. One of the profound turning points in my life as a fetishist came in my late teens when I watched my skinny boyfriend nonchalantly eat three or four pieces of pie at his family's Thanksgiving dinner, leaving me so addled I could barely contain myself in front of all his assembled cousins and relatives. Another big moment for me came in my twenties, when I took a vacation to a hot climate where the local men tended to have stocky physiques and round, tanned bellies , which they would proudly bare in the sun. The sight of them kept me in a constant state of horniness.

One fetish that has always made sense to me even though I don't have it is somnophilia: excitement derived from watching other people sleep or fall asleep. I think the reason I get it is because it has much in common with my fetish for happily drunken people: both drunkenness and sleepiness can be delightful states of being, and some of us fetishists find that kind of delight arousing. As always, consent comes first, so even though these fetishes are predicated on one partner being in an altered state of consciousness, resist the urge to act out your desires on someone who is tired or inebriated to the point of semi-unconsciousness. Instead, partners of such fetishists can agree to exaggerate their actual incapacitation, pretending to be much more drunk or asleep than they are, or they can role play these states. Remember, all kink is a kind of pretend play!

FETISHIZING THE EXTREME: CAR CRASHES, FOOD FIGHTS, FALLING ASLEEP, AND OTHER "ATYPICAL SITUATIONS"

Beyond fetishes that focus on common sensory experiences and activities like the feel of leather or the sound of whispering, there are also fetishists who lust after more extreme corporeal phenomena. I first found out about "sploshing," also called WAM (or "wet and messy"), way back in the 1990s, when, in an underground bookstore, I came across a magazine full of pictures of pretty girls covered in paint, cake frosting, and other sloppy substances. In a 2013 piece for *Vice*, Monica Heisey investigated this fetish, which can include fantasies about being doused with—or watching someone else get doused with—everything from mayonnaise to mud. She interviewed a man named Stephen, who can chart his WAM fetish back to childhood, when he found himself aroused while watching a cute woman on a British children's show get slammed with custard pies in good fun. To this day, his "number-one turn-on" is "a good old-fashioned Lady Getting a Pie Directly to the Face," preferably after the woman taunts him, saying that he wouldn't dare do such a thing to her. And like most self-respecting fetishists, Stephen could describe in detail both the things he was absolutely mad for (like a playfulness around the activity reminiscent of his childhood TV show) and the things he found unappealing (like humiliation and the use of baked beans).

I would also include in this category of "humans in extreme and atypically sexual situations" people who are into car crashes. This fetish is notably explored in the subversive fiction of J. G. Ballard, whose car-crash survivors are sometimes amputees (who, as we have seen, can also be objects of fetishistic desire). Ballard's work, critics will tell you, is about exploring the toxic relationships humans have with our technological devices. Or a metaphor for our death-wish natures. Or perhaps it's all an allegory for the impact of celebrity culture on us, and how, as novelist Zadie Smith puts it, "our worship of the famous and beautiful (with their unique bodies and personalities) [can result in] nothing less than the bloody sacrifice of the worshipped themselves." But I'm not entirely convinced that Ballard himself isn't an actual car-crash fetishist. I tried to read *Crash* and while I couldn't quite stomach it, I recognized in it the obsessive, detail-oriented perversity I know well from my own fetishistic mind, and which also shows up in the literary style of Sade, Sacher-Masoch, and cult filmmaker and infamous cross-dresser Ed Wood (whose essays are stuffed with excruciatingly detailed references to angora sweaters, his personal fetish). While some *Crash* fans don't believe anyone IRL has such a fetish, evidence proves otherwise. In a 2013 article for *Scientific American*, psychologist Jesse Bering (author of the book on sexual deviancy called *Perv*), reminded us that there was a "20-something masochist described by the psychiatrist Martin Keeler in 1960 . . . in a long-forgotten issue of *The American Journal of Psychiatry*" who felt that "nothing was hotter than the thought of a beautiful woman hitting him with her car."

FETISHIZING THE BODY'S FLUIDS

Last but certainly not least for this chapter on fetishes are bodily fluids, perhaps the most literal kind of paraphilia—"next to" or "of" the body—as you can get. As kink-educator superhero Tina Horn puts it in an excellent piece she wrote for *The Establishment* in 2017, "Piss and milk. Snot and tears. Cum and sweat. Spit and blood. . . . Every body fluid has its own devoted fetish fan base."

It stands to reason that if people fetishize *parts* of the body (such as the feet), things put *on* a body (such as shoes or chocolate syrup), and things that can happen *to* or *with* the body (such as sleep or a car crash), then of course people also fetishize the very matter that our bodies produce. As Horn writes, "Fluids are bodies in action, the parts of the body that no amount of socializing can contain." This is also what makes these some of the most taboo fetishes of all: vanilla folks tend to see piss, breast milk, snot, and blood not simply as *non*-erotic but as *anti*-erotic—shameful, repulsive, and repellent, and the last thing you want to engage with during sexy time.

And yet piss is a relatively common kink: about a million respondents to a 2016 survey on sexual desire in the United Kingdom reported having a thing for watersports. A lot of non-fetishists can get off on using urine as part of a D/s scene or a simple act of outré sexy fun. In the gay male community, piss play isn't even considered particularly kinky (and neither, of course, is anal sex, both of which still hold a taboo mystique among many heterosexuals). Chris Hawke, who organizes piss-centered events, has found there are "two reasons people are into watersports": One is "the dominant/ submissive path where guys want to pee on you to degrade you." The second is the intimacy path, where you are "relaxed enough to pee, and [exchange] fluid that has been throughout [someone else's] entire body . . . you're taking that in or it's getting on you or whatever: I find that very intimate and erotic." But no matter the reason, he says, the activity is the same.

Psychological researcher Raymond Denson would concur. He found, in a 1982 Canadian study, that pee fulfilled different functions for the various kinky folks he interviewed, and as part of his analysis, he argued that the kink might be better understood by organizing it into more specific sub-labels like "uromasochism." In other words, not all people who are into pee are urolagnia fetishists. And even for those who *are* urophiliacs—actual fetishists—there is great variety in how the fetish manifests. Some might be into wetting their pants and smelling it afterward but don't ever want to taste it, while others are into having their lover piss into their open mouth. (There's also a subcategory of urine fetish called *omorashi*, which is when you get turned on by having a full bladder and a desperate need to pee. Until I started working on this book, I never knew this term, but I now recognize that I have a mild version of this fetish. The origin might have been in childhood when I discovered that masturbating with a full bladder made my orgasms more intense. I'm also drawn to the control/teasing/torture aspect of omorashi.)

The air of taboo—heightened, of course, by very real health concerns about the infections that can be transmitted by swapping fluids—is exactly why some fetishists go cuckoo for it: this is a heady, edgy kind of play. But there are other reasons, too. Connecting with someone's fluids is a shortcut to intimacy, an act of enormous trust given and received. Horn again: "The wet parts of the body are the most fascinating to us. . . . Fluids, especially ones we've lost control of, are the body's way of expressing itself; they tell the truth."

I theorize that underlying all deep-seated paraphilias is a sense that the fetishized object, action, or state is a way of telling a truth, or communicating another kind of pure energy or message. There's a thing I like to do in bed with my lover: First, I touch his chest and say out loud, "This is safety." Then I touch his cock and say, "This is sacred." Then I touch his belly—my fetish—and say, "This is power." It is not unlike a religious ritual, wherein I am naming and physically making contact with something holy and magical. That is the original meaning of a fetish, and it's what we paraphiliacs experience, blissfully, every time we get in proximity to the object of our love beyond.

CHAPTER 7

I WILL BE YOUR FATHER FIGURE

On Role Play

*The possibilities of role play — race play, age play,
and other fascinating scenarios — Littles and ABDL —
a Daddy/girl age play mixtape — how much is that doggie
in the window? — furries: a que(e)ry — a call for a
new word for "nonsexual kink."*

As we've already observed, sex can be a terrific escape pod: a way to temporarily stave off ennui, existential dread, and house chores. Freaking out about the melting ice caps? Bad day at the office? Try consensual sex! It's a no-cost recreational activity that can double as a workout! And kinky sex—which often involves novelty, mind games, extreme sensation, and other engrossing elements—can be an *especially* diverting pastime.

But it can be hard to leave all the daily grind stuff behind and simply dive into erotic joy. We carry our anxiety-ridden selves with us into the sexual moment. Which is why this chapter is all about checking our own identities at the door, and with them our stresses, through the magic of *role play*. If you think you're feeling too tired or stressed for sex, pretending to be someone else for a minute or an hour can do wonders to shift your mood. You are no longer Kim Doe, panicked about bills and work and climate change. You're a swashbuckling vampire, or a swaggering basketball star, or a sweet dolphin, or an end table, and all your quotidian concerns have been momentarily vanquished.

THE WONDERFUL WORLD OF ROLE PLAY

On its own, kinky role play is pretty harmless stuff—much less threatening, you'd think, than the things with needles and cattle prods and such that BDSM people do. And yet role play is widely seen by the vanilla world as one of the weirder types of kink out there—a genuine taboo, even when all it involves is a game of pretend.

TV shows, mainstream movies, snarky birthday cards: joking and dismissive references to role play are rampant. Just yesterday my partner showed me the daily strip from the wholesome family comic *Foxtrot*: the long-married white suburban couple seem to be discussing a role play in bed—only to have it turn out to be a joke about how the husband is really lusting after a game of chess.

Maybe it's *because* it's a game of pretend that role play is so widely mocked. This probably comes from a deep sense of shame: not just shame about sex and desire, but also about *play*, about *acting*, about taking on a character. That shame is sad enough, but I also feel glum about how stereotypical and unimaginative the usual representations of erotic role play are. In almost all mainstream sex-advice articles that gently recommend trying it (and they are legion!), the same common tropes are trotted out. Among many other similar pieces, a 2015 article in *Bustle* by sex columnist Aly Walansky dutifully lists them off: cop and criminal, doctor and patient, two strangers meeting. Such off-the-shelf scenarios are popular for good reason: they embody potent power dynamics most of us are familiar with, and they can be fun and rich. Many experienced, lifelong kinksters find nothing more satisfying than a good nurse-and-invalid role play. Remember, though, that characters found in the sexy Halloween costume aisle are not all role play is or can be.

Much of what deeply kinky people do for role play is weirder and more specific than the run-of-the-mill pizza delivery–type scenarios we've all heard about. I once attended a workshop on incest role play—already a niche category, though one frequently depicted in porn—and was downright inspired by the variety and creativity on display as the participants in this small group shared their favorite role play flavors. One triad of lovers had an incredibly complex siblings/parent dynamic, complete with a long backstory featuring a mean, bullying sister and a kinder, downtrodden sibling who none-theless helped the sister "gang up" on their unsuspecting dad. (In actuality, all three of these people were roughly the same age.)

The great thing about truly creative, customized kinky role play is that it can slice through age, gender, and every other construct you can imagine: you can become completely unbound by what you actually look like or what your personality is or what "real" roles you are accustomed to playing in your nonerotic life. Choose your desired tone or persona and customize to your heart's content! Weary parents can become children or pampered pets. Humans can become birds, or aliens, or objects. Quiet, timid types can become raging tyrants. Successful overachievers can play at being lazy scoun-drels. Breadwinners can become submissive maids. You are limited only by your ability to come up with ideas—and even there, I'd say *push further.*

You can start small. If you've already tried a pool-boy-meets-MILF game, try it again with a different tone or twist: maybe the previously shy and obedient pool boy is now bratty and assertive. Maybe it's a really hot day, and you both need to get into the shower. Maybe the MILF is vacuuming in only a ratty t-shirt when the pool boy comes to the door. Maybe there's a skulking jealous spouse nearby. Maybe you switch roles. Think about what naturally appeals to you and your play partner, and what works with—or, for fun and an additional challenge, against—your existing dynamic. Any scenario has endless potential for variation and expansion, and even subtle tweaks can open up whole new realms of arousal.

Role play can be awkward and intimidating at first. For a long time, I felt too inhibited to dive into it, so even though my mastur-batory fantasies were *full* of elaborate characters and scenarios, I never was anything but myself during partnered sex. That changed once I was with a partner who was as committed as I was to exploring new sexual avenues. We began to try role playing, though it wasn't immediately easy for either of us. I was overthinking it, worrying whether I was in character, as if I was starring in a Broadway play rather than just fooling around in private. My partner is, in real life, a shy person who does not enjoy performing, and it was also hard for him to loosen up and have fun. Even as we started to get more comfortable, we often would shed our roles before either of us was ready to orgasm, because it felt too strange to do *that* while pretending to be someone else.

But we were committed to expanding our sexual range, so we kept at it: *if at first you don't succeed*, right? We practiced and laughed at ourselves and refined our tactics, exploring new games and new roles. And soon we learned how mind-altering role play can be. Now we slip easily and happily into role play on a regular basis, and we do not break character when we pass GO. Believe it or not, by this point my partner and I have found that when we get into a good role play, something akin to Method Acting happens for him, so that if he's enacting the role of a teenaged boy, he will ejaculate like a teenaged boy, quickly and suddenly, even though he is actually fifty and orgasm usually takes a bit longer these days. I'd be thrilled to hear what transformations happen for you and your partners when you get deep into a role play.

Some role plays demand or can be enhanced through props, costumes, and other accoutrements, and for some people this is a big part of the fun and the arousal. I know someone who sewed elaborate matching outfits for herself and her partner to suit their baroque and pervy scenes, which included highly conceptual per-formances such as enacting a hazing ritual between 1920s fraternity snobs. If you are into props and costumes and can make or afford them: go for it! But please know that role play does not require you to spend a penny or a minute more of your time than you want to. Role play can be done using only your mind and some form of communication.

In longer-term relationships, clever perverts can figure out how to meld and melt a role play dynamic into their daily noneroptic lives as a kind of omnipresent long game. For example, a discreet pair of frilly panties worn daily under a Brooks Brothers business suit at a high-powered corporate job can be a potent reminder of the very different role one plays at home. A scolding text received every morning from a long-distance partner can serve as a reminder of one's servitude. A cute cat-ear headband worn to the supermarket can be a subtle indicator of the purring kitten you turn into when alone with your lover. Here too, you need only commit in the ways that work for you. Your dips into role play can be fleeting and rare, and you can make them as simple or as complex as you like.

It is nobody's business but your own how filthy or bizarre your role plays get. Role play is the space in which you or your partner can pretend at being a corrupt cop, child molester, rapist, or an otherwise wildly inappropriate and repugnant character. In addition to being exhilaratingly edgy, "dark role play" (as it's sometimes called) can be a safe way to handle our more fraught and troubling urges. A caveat, though: when played out in full view of onlookers at a kink event, good BDSM etiquette holds that role players never force bystanders to participate in their scenes, nor should the "audience" ever interfere with or try to jump into a role play in progress. There is absolutely nothing wrong with two or more consenting adults acting out a taboo, impossible, or unethical fantasy as a game of pretend, as long as those involved all *want* to be involved. Because—and it bears repeating—that's what role play is: an enthusiastically consensual *game of pretend.*

We are truly only limited by our imaginations and our ability to find someone who is as eager to do this weird stuff as we are. On the BDSM website FetLife, a recent peek at a forum for people seeking role play partners turned up the following posted desires:

— Someone looking to play a boy living with his stepmother. Okay, nothing so unusual there, except that this person was looking for someone to play not the stepmother (she would be "offscreen" and only mentioned, it seemed) but a wealthy neighbor who *blackmails* the boy and eventually joins forces with the stepmother to turn the boy into a "sissy" with all manner of brutal sex toys.

— Someone who wanted to be a unicorn. But not just a unicorn: a black-furred unicorn with cyber components. This unicorn-hopeful was trying to find a "captor" to own them and demand their total obedience.

— Someone looking to do a long-term Bonnie and Clyde–type role play of young lovers on the run, committing pretend robberies.

— Someone who wanted to play out an execution scene in which the executioner would be in an all-leather outfit, complete with hood, opera gloves, and "leather-covered English judicial noose" (I had to look it up), and the tortured soul would dress in a long silk skirt.

— Someone who wanted to play the Black mistress who then becomes the trophy wife of a racist white man.

SOME PARTICULARLY FASCINATING ROLE PLAYS (INCLUDING RACE PLAY, ADULT BABIES, LITTLES, FURRIES, AND MORE)

Perhaps some readers paused when, just above, they read about the person seeking to play a Black mistress to a racist white man. I know I did. As we've already noted, because role play is often fueled by inhabiting dynamics and roles that would be extremely problematic or even illegal in real life, there are entire subcategories of role play that many (even many hardcore kinksters) find baffling and disturbing. But in my research, I've found that the more politically fraught and taboo the category, the more likely it is that there are people exploring it.

Race play is one of those categories. "One of the most dramatic" kinds of role play out there, "the most taboo of taboo," in the opinion of BDSM scholar Stephen K. Stein, it "eroticizes racial difference," thereby upping the stakes and the intensity of the play for all involved. As Stein writes, some race play "mirror[s] historical disparities of power," such as a scene in which a white person would play a Southern plantation owner and a Black person would play their enslaved "property," while other race play scenes "reverse" those historic dynamics to enact fantasies of vengeance or reparation.

As an American white woman who cares about racial justice, the very idea of race play is deeply off-putting to me, and I have zero interest in participating in it. It's likewise difficult for me, as a Jew, to be at the occasional kink event where people in Nazi regalia happily stomp by to play out some dirty scene in a sex dungeon. As with any kind of kink I find disturbing, I find that I can simply choose to look away or walk away. I understand that playing out extremely tricky emotional terrain around racism and bigotry within the carefully negotiated, enthusiastically consensual, play-acting confines of a BDSM scene can be extremely fulfilling—even healing.

If you are interested in learning more about race and role play in BDSM, I recommend looking up Mollena Williams-Haas. An American Black woman known as a brilliant BDSM educator and highly respected member of the leather community, Williams-Haas has been interviewed on many sex podcasts, speaks regularly at kink events and panels, and has had her written work anthologized in several good-quality kink anthologies. She calls herself "an Award-Winning Executive Pervert" who is "owned and collared" by—and legally married to—a successful white and Austrian-born composer, Georg Friedrich Haas. As she wrote in her essay "Stop, Drop and Role! Erotic Role Playing" in the anthology *The Ultimate Guide to Kink*, she has found that there can be much satisfaction in "playing with real, structural inequalities in safe and pleasurable ways." In 2012, she spoke to a writer for *Jezebel* about her role play origins, reporting that she has early memories of getting turned on by depictions of Confederate masters and slaves. As a feminist and confident woman, she feels strongly that it is an act of defiance and self-actualization to explore such taboo fantasies, to choose what she does with her body and her erotic life. In a piece about her marriage in the *New York Times*, Williams-Haas said, "To say I can't play my personal psychodrama out just because I'm Black, that's racist." She makes the point that anytime she plays with a white man, it's inherently "race play" in some way. In a piece in *Bitch*, Williams-Haas said, "I show my respect [for my ancestors] by living fearlessly. I firmly believe the people who fought and died for our freedom weren't sitting on the front lines worrying about how that freedom would be used."

Despite—or perhaps entirely made possible by—the ways in which Williams-Haas and her husband reenact the history of racism and slavery in their erotic relationship, in his professional life as an artist, Haas composes pieces about and in honor of the victims of racist police brutality. To my mind, this is a testament to how thoughtful both partners are about the kinds of racist dynamics they explore in their romantic relationship. And it is a reminder of how race play and other highly taboo and involved role plays can only work if, underneath it all, there are enormous amounts of enthusiastic consent, mutual respect, and deep communication and understanding.

I believe that kinky people who are role playing in semi-public places such as sex parties ought to follow the same kinds of guidelines that apply to dress codes at other kinds of costume parties: don't appropriate the cultures of marginalized people; don't do blackface, yellowface, and the like; and generally, follow a code of ethics informed by cultural sensitivity—which would probably preclude Nazi play. (What you do in the privacy of your own home or mind, of course, is your business, as long as you don't record and post it!) One prominent BDSM educator, Midori, has said that race play is best reserved for those at an "advanced" level of role playing, and Stephen K. Stein points out that in decades past, you would rarely see workshops on it or scenes held at play events. And while BDSM gatherings sometimes offer workshops or panels on race play, there aren't really active, IRL *communities* of responsible race players: as we just noted, it's something best explored between very trusting partners.

Perhaps not quite as controversial as race play, but still definitely taboo, is age play, in which you and/or your partner pretend to be an age other than you are, often in a relationship dynamic other than the one you actually have. Casual age players will occasionally bring an "as seen in porn" stepdaughter fantasy to their bedroom with a romantic partner while more hardcore practitioners may find bliss in a relationship that incorporates 24-7 Mommy/boi or similar D/s power exchanges. Many of these age players do not discuss their kink with anyone other than their sexual partners.

Other kinds of age players, however, take their kink beyond the privacy of their home and seek out in-person community, despite the controversial nature of their fantasies. An example of such age play-ers are Littles, a subset of age play that contains further sub-subsets. In chronological order of age, these subsets include:

Adult Babies and diaper lovers. (The two kinks are often combined and abbreviated as ABDL.) Adult Babies usually identify
with, and want to enact behaviors of, children ages "infant" to
"toddler." (Note that I'm using quotation marks to indicate that
these terms refer to *adults* playing pretend.) Within this group,

Adult Babies who identify as infantalists may seek out caregivers to satisfy their desire to be swaddled, fed, and changed. Diaper lovers, on the other hand, may focus mostly on the sensations of diapering—and the piss and scat play that may naturally follow. This fetish is more frequently erotically charged than it is for those practicing the Adult Baby kink, though ABDL players of any kind can also explore their fetish on their own, without a partner. ABDL players may or may not incorporate overtly sexual activities with others into their role play. (When they do, this is often called "dark age play.")

While one certainly can wear a diaper or curl up in a play-pen—real or imagined—in the privacy of one's own home, for whatever reason ABDL is one of those kinks that seems to lend itself to community. There was a monthly party in London for Adult Babies that ran from at least 2008 until the COVID pandemic hit, and around the world ABDL fetishists can attend tricked-out "nurseries" at BDSM clubs. A small but thriving cottage industry of independent businesses produces the paraphernalia ABDL age players seek: fleece blankies, changing mats, and, of course, cute disposable diapers, all big enough to fit grown-ass people. There's an ABDL brick-and-mortar store outside of Chicago, complete with an adult-sized rocking horse, high chair, playpen, wooden crib, and other things that create a nursery atmosphere for those shoppers who wouldn't otherwise have access to one. And there's a professional "baby-care" facility outside Los Angeles for people who want to pay $150 an hour to be babysat by a "mommy" who will provide sippy cups, arts-and-crafts time, cuddling, and a diaper change—but no sexual contact. (All-inclusive overnights can cost $2,000.)

Littles. Though the term "Littles" is often used broadly to refer to anyone doing underage age play, the core group of Littles tends to play at ages ranging from toddler through elementary school, and that's the meaning I'm referring to here. (Not everyone capitalizes the term "Little," but I'm doing so here to distinguish the term from other meanings of the word.) Littles identify as having not just a fun fantasy character but often a psychologically meaningful *alter ego* who is a child, often of a very particular age and personality.

Littles may enjoy activities such as wearing onesie pajamas, drinking from juice boxes, using pacifiers, coloring with crayons, watching cartoons, cuddling with stuffed animals, and otherwise indulging in the sensory pleasures of childhood. As with Adult Babies, some Littles view and enact their kink as a nonsexual outlet that provides a sense of security, safety, comfort, and relaxation, while others seek out very erotic scenes or relationship dynamics as part of this expression. While many Littles seek a partner with whom they can explore their persona, some Littles use this mode of expression whether they're in a relationship or not: being a Little (like being an Adult Baby) is something you can do solo.

Some Littles go into their "Little headspace," or persona, only during specific times or scenes (erotic or otherwise). For example, a hardworking adult might manage a busy daytime schedule full of responsibilities without once thinking of their Little persona, but finish every evening with a relaxing coloring session just before bedtime, during which they imagine themself to be a child again. Other Littles, however, who sometimes call themselves "lifestyle Littles," strive to carry a spark of that child self with them no matter what they are doing. This might manifest in something as simple and vanilla-seeming as carrying a Disney-themed phone case or choosing to skip in a grocery store parking lot. As one Little puts it, "it's a mindset." Sassafras, a queer lifestyle Little who is also part of the leather community, writes on their author website, "Being little is the core of who I am, . . . central to the way that I walk through all aspects of the world and work that I do. [I try to find] ways to stay true to my littleness even when I am interfacing with the big and complicated world." To do so, Sassafras mentions "finding magic" in everyday routines as a way to stay connected to the Little identity, and talks about enjoying activities such as building sandcastles or going to the zoo.

Middles. These folks role play a romanticized and seductive teenaged self, often one who seeks adult attention, as embodied in movies like *Lolita* (1962, and the 1997 remake, though the OG is far superior), *Pretty Baby* (1978), *Poison Ivy* (1992), *American Beauty* (1999), or many early Lana Del Rey videos. (Note that these depictions all revolve around conventionally attractive white girls: movies that glamorize inappropriate relationships between adults and BIPOC girls, or boys of any race, are far less common, because the default construction of "pretty teen" in our racist, patriarchal culture is white, female, thin, doe-eyed, pouty-lipped, and so on. In age play, of course, a Middle can be any race, size, gender, or style.)

Role plays for Middles often involve knee socks, ponytails, or similar markers of objectified adolescence: the Middle scene is known for being a more sexualized space than that of other Littles. Some Middles identify as nymphets, as babygirls (in a "spoiled teenage princess" way, not an infant way), or use the term "Lolita." All of those terms (and the reference to Nabokov's character) convey the erotic, sugar-daddy-flavored power exchange inherent in these archetypes: there is almost always an eyelash-batting dependence on an "older" figure who provides attention, gifts, care, and pampering, but who in turn is besotted to the point of capitulation to the Middle's demands, so that the power dynamic is, in its way, balanced. You will often find Middles acting out bratty or rebellious roles, which are ripe with sexy possibilities. As Amy Martin, who writes the BDSM blog *Beautifully Broken Submissive*, rhapsodizes, "The Babygirl/Lolita is the maiden, the sacred whore, the priestess, the ritual font from which all carnal knowledge is drawn. A Babygirl/Lolita is also about a display of submissive power . . . submitted to the Caregiver counterpart."

While one might assume that Littles of all types take on a submissive role in their relationships, in fact there are consensual power exchange relationships in which the Little (or Adult Baby or Middle) has the control. There is also a category of "brats" who enact their Little personae through sulking, mischief, teasing, whining, etc. And just as every Little has their own vision of the perfect Daddy or Caregiver or Mommy, every Daddy or Caregiver or Mommy has their own vision of the ideal Little.

And where to find this perfect role play partner? Age players of all varieties are welcome at community gatherings like CAPCON, the Chicago Ageplay Convention, which has for ten years been transforming bland, corporate hotel-conference spaces into changing rooms, play areas, and nap rooms for excited adults. Similar gatherings are held each year in the UK, Switzerland, and elsewhere, featuring story times, vendors, and other resources for age players. And there are, of course, websites (and apps) for age play as well.

Most people in the age play community share the ethical clarity that their identities have nothing to do with pedophilia. Anyone under eighteen—and in some cases twenty-one—is strictly barred from all kink events, including age play, and are also barred from accessing any of the vast age play–related content on FetLife (they're not allowed to be members, nor are any members allowed to discuss actual children in any context, including nonsexual references to their actual family members or their own memories of childhood). But some underage individuals fake their ages and sneak onto restricted websites, as I imagine happens with all online porn. Amy Martin (who is, in real life, also a wife and mother) wrote on her blog in 2016 that she has noticed more adolescents on mainstream social media identifying as Littles.

Perhaps—and this is my theory—this is due in part to the rise of singer-songwriter Melanie Martinez, who appeared on the television show *The Voice* at age eighteen in an oversized hair bow and schoolgirl skirt, playing a toy piano. Martinez released her first full-length Little-themed album *Cry Baby* in 2015 at age twenty (but looks and dresses younger than she is, and her music and videos are popular with teens. One can understand the appeal of this aesthetic, which is also reflected in Tokyo street style and other teenaged subcultures. But as Amy Martin writes, relationships between Little-identifying teens and adults are "not BDSM, not age play, not role play." To state the obvious, if you are actually fifteen, you can't *pretend* to be fifteen. No minor can be a Middle while they are, in fact, still in their adolescent years, nor should any adult engage in an age play dynamic with someone under the age of consent. Relationships—even just online flirting or commenting—with actual minors is immoral and illegal. Don't do it.

A DADDY/GIRL AGE PLAY MIXTAPE, WITH LINER NOTES

Sometimes my primary partner and I play dirty Daddy-girl role plays. I don't identify as a lifestyle Middle, but I occasionally like to slip into that persona, among others in my repertoire.

But here's a potentially confusing fact: even when I'm *not* age playing a teen, I call this partner Daddy. I like to say that I call him Daddy the way that women in early twentieth-century blues songs call their men Daddy, or the way gangster molls in noir films call their men Daddy, or the way the pampered mistress of a sugar daddy might answer her lover's call: as a term of subversive endearment and playfully submissive enticement.

I'm not alone. I'm fascinated by how much evidence there is that people of all genders, races, classes, orientations, ages, and backgrounds call their partners Daddy (or Papi, or some variation thereof) as a sexy, edgy pet name. This playlist is evidence of that.

1. "My Heart Belongs to Daddy," Eartha Kitt (1953 and numerous subsequent recordings)

   Probably the most famous Daddy/girl song, purred to purrfection by Catwoman herself. The brilliant lyricist Cole Porter wrote it for *Leave It to Me!*, a little-known musical. In this musical, the song is sung by a stripper who is talking about her millionaire sugar daddy, even though the lyrics never make it totally clear if the singer is talking about her actual father or her boyfriend. (Porter was gay, and one might say that gay men know a thing or two about the delights of a sexy Daddy.) The song has been covered many times, including by Ella Fitzgerald, Ariana Grande, and D/g icon Marilyn Monroe, who sings it in her movie *Let's Make Love* (and who treated every man she appeared with on screen like a Daddy she was hoping would rescue her).

2. "Partition," Beyoncé (2013)

   What I love about this song is that Beyoncé makes it very clear in the intro that she is a confident, successful woman and Jay-Z's wife—"Say 'hey, Ms. Carter!'" she instructs her audience—but she also embraces her erotic submissive side, telling us how she likes to get "on her knees" in the back of a cab for her husband. "Daddy didn't bring the towel," she slyly reports.

continues

3. "Sweet Daddy," Storey Sisters (1958)

This obscure song was recorded by an early rock 'n' roll/R&B girl group made up of two sisters from Philadelphia, also known as the Twinkles. It's a devoted ode to a lover who is "my daddy" in the morning, evening, and "late at midnight," followed by a knowing erotic wail. Their bigger hit was a song called "Bad Motorcycle," a euphemism for "bad motherfucker," so clearly the ladies were okay with walking right up to the line of what was inappropriate.

4. "I Know What Boys Like," The Waitresses (1982)

This is not specifically a song about a Daddy/girl relationship—in fact, the lead singer, Patty Donahue (RIP) describes the *men* as behaving like "pouty children denied their candy." Nevertheless, this New Wave hit gets bonus points for Patty's disaffected and smirky Middle-esque vocal performance. I always think of it as the personal anthem of cockteases everywhere: "I *might* let you," Patty intones, before mockingly laughing and calling out, "Suckers!"

5. "Babygirl," Charli XCX (2017)

In my humble opinion, this song by the contemporary English pop star is a total rip-off of the Lana Del Rey aesthetic: the delivery, lyric content, and general vibe are all simply a more upbeat, mainstream take on what Lana's been doing all along. But I'm biased toward Lana. (See track 10.) The singer does call herself a "pinup princess" and repeats "I'll be your baby girl" as the chorus, so I guess it gets to go on this list.

6. "Give It to Me, Daddy," Hartman's Heartbreakers (1937, rediscovered and re-released in 1981)

A weird little treasure, this is a hillbilly tune sung in a cutesy-pie voice by a certain Betty Lou deMorrow, who cheerfully implores her "Daddy" to "give it to her every night." (In another of her songs, Betty Lou tells her lover—in an almost identical melody—that if he lets her play with his little yo-yo, she'll let him play with hers.) Music writer Mark Armstrong, in his liner notes for the 1981 Bear Family Records re-release, called the song "the crème de la crème of smuttiness" and said that back when it first came out, it would have mostly been played and sold at brothels, where one can assume clients could also indulge in some age play if they so chose.

7. "Cherry Bomb," the Runaways (1976)

Lead vocalist Cherie Currie—who was only sixteen when she recorded this classic—often did live performances of the song while clad in lingerie, which makes her ferocious growling of the line "have you and grab you until you're sore" all the more impressive—and all the more Lolita-inflected. I love the way she lingers over the phrase *Hellllllo Daddy*, and I love that ultimately, it's a defiantly proud song about the singer's sexual agency.

8. "Daddy," Julie London (1961)

The first of songwriter Bobby Troup's works to become a hit, written while he was still a student at the University of Pennsylvania in the late 1930s, the original version was recorded as a big-band narrative about a girl named Daisy Mae and her exploits with her sugar daddy. Troup's wife, Julie London, later rerecorded it and chose to emphasize the seduction in the materialistic lyrics. "Won't I look swell in sables, clothes with Paris labels?" she coos, enticing her lover to pony up.

9. "Daddy Issues," the Neighbourhood (2015)

The rare song from the Daddy-type's point of view, this 2015 track is ostensibly about the male singer's own issues with his late father but addresses a "crying" girl and includes the lyrics: "if you were my little girl / I'd do whatever I could do." I'm not sure if it's generally a great idea for both members of a D/g relationship to be seeking a father figure, but hey, I hope they can work that shit out.

10. "You Can Be the Boss," Lana Del Rey (2010)

Lana is the undisputed queen of the Daddy/girl song.* From the very start, she adopted a lollipop-licking, pouty-voiced, Lolita-inspired demeanor, even when singing about men who seem to be the same age as she is. Notably, though, she briefly dated—or led the public to assume she was dating—Axl Rose of Guns N' Roses, who is twenty-five years her senior. Before she ever met him, she wrote a song called "Axl Rose Husband," in which she sang, "You're my one king daddy / I'm your little queen." Later, in early 2020, she was in a relationship with a beefcake police officer a dozen years her elder.

continues

You could choose any number of Lana songs to put on this list, but my personal favorite is "You Can Be the Boss," probably because it also fetishizes a boozy Daddy, which is one of my kinks. The title of this song alone is a great encapsulation of the consent and negotiation required in D/g or any other erotic role play/power exchange relationship: the daddy gets to play the boss only because his girl says he can.

*It's worth noting that Melanie Martinez is also big in this category—she has built her entire musical career on a Little persona, her songs replete with baby and kindergarten imagery and references. But she seems to use girlhood exclusively as a metaphor for adult problems and relationships, and does not delve into role play in her song lyrics, despite the kinky, Littles-inspired world her songs and videos create. There's something I find problematic about Melanie Martinez's use of these motifs that I can't quite put my finger on—maybe it's the fact that, as I mentioned earlier, she first achieved fame while still in high school, and therefore lacks the chronological distance required to make her age play a fantasy rather than an enacting of sexualized adolescence.

HOW MUCH IS THAT DOGGIE IN THE WINDOW?

There are kinks I have and kinks I don't have. Among the kinks I don't have, there are some that I find hard to understand—though I try! And then there are kinks I don't have that nonetheless make total (and appealing) sense to me. Pet play is the latter.

Maybe it's because I've always been an actual animal lover who finds creatures of all kinds—koalas, gorillas, rabbits, seals, deer—adorable and worthy of empathy. I know that people who dress up in horse bridles and dog collars are not actual animals, but when they melt into those personae, I am totally there for it, viewing them as just as cute and delightful as the real thing. Even though I'm not a direct participant, I absolutely love to be around people who have gone into character as a kinky puppy, fox, or kitten.

Puppy play has a long legacy within the queer, leather-aligned parts of the BDSM community that are rooted in the domain of gay men. It's impossible to chart the exact history of animal role play, but we do know that gay leathermen have long donned dog collars and leashes. And as far back as the 1940s, there has been pornographic art of people dressed in pony regalia, most notably in the photography John Willie created for his fetish magazine, *Bizarre*.

After a few decades of being relatively untrendy, this kink has undergone a recent resurgence and is enjoying new attention. The artist Zak Krevitt, who has made photographs of people who do this kind of role play, told the *Huffington Post* in 2016 that puppy play, which is "largely made up of LGBT folk," may not be "queering sexuality or gender per se," but it does "[queer] one's humanity" in a "rejection of the human and an adaptation of the primal."

An annual event called Ponies on the Delta sounds like a BDSM animal role play paradise. It's a three-day in-person gathering that takes place (when there's not a pandemic) on a campground outside of New Orleans where, according to the website, attendants can "come find their herd" while discovering "how pony-like" they can be. Activities include a variety of field events for hard-working human horses and their handlers, including dressage (complete with judging and ribbons), sheep herding, a fox hunt, and more. For those without their own horse tack, which can be very expensive, some is available on hand to borrow. Other kinds of animal play and kink beyond pony-centric ones are also welcome: there is a puppy obstacle course and a fully equipped dungeon on hand, plus a Burning Man–style after-hours dance party. Ponies on the Delta has attracted pony players from around the world, who arrive with fully developed horse alter egos, beautiful leather masks, bridles, and furry hoof hand-coverings. As one German attendee said in a video on the YouTube cultural documentary channel iWonder TV (formerly known as Wizard of Odd), "My pony is a second character inside me, and [here] I can let it come out." In the same video, another attendee points out, "Ponies like a lot of attention and affection. For some people, it might be totally nonsexual role play, where they just want to pretend to be a horse. Everyone has their own style."

Attending group events is something that age players, pet players, and furries (see below) all have in common. Because real-life children and domestic animals are dependent on adult human companions, people role playing those personae tend to be socially driven, making the kinks particularly well-suited for events—and the natural capitalist outgrowth of events, commodification. The ABDL, pet play, and furry communities all tend to organize social gatherings such as play dates and parties, and many of those gatherings revolve around commercial enterprises. As George Gurley points out in a 2001 article for *Vanity Fair* about furries, the Internet began making it possible for these role players to connect and organize with others. In recent years, furries conventions have been held all over the world, easily drawing over a thousand attendees each; to put those numbers in perspective, many smaller niche conventions for BDSM and other subcultures typically attract only a few hundred folks. One reason for these large turnouts could be that Littles, pony players, and furries all tend to covet dedicated resources that (a) are not easy to have at home, and (b) are not the dungeon-like spaces usually found at broader kink events. These communities seek out adult-sized playpens, special obstacle courses, and large meadows for romping.

FURRIES: A QUE(E)RY

Furries are people who role play as *anthropomorphized* animals. If you think of a puppy player as inhabiting the role of a pet dog, then think of a furry as playing (and taking inspiration from) figures like Bugs Bunny, Minnie Mouse, Pinkie Pie from *My Little Pony*, or another animal character from kiddie cartoons. (There's that wellspring of kink again!)

Most often and most famously, furries get into character by dressing up in costumes called fursuits. While these costumes are often of the full-body sports-mascot variety, some furries (whether out of preference, necessity, or practicality) go with a more subtle tail and/or animal ears added on to their regular human outfits.

And while costumes are important in the furry subculture, they are not a necessity. The only vital aspect of being a furry is having a developed "fursona": an animal self with a name, species, personality, body movements, and backstory. A furry's role played character is

a fully realized alter ego. To my mind, this is one interesting com-
monality between the role players who identify as Littles and those
who identify as furries.

Furries both are and are not part of the larger kink scene. It's my
sense that before the Internet allowed the furry subculture to flourish, many furries found refuge in events and online forums aimed
at kinky folks who shared their interest in dressing up in strange
costumes and escaping into an elaborate fantasy persona. Some folks
consider their furry play to be an extension of puppy and pony play
historically rooted in the kink community and there are others who
rather see it as a wholesome, nonsexual expression of an alter ego.

Either way, identifying as a furry seems to be trending: in 2015, a
Bloomberg news article cited an online geolocator that allowed over
7,500 self-identified furries worldwide to map themselves; at this
writing, Furmap.net (which replaced the earlier version Furrymap.
net) shows almost 17,000, with furry "hotspots" in Central Florida,
Mexico City, Sao Paulo, Krakow, Moscow, and Jakarta, to name a
few. In 2017, a single furry convention, Anthrocon, drew over 8,400
attendees to its annual event in Pittsburgh. Meanwhile, furry media
personalities are attracting large audiences, such as YouTuber Pocari
Roo, who wears a bright-blue kangaroo fursuit and currently has
over two hundred thousand followers. (The Netflix show *Glow*,
which also came out in 2017 but is set in the 1980s and is based on
real events and people, features the character of Sheila, a wrestler
who never removes her wolf costume or makeup: I think of her
character as a proto-furry.)

Like many other subsets of kink, the furry world is a full-fledged
subculture, complete with slang and magazines. And, as we've seen,
some in this world lean into kinky/sexy territory, and some decidedly
do not. A 2015 article by reporter Dylan Matthews for *Vox* noted
that "while sexual activity with other furries (known as 'yiffing,' after
the sound foxes make during sex) is part of the subculture for some,
others maintain a non-erotic interest in the subject." While it may
have originally begun as part of the kink community, and though
there is certainly no shortage of furry-driven porn, the furry sphere
is now known more as a fandom, with an emphasis on costumes, art,

and play-acting a persona in a way that's meant to be more about humor and entertainment—or tapping into a profound and deeply satisfying sense of nonhuman self—than it is about eros.

And this is another way in which they are much like Littles. As we've discussed, some Littles are very clear that their Little personality is *not* sexual and therefore they are not to be sexually approached.

I have a lot of empathy for Littles, furries, and others who want to explore things we call "kink" without the sexy parts: who am I to say that someone can't dress up as a toddler—or, for that matter, as a kangaroo—just for the sheer, wholesome fun of it? If I believe people should be allowed to do these things sexually—and of course I do—why would I not believe they should be allowed to do them non-sexually?

My problem comes with using the term "kink" when the tone around the identity, activity, or behavior is nonsexual. I'm also frustrated by people with these nonsexual kinks showing up at kink events where sexual expression is clearly the primary objective and then getting upset by any erotic assumptions made about them. Context is everything, and if you are categorizing your quirky behavior as a *kink*, either by showing up at a kink event or posting on FetLife or otherwise putting yourself out there in a sexualized space, I don't think it's reasonable or realistic to ask others to avoid sexualizing that behavior.

As an alternative, I hope that we can come up with another term for these powerful kinds of nonsexual adult play, and that other kinds of nonsexual gatherings, communities, and the like can continue to flourish. My guess is that if there was a better, more distinct term for such passions—a better "brand," if you will—even more people would find solace and resonance with them.

CHAPTER 8

CAUGHT UP IN YOU

On the Kinks of Attention and Neglect

*The eros of attention — voyeurship and exhibitionism —
the art of sex in public — hotwife and other ways to turn
jealousy on its head — in the realm of no senses — a case
for reverent objectification — hypnosis, bimbofication,
feeding, and other forms of control.*

I was an angsty twelve-year-old in 1984, the year that Animotion's hit single "Obsession" came out. I had barely started to delve into the world of relationships or sex, but I *loved* this New Wave song, which was infused with both. Its lyrics, by Michael Des Barres, were—and are!—completely inappropriate for an impressionable pre-adolescent: they were inspired in part by the notorious John Fowles novel *The Collector* and the British film adaptation of it, both of which tell the story of a lonely and deranged man who kidnaps women hoping to force them to fall in love with him. But the song felt utterly romantic to me, and I relished the idea of someone being a "possession, unopened at [their lover's] feet," and experiencing an adoration that "consumed [the] soul" to the point where I had "no control."

Several decades later, with a few codependent relationships and rounds of therapy under my belt, I can say that no one ought to aspire to what this song describes: this kind of dynamic is toxic, dangerous, and unhealthy. And yet, I think that even when we know this intellectually, many of us still equate full-on obsession with love, or at least attraction. And we think it's something we want. A host of movies and romance novels reinforce this idea: "true love" means utterly sacrificing one's identity and abdicating all responsibility in the face of burning desire.

A truly obsessive relationship, as anyone who has been in one knows, isn't fun: it's exhausting and humorless, icky and suffocating. One thing kink gives us is the space to explore, in a temporary and make-believe way, that level of romantic entanglement in a manner that is safer, saner, and more playful. Which is important, I think, because the *idea* of obsession is, after all, quite sexy. It's sexy to want something or someone with a desperate, adolescent yearning. It's sexy to *feel* wanted that way, too, at least for a few minutes or hours. Desire of this type is an adrenaline rush; it's an energizing jolt.

Obsession. Surrender. Control. Attention. There is an undeniable power in these emotions, because they are ultimately about experiencing what it means to be fully alive, in thrall. They are also ways of feeling *seen:* a bit of obsessive attention, or surrendering of control—administered in small doses, without the abusive behaviors evoked in those song lyrics—can help us feel taken care of and appreciated.

Obsession, surrender, and control are also delicious flavors of overwhelm, which is an experience that humans crave. If we didn't, there would be no need for horror movies, roller coasters, spicy food, or race cars, much less kink.

In this chapter, I'll look at some of the kinks associated with paying, seeking, or denying attention, such as voyeurship and exhibitionism, hotwife and cuckolding, orgasm denial, human furniture, and sensory deprivation. I'll also talk about kinks that are related to control but that don't fall under the more common categories of D/s or S/m: erotic hypnosis, bimbofication, and feeding/encouraging. I wanted to make sure to touch upon some of these lesser-known alternative sexual practices, and in a broad sense I think of all these kinks as related to our ability to succumb, for a moment, to a mind-altering void that transports us from our daily routines into a feverish, trance-like state of arousal.

ARE WE *ALL* VOYEURS?

I can't even count the number of times a person on a TV show or movie—or at a real-life party—has seductively lowered their voice to utter the words "I like to *watch*" as a kind of eyebrow-raising joke. It never fails to seem a little deviant.

But *is* it deviant? Or is "liking to watch" one of the most vanilla pleasures out there? Don't get me wrong: vanilla pleasures are hot, yummy, valid pleasures! And since most of us want to feel *seen*, it's a very good thing that so many of us enjoy watching.

I've long wondered, though, if voyeurism, also known as scopophilia, gets overplayed as a kink. Those of us who are sighted tend to enjoy using our vision to make meaning of our world and help us decide what interests us. "Liking to watch" isn't really unusual. If it was, there wouldn't be a multibillion-dollar porn industry.

Scientifically speaking, humans are a sight-driven species, possessing color and stereo vision and depth perception. We rely on sight, and we also find pleasure in it. We love looking at art, watching movies, gazing out at the beautiful natural world. Looking at beautiful people ain't bad, either. The meaning behind idioms such as "head-turning," "good-looking," and "love at first sight" are all rooted in the functions of our eyes and the ways they connect to our brains. In a 2007 article for the *New York Times*, science writer Natalie Angier reported on a series of studies that "demonstrated that the body's entire motor system is activated almost instantly by exposure to sexual images, and that the more intensely sexual the visuals, the stronger the electric signals" that resulted. (This is the reason, one can presume, why so many men assume that dick pics will be appreciated.)

Is it kinky if you want to get all *Sex, Lies and Videotape* and watch your partner masturbate? I'd propose that when someone you already find attractive invites you to watch them touch their own gorgeous body while you watch them get more and more aroused, that's just good old-fashioned sexy stuff. I don't think there's anything particularly kinky about it. The authors of a *Kinkly* article on the subject write that "most people feel aroused observing others when they are semi-clothed, nude, or receiving sexual pleasure." So where is the line between completely typical human responses to visual stimuli and the kink that gets called "voyeurism"?

Perhaps the problem lies in the evolution of the term. Like "sadism," another term that has become over- and misused, "voyeurism" originated with turn-of-the-last-century Freudian psychologists, and it referred to a specific pathology: voyeurs were people who got their erotic kicks from watching or capturing images of someone who doesn't know they are being watched. The *DSM-5* now calls this condition "voyeuristic disorder," defined as a condition in adults (almost all male-identified) who "continuously experience strong sexual arousal from observing an unsuspecting person who is either naked, undressing, or engaging in sexual activity" and who act on their urges. Those actions can be criminal offenses. Under this medical definition, voyeurism can't be done as a healthy kink, because being a "peeping Tom" is inherently unethical and non-consensual. If you *pretend* to enact such a scene—by, say, staging a negotiated tableau in which your lover makes believe that they don't know you're looking at them—then that could be really fun and hot. But creeping up on strangers, which is what "voyeurism" originally meant, is never okay.

These days, talking about voyeurism can be confusing, because the original definition of the word "has survived alongside newer uses," as a 2021 article by the editors of the medical site WebMD states. We now say someone is a voyeur when they show interest in looking, non-sexually, at celebrities, car crashes, and what have you; we also call watching striptease voyeurship, even when the stripper fully knows that they're performing for others. When it comes to ethical, healthy voyeurism, I'd argue that what distinguishes normative sexual behavior from kink is how extreme the preferences are. A kinky voyeur may like to watch *to the exclusion* of almost all other activities: they want to *only* watch, or enjoy watching more than they enjoy participating, and the voyeurship could thus be categorized as a fetish. And a fetishistic voyeur might best get off if positioned behind the lens of a camera, or across the room from the action, rather than directly in the thick of it.

As with all kinks, having specific, taboo predilections such as voyeurism can cause guilt, shame, or distress in a relationship, especially if a partner finds your interests odd. The intensity of a voyeur's gaze may feel off-putting to the person being watched, no matter how consensually. To all voyeurs, though, I'd offer this good news: there are a multitude of exhibitionists out there who might absolutely love it if all you want to do is watch through the shower door or replay their homemade video. Like a masochist who has found their dream sadist, or an age playing submissive boi who has found their perfect Mommy, a voyeur can seek out just the right exhibitionist to make all their wildest fantasies come true.

THE GENTLE ART OF SEX IN PUBLIC

There are some kinds of outré sexy activities that get talked about a lot more than done. I've been lucky enough to get to do a lot of wild, adventurous things, but I've never, for example, joined the Mile High Club. I honestly can't figure out how one would really do this. Those airplane bathrooms are tiny. And smelly. Maybe that's part of the appeal, but the idea sounds better than the execution to me.

I've also always loved the idea of outdoor sex in public places, which, sex educator Kenneth Play points out, makes sense: for much of our existence as a primate species, outdoors was the *only* place we had sex. But in this century, it, too, seems hard to pull off. Of course, most kinks involve some thrill factor, and I understand that the risk of getting caught, or even arrested, might be arousing to some. Besides, public sex *looks* great in the movies: up against a brick wall in an alley with a hoisted skirt, or on a picnic blanket in a meadow, or rolling around in the waves, the fast and furious nature of it all. I just wonder how many times the sensory experience delivers on the promise. Combine potential embarrassment with wet grass or dry sand, bugs, dumpster stench, and sweat, and it makes sense why most of us end up in a nice, clean bed.

To each their own, though, and sex in public is definitely a common kinky fantasy. Public sex bonds the participants in their outdoor (ad)venture. Certainly there's a hint of exhibitionism in it, and like voyeuristic acts, exhibitionism requires thoughtful consideration around the question of consent: you should plan to exaggerate the exhibitionistic circumstances of your play to avoid actually exposing an innocent and non-consenting bystander to your body parts of sexual conduct. Hot public sex can quickly become a very troubling case of indecent exposure.

So how to walk that fine line between thrilling tryst and lewd misdemeanor? I found a helpful 2019 article by journalist Alyssa Girdwain in *Women's Health* that had some smart recommendations. For one, you could employ a semi-public location such as your own patio, rooftop, outdoor shower, shed, or backyard. I'd suggest that you aim for a time of day, such as late morning or in the middle of the night, when the neighbors—especially minors—are unlikely to be around.

Girdwain also mentions car sex, a go-to for many teens and still exciting for adults. I recommend using a car with bench front seats and no stick shift for maximum comfort and ease. Don't have access to one of those? You can always head into the backseat, or into the tinted-glass rear of an SUV or minivan. Where to park it? I live in a state that has small parking lots along rural roads meant for quick stretch breaks, and let's just say I am fond of those. If you are more of an indoor sort, Girdwain suggests scoping out a single-stall bathroom. My personal preferences run toward roomy, nicely-lit lavatories at elegant restaurants and the like: even though I've never done this (yet), I still evaluate every lockable public restroom I enter for fuck potential.

Here's a favorite of my exhibitionistic partner, who absolutely loves the thought of being watched: book a hotel with floor-to-ceiling glass windows and/or a balcony, and go to town. Most likely, no one is really looking, but there's always the possibility!

GETTING NAUGHTY IN NYC

The luxury Standard Hotel in New York City was built to overlook the High Line, a former elevated train line converted into a delightful walkway filled with pedestrians. The Standard has nonreflective glass windows, and that's no accident: a 2009 *New York Magazine* piece by Coco McPherson called "Public Sex and the Standard Hotel" reports that the hotel took out risqué ads basically inviting people to put on a show for the folks on the High Line below. When the Standard first opened, Ricky Serling, a worker from the neighborhood, told McPherson, "I've seen men and women, women and women, men and men, lights, leather, chains, everything." Fast forward to 2017, and the locals were getting a little sick of the hotel guests' "sex-crazed antics," according to a finger-wagging piece in the *New York Post*, which then ran a bunch of peeping photos they'd taken to illustrate the story—you know, to be responsibly journalistic about it. The photos show a telescopic shot of an illuminated room at the Standard in which three comely people cavorted around in lingerie, unaware of the "journalist" snapping away below—*or were they?*

A more rustic version of semi-public hotel sex is sex while tent camping, which Girdwain also mentions. As long as you're the outdoorsy type, this can be fun, because it's generally considered totally fine to do whatever you want within the confines of your own tent (as long as you obey quiet hours and aren't obnoxious about it), but you can get down while knowing that your "walls" are just nylon and there are strangers close at hand who can guess what you're up to.

And if you're able to shell out some cash, most major cities are home to underground "on-premise" sex events: parties where you are allowed to fuck people right at the venue, which is often a designated club, hotel, or private home. (Join a swinger site or app such as Swing Lifestyle [SLS] to find listings and recommendations, or search for "adult-only resorts" and read reviews by swingers.) You may think you have to have sex with strangers at these clubs or parties, but that's not true: many people go to sex events just to put on a show with their partners in an erotically charged atmosphere. However, if you're looking for an exhibitionistic fix, keep in mind that if it's a couples-only party, everyone might be too busy getting it on with their partners to pay any attention to you. On the flip side, sex clubs that have nights where single men are allowed in can translate into being encircled by an overeager mob of leering strangers, which is sometimes hot—and sometimes really not, depending on your tastes and mood.

One final word of advice: if you want to take to the woods or beach for your romp, as Girdwain suggests, be smart about it. Pack a lightweight, washable blanket, wear tick and bug repellent, and dress for ease and speed of access.

HOTWIFE AND OTHER WAYS TO TURN JEALOUSY ON ITS HEAD

Watching or being watched in an erotic manner is a particular kind of paying attention. Kinks like hotwife (in which a partner feels pride and arousal by the thought of their wife-type stepping out), cuckolding, and consensual gang bangs play with this type of attention, much like voyeurship and exhibitionism. But they also add the variable of nonmonogamy: watching others check out your hotwife, watching your partner "cheat" on you, watching others have sex while you "wait your turn." Sometimes these scenarios don't involve watching at all, and instead the partner is told about the sex they didn't participate in. In either case, these scenarios are meant to evoke titillating and arousing feelings of humiliation, shame, pride, or sluttiness.

Note that I am speaking here about *kinky* ways to play with nonmonogamy. Many polyamorous and ethically nonmonogamous couples—swingers and people in open relationships, for example—conduct their business in sincere and serious ways that emphasize the wholesomeness of the arrangement: they may invite their lover along for apple-picking with the kids and wife, or all play poker together every Thursday. That's fabulous—and something I myself have found very rewarding—but I don't think of it as kinky, as it seeks to recreate a normative nonmonogamous relationship model, rather than heightening what feels "dirty" or "wrong" about it.

It's also vital that we separate out consensual kinky behaviors from yucky, problematic behaviors. "Cuckold" is a term that has been used since at least the thirteenth century to insult a man whose wife is cheating on him; it shows up as a bawdy word in the works of Chaucer and Shakespeare. (The etymology comes from the fact that cuckoo birds raise hatchlings that other cuckoos have laid in their nest, which has actually made cuckoos an evolutionarily strong species!) In a blog article for the sex-toy company Lelo, researcher Stuart Nugent notes that "a cheating wife generally renders the man a pariah, or a punchline," in ancient cultures from Rome to China. During the 2016 election cycle, American white nationalists took to calling any Republican who was not reactionary enough for them a "cuck."

Now, if someone feels genuinely humiliated and betrayed by their partner's philandering, there is no kink in that: that's just plain old boring, hurtful adultery. Yet 1.75 million people—mostly heterosexual men, who, one could argue, have the most entitlement, and therefore anxiety, about their status—use "cuckold" as a search term on porn sites every *month*, according to a 2016 data report from the analysis team at PornHub. So clearly the fantasy of watching one's wife get banged by another guy while you sit passively in the corner is pretty exciting.

Which brings us to this point: all of these infidelity-based kinks are rooted in a bunch of toxic-masculinity nonsense about wives as property—notions that reduce men either to virile studs or passive doormats, and women to either wholesome saints or sinful hussies. Many of the kinks that play out these roles seek to turn those notions of jealousy and sin on their heads, but without the underlying patriarchal paradigms, there would be no taboo and thus, no kink.

This shouldn't surprise those of us privy to the machinations of the kinky mind. We know that for every person who, in their daily life, wants to feel empowered, respected, and worthwhile (and that's pretty much all of us, no?), there are many pervy folks who want to experience, in our erotic lives, within the safe and negotiated space of enthusiastically consensual play, feelings of degradation or inferiority. When someone *chooses* to play the cuckold, they are getting aroused by their partner getting well-fucked by someone else—maybe even someone better looking, wealthier, or more charismatic, and with a bigger, thicker cock. The turn-on is *in* the emasculation: a husband can choose to play up his status as a "sissy" and the wife's fuck buddy can play up his superiority as a "bull." A happily cuckold-centric kinky couple will pile on the taunting and humiliation for all its worth, knowing that underneath it all is a rock-solid relationship built on trust and honesty. This kind of kink can also be a way to heal from past trauma or baggage around infidelity: a man identified as Peter in a 2016 article by Charlotte Shane in *MEL Magazine* says that he began fantasizing about women who slept around after being in a hurtful relationship with a chronic cheater. For him, it felt extremely reassuring to find a partner with whom he could play out that same scenario with his consent and participation.

Because of the potential for genuine insecurity in such a situation, cuckolding is a very high-stakes kind of role playing, and certainly all involved should be extremely clear on the parameters of the game.

The emotional elements tied into cuckolding—virility, masculinity, fidelity—are deeply fraught in most cultures, which means that as a consensual kink, it has the potential for being very naughty fun indeed . . . but it can also go south.

If you're not totally sure you want to delve into cuckolding, yet something about this scenario gets you hot and bothered, there is a way you can play with the idea of being a slut without involving any other sexual partners: just use your filthy imagination! The "slutty" partner can wear a revealing outfit under their coat and lean over their beloved—and maybe some nearby strangers. They can surreptitiously let their partner know they aren't wearing any panties out in public. They might flirt with the bartender, car mechanic, or delivery person and tell their beloved *all* about it—or do it in front of them. They could dance up on a willing stranger at the club. Basically, they can do anything they want short of actual sex to remind their partner or spouse of what a brazen little tart they are.

Those seeking a less intense variation on cuckolding may also want to look into its sister kink: hotwife. The term and practice come from the hetero-centric swinger community where, for some couples, a big part of the thrill is for both the woman and her man to think of her as insatiable, sex-crazed, and highly desired by others. In a dramatic reversal from how such a dynamic has *usually* played out throughout the history of heterosexual marriage, the hotwife's innate sexual power is celebrated and encouraged, and it can be done without the humiliation factor inherent to cuckolding. Troy, also interviewed for Shane's *Mel* article, put it this way: "I love the idea of my wife's deepest, truest state being purely wanton." He also sees hotwife as helping him maintain his competitive edge as a man, saying, "I always need to be smarter, funnier, more engaging, more attractive. . . . I constantly strive to be a better partner for my wife, and I get the thrill of winning her over, time and time again."

As with any kind of kink, there are innumerable ways you can spin your particular take on hotwifing. Cuckold kinkster Adam MC Amen, on his site Cuckold Club—a (free, ad-supported) clearinghouse of cuck-related videos, stories, and other resources—describes eleven types of hotwife dynamics. Among them are "stag and vixen" relationships, in which a Dominant-type husband maintains control by deciding who his hotwife will fuck and when, and is usually there with her when it happens; the "Mistress hotwife," in which the wife acts as a Domme who teases, feminizes, or denies orgasms to her submissive husband; and the "slutwife," who prides herself on indiscriminately taking all comers.

Of course, all of this only works if both parties are equally pumped about it. If the cuckold actually feels shaky or left out, or if the wife-type feels forced into the situation or made to feel bad about it afterward, that's not enthusiastically consensual kink and we're right back in a medieval play full of marital strife. If either you or your partner are uncertain about wading into these deep waters, go slowly and communicate a ton—or forego the actual thing and just watch a bunch of hotwife porn together!

I also want to offer a word to the wise about kinky gang bangs and the role of the penis-owner in such a scene. A huge draw on porn sites, a gang bang begins with the premise that one person— usually but not always a cis woman—enthusiastically invites a group of people—usually but not always cis men—to fuck her. My sweetie used to think he would be really into a gang bang, as the idea of sexually insatiable women is extremely arousing to him. But when he finally got the chance to participate in one, carefully orchestrated at a kink event and "starring" a woman with whom he had an established sexual relationship, he found it disappointing. The truth of the matter is that the "bangers" don't get much attention at a gang bang. Generally speaking, the identity of the individual bangers is somewhat anonymous or irrelevant to the bangee, since the whole scenario is about raunchy, group-oriented quantity over intimate quality. And because what turns my sweetie on more than anything is feeling secure that his lover is *extremely* into him—even if only physically or only for that moment—he just couldn't get comfortable in the rushed, high-pressure atmosphere of a gang bang. He wasn't the only guy with this problem: I saw many of the participants at this event having a difficult time maintaining their erections when surrounded by other men anxiously awaiting their turn and trying to stay in the zone. My guess is that gang bangs are one of those things that look at lot easier and better when performed by adult entertainment professionals than they do IRL.

IN THE REALM OF NO SENSES

We've spent much of this book talking about the various ways kinky people get off from textures, tastes, smells, and physical sensation, and in this chapter we've been looking at some of the ways that "paying attention" can be a huge turn-on. But what if your thing is being *deprived* of sensory experience and/or attention?

Welcome to the world of human furniture, mummification, chastity devices, ruined orgasms, and other ways that wonderfully freaky people can turn normative notions of pleasure on their head.

I think of all these kinks as holding commonalities with masochism: arousal that stems from a deliciously torturous sense of denial. Although many folks can think of nothing worse than having our needs ignored by a lover, for people into these kinds of pervy pleasures there is a powerful high associated directly with these kinds of psychologically (and sometimes physically) painful experiences—providing, of course, that it is done only within a negotiated and fully consensual erotic space.

Edging (also called orgasm control, orgasm denial, or even just "teasing") is one example. Edging is the art of staving off sexual release: when one chooses to stay instead in the zone of sustained but unresolved arousal. It's my sense that many vanilla people have had some fun with edging without even knowing it. I'd argue that anytime someone starts messing around (solo or with partners), gets turned on, and then stops because circumstances or emotions preclude orgasm or an otherwise satisfying outcome, it's a kind of edging. Personally, I remember being a teenager who hadn't started having sex yet and walking around in a kind of glazed stupor, all revved up after a session of heavy petting or even just a hormonal surge of horny desire: it was frustrating but also kind of fantastic. One could also think of the thrilling crush energy that one gets from just starting to text or flirt with a new partner—those moments before anything sexual has happened that hold the promise that it *could*—as a kind of emotional edging.

To my mind, intentional, kinky edging is a way of getting back to, and dwelling in, that stimulating headspace, and making it last as long as possible. As writer Haley Lyndes put it in an article she wrote for *Popsugar* in 2022, "Edging is everything you're looking for in an orgasm: a longer time spent . . . turned on, an intense climax, and a period of total exhaustion from the thrill of it all." Lyndes interviewed sex expert Emily Morse, who points out that edging can even be educational, as it can help us learn about our "orgasmic thresholds." Most people who practice edging can vouch for the fact that it often produces an extra-strong release when they do finally cum; it can also help two or more partners better synchronize their "finishes."

Those into ruined orgasm, orgasm denial, and chastity devices take the practice of edging into a more intense, BDSM realm. Most of us have probably heard of a chastity belt, a device that "locks away" the genitals, which is mentioned in various historical accounts and fantasy novels. But the truth is, as far as scholars can tell, no one ever actually locked up their wife or daughter's vulva in a piece of mechanical gear, nor was such gear used on men, either. Scholar of medieval studies Albrecht Classen even wrote a book that busts through the myth that such things were ever used (other than perhaps by serious, enterprising sexual deviants, who have existed throughout history but whose stories we often don't know!): literary and artistic representations of chastity belts, he says, are likely purely allegorical.

But just as contemporary dungeon-dwellers use medieval torture implements such as whips and St. Andrews, crosses for deviant fun, so too have they designed real-world orgasm-denying devices modeled after the mythological ones. You can easily buy a chastity belt online these days, although the ones I've seen seem more decorative than functional. Sure, it can look sexy to wear a leather thong with a big padlock on the front, but such gear sounds as likely to *cause* an orgasm to the wearer as to prevent one—especially if you buy the kind I saw on a website that has one hole that a clit can stick out of and another for the vagina!

Contemporary cock cages, on the other hand, are designed with actual orgasm-denying functionality in mind. For someone like sex educator and chastity enthusiast Dainis Graveris, feeling "truly trapped" in an inescapable device that is also comfortable enough for extended wear is the whole point, and he swears by the "intensity of feeling" he gets when, after serving a period of "patience and gratitude" for his D-type, the device is removed. On his sexy-toy review site Sexual Alpha, Graveris evaluates the cock cages available on the market, which offer features such as lock-and-key sets, smooth inner surfaces, air vents, holes for urinating (and ejaculating), and spacers to adjust the size and squeezing sensation. Graveris recommends the Dominix Deluxe for the delight of "cold hard metal bars" against one's cock, and notes that it's very difficult to get an erection with it on—which he considers a plus. The best part about the Dominix Deluxe, he writes, is that "the open spiraling design is awesome for teasing." Graveris describes another device, the Holy Trainer V4 (which Jeff Bezos is glad to have you buy on Amazon, believe it or not, and where you can read reviews by other satisfied customers) as having an enclosed space that "feels extra restrictive and frustrating," which, he notes, is another one of its advantages.

And what about the ruined orgasm? Exactly what it sounds like, a ruined orgasm is one that happens but doesn't produce a satisfying feeling, usually because the person is denied some basic need at the crucial moment. A kind of failed edging, in a ruined orgasm a body (of any gender) spills over into release, but it's not a *good* one, and it leaves one disappointed, restless, or achy. If you're into this kink, that's exactly how you and/or your partner want it! Ruined orgasms can be achieved (if that's the right word!) by having the porn images you're viewing disappear, or someone grabbing away your vibrator, or forcing your body into a position that is less pleasurable, all at the moment of truth. Wearing a cock cage can also foster it: Graveris notes that with the Dominix Deluxe, you're strapped into a device that allows you to cum while wearing it, but "it won't be satisfying for you," which is perfect for kinksters like himself and their "sadistic keyholders."

If you seek a sense of emotional denial along with the physical, you may be into kinks such as human furniture (aka forniphilia), in which someone is "used" as a side table or footrest by a partner who treats them with the same disinterest as one would treat an inanimate object; or ashing, in which someone is used as an ashtray for a cigar-smoking hottie. There are also mummification and other sensory-deprivation techniques in which a partner can learn how to wrap their lover in plastic wrap, cotton, duct tape, or other materials and either "leave them for dead" (for a previously agreed-upon amount of time, and with an emergency plan in place) or expose certain body parts for cruel, teasing fun. *Learn* is a key word here:

sensory deprivation is one of those kinks that requires study and planning, as body position and materials must be carefully managed in order to prevent allergic reactions, loss of circulation, dehydration, panic, and other serious problems. Do your research and proceed with caution when practicing any kind of sensory deprivation; never play while stoned, and never leave your partner unattended or without a way to communicate a hard stop.

Whether physical or mental, deprivation provides its own sensations: as blogger Robyn notes on the sexuality site Lovense, being mummified or serving as a table or toilet (for folks seeking pee or scat play) can bring up feelings of complete surrender, helplessness, and humiliation, and can be played by the Dominant/depriver in whatever tone they like, from affectionate to cruel. One can reach a level of submissiveness equal to the most elaborate chains-and-whips S/m scene without the use of specialized equipment. Many folks find an intense, even hallucinatory, bliss—an intense version of "sub space," not unlike the relaxation one gets from the flotation tanks offered in some spas—when given the chance to mentally float away in a level of confinement, darkness, and silence that they haven't experienced since leaving the womb.

All of these techniques and games are ways to temporarily and consensually surrender one's sense of humanity and dignity in exchange for a taste of what it's like to be "nothing but an object." While this may seem like an odd desire, I think it's precisely *because* we spend so much time fretting about how we're seen and how seriously we're taken that some of us choose to cathartically, erotically enact the worst-case-scenario of those anxieties on our own terms—a situation in which we're completely disregarded as an individual. Just as someone with a "getting beat up" kink wants to experience a negotiated version of an otherwise dangerous and miserable scenario, people with a desire to be erotically ignored or subjugated are able to face that situation knowing they are in full control.

A CASE FOR REVERENT OBJECTIFICATION

Most of the kinks discussed here involve people being consensually "used" in some form or another. This raises ethical questions. Isn't it inherently *wrong* to use people, especially if those people are women or people of color or otherwise historically marginalized folks who have to continually fight to be taken seriously? Isn't objectification the kind of misogynistic, racist, and sexist crap that activists have been trying to help us overcome?

It can be difficult to explain why someone—especially a feminist, woman-identified person like myself—can be okay with certain kinds of objectification. The devil, of course, is in the details: tone, context, approach, and situation. For example, I make an effort to look nice when I go out in public, and it feels validating when that gets noticed with a few thoughtful words. But I don't want anyone to ask for or expect anything in return for those words—if they do, then their action crosses the line into street harassment. Compliments should be given generously and respectfully, not crudely or with strings attached.

Inside consensual erotic spaces, I crave an even more intense version of this: I want to be told, by someone I like, that my ass looks incredible or that the way I look is getting them all wet. Within this context, I love nothing more than to be admired as a glorious objet d'art, and used accordingly—as long as, in other aspects of the relationship, I am also revered for my brain, personality, and hard work. My guess is I'm not alone in this.

That's why I like to use the term "reverent objectification": I believe there is a way to both recognize someone's humanity and also paint them as a luscious plaything. First, of course, make sure that your partner is seeking this kind of attention. Then play it up for all its worth: shower them with dirty talk about how you've been staring at them for hours, how you're going to use them all up, how they are nothing but your toy. In the right context, this can be a marvelous way to treat a lover to some much-wanted attentiveness.

HYPNOSIS, BIMBOFICATION, GAINING, AND OTHER FORMS OF CONTROL

There are attention kinks that overlap with D/s in the sense that, at their core, they are about taking or surrendering control. Erotic hypnosis, bimbofication, gaining, and other lesser-known deviant sexual expressions—all of which focus less on typical domination and submission and more on very specific scenarios and outcomes—can fall into this realm. Because they are so specifics-driven, it might make sense to also think of these as part of the *fetish* subcategory of kink.

Internet culture writer E. J. Dickson, in a 2020 article for *Rolling Stone* on bimbofication, calls it a "fetish that involves the transformation of an understated, normal-looking [person] into a surgically enhanced, spray-tanned camp icon" of the Paris Hilton/Ariana Grande type, which implies that others are witnessing, if not facilitating, that transformation. (Ironically, the fetish has recently become a trending "aesthetic"—or #aesthetic, a Gen-Z slang term referring to posted images of niche fashions and lifestyles made popular through online communities—and enjoys a viral following on TikTok. The *Rolling Stone* article called BimboTok "a collective performance of hyperfemininity" and reported that its proponents are all about agitprop, agency, and self-empowerment.)

Bimbofication can be explored either because someone really wants to help transform their partner into the vapid sexpot of their dreams and that partner enthusiastically agrees, or because someone wants to mold their own image in this style and allow others to enjoy that image. It can be performed fleetingly or occasionally in play sessions, or adopted as an ongoing personal style and attitude. At its core, bimbofication is another kind of role play: just as powerful businessmen may want to don frilly panties to enact a persona quite oppositional to their standard one, some bimbo fetishists are serious intellectuals who see their play as a kind of performance art, emotional release, or fun, experimental game. One could think of bimbos as cotton candy–flavored submissives: a lighter and sweeter way of engaging in D/s, and, debatably, a way to harness misogyny and transform it into female empowerment—a "fresh approach to intersectional feminism," according to Arielle Richards, an Australian journalist and author of a 2022 piece on the trend for *Vice*. One of BimboTok's biggest and longest-running stars is Chrissy Chlapecka, a self-identified "radical leftist" whose skimpy neon pink outfits and cartoonish voice are used to forward a queer, anti-racist, anti-capitalist agenda centered around loving yourself for who you are and refusing to let the system get you down. TikTok user Isa (@subversivenotbasic) calls bimbofication "weaponized incompetence."

I used to correspond with a man who was interested in using erotic hypnosis to help women like me—opinionated, brainy—let their inner bimbo out to play. As long as it's done ethically, with plenty of discussion and consent happening ahead of time, erotic hypnosis can be used for all kinds of sexy mental suggestions, including vanilla goals such as maintaining a harder erection, being able to feel more aroused, or achieving a hands-free orgasm. Hypnosis is a skill which must be learned and honed (there are plenty of YouTube videos and books on how to do it), and it can allow us to imagine ourselves as capable of things our doubting minds restrict. In the kinky realm, perhaps its most common utility/fantasy involves helping a submissive type melt into that role. (There are also folks who find the very process of hypnosis arousing; this is known as "hypno-kink.")

Although I didn't personally give hypno-bimbofication a whirl, I see the appeal of simultaneously enacting the roles of smart feminist and space cadet. As a child of the 1970s, I was exposed to many adorable representations of the bimbo on television: I had a crush on Goldie Hawn's giggling hippie on *Laugh-In*, the earnest and buxom country bumpkins on *Hee Haw*, and the airheaded and carefree Melody on the *Josie & the Pussycats* cartoon. They all looked so happy and relaxed, and everyone around them seemed to find them irresistible. Dickson's *Rolling Stone* article cites Kate Muir, aka @bimbokate, who has this caption on one of her most popular TikToks: "Being a self-aware bimbo is amazing: you become everything men want visually while also being everything they hate (self-aware, sexually empowered, politically conscious, etc.)." I was fascinated by a 2020 piece by erotica writer Max Bliss for *Medium* in which he describes how he and his PhD-holding girlfriend were able to "temporarily [replace] her intelligence with bubbles and sex" through the power of induced hypnotic trance-states.

I'm interested in this kink most likely because, as with the gaining fetish that I have always had, bimbofication involves a defiantly unabashed attitude toward hedonistic pleasure. In both kinks, the object of affection flaunts their taboo conduct, whether that be acting like the ditzy, slutty self they've previously sublimated or eating more than they "should." They are *proud* to be a dumb blonde or a glutton, and it's that smug pride and pleasure that I find arousing. And while tickling (discussed in a previous chapter) isn't my primary fetish—it's not even really in my top five—I'm definitely oriented toward the "lose control" part of it. As a kid I masturbated to a recording of the song "I Love to Laugh" from the original 1960s' *Mary Poppins* film. Even though there was nothing about the wheezy old man who sang it that I found physically attractive, I got turned on when he was literally floating with joy from out-of-control laughter. The idea of being overcome with "glee," as he calls it in the song—being unable to stop the sensations of reckless delight, just as happens in orgasmic release—is central to my kink for other people's hedonistic indulgence.

Which is probably why I love that in the gaining community— which is mostly populated by gay men and elevates "gluttonous" men to the height of desirability—the guy "paying attention" to the gainer is called an "encourager": the idea of *encouragement* really gets at the heart of the subversive nature of that role. (In the gaining fetish, sometimes those involved are also called "feeders" and "feedees.") A 2020 Tumblr post by @buildabhm (or "build a big handsome man," BHM being common Internet parlance for beefy guys) reminds encouragers that there are many ways to enact the role that go beyond, say, baking and feeding someone a cake: you can praise their appetite, rub their belly, and tell them how gorgeous you think they are. Or, conversely, you can call them a greedy pig, if that's more their speed.

Of course, you should always remember that no matter who you are helping to "lose control"—be they a gainer, a bimbo, or any other erotic persona—ultimately, their body and mind are their own. Outside of consensual and negotiated role plays, you have no right to tell them what to do. But if you are fortunate enough to hook up with a kinky fucker whose peccadillos are a match for your own, hopefully you will be invited to spend many hours ignoring or lavishing them—or being ignored or lavished—with exactly the kind of obsessive attention you both crave most.

CHAPTER 9

SUPERFREAKY

Kink History and Icons

*Icons and milestones of kink history—sexual deviance and
the birth of the Internet—a highly personal roundup
of representations of kink in the movies.*

Although I cannot for the life of me find it, I have a vivid memory
of reading an account—I thought it was in the *New Yorker*—about
the notorious and brilliant D. H. Lawrence, the early twentieth-
century British author of *Lady Chatterley's Lover* and other groundbreaking, sexually explicit literary works. By all accounts, Lawrence
was an angry, difficult man and a rampant misogynist, and many
people have said that his treatment of his wife, Frieda, was abusive.
There are other accounts that say she fought vigorously with him,
too, both physically and verbally—and since she was a hearty woman
and he had tuberculosis, that she was stronger and bigger than him
for most of their relationship. It's also an accepted fact that Frieda
had sex with many other men while married to Lawrence—and that
he didn't seem to mind.

Most people who witnessed their relationship dynamic seemed
horrified by it, concluding either that D. H. was a cruel, mad artist
who demeaned and beat his poor wife, or that Frieda was a stupid
and obnoxious boor who tormented her poor husband. The account I read—I think it might have been gleaned from the diaries
or letters of the novelist Katherine Mansfield, found and published

posthumously—gave a first-hand account of visiting Lawrence and Frieda at their home, watching as the couple fought violently and, one could argue, performatively: I recall an anecdote about D. H. smashing a piece of pottery on the floor in anger, and Frieda crawling around on all fours in front of the guests, picking up the shards at his demand. Or maybe the story depicted Lawrence himself scrubbing the floors while Frieda berated him? Another story I read, in a 2021 article by Corinna Honan in the *Daily Mail*, reports that, while entertaining another literary couple, D. H. began to hit his wife and then chased her around the table, until they both fell into their chairs and then began chatting fondly about some mac and cheese they'd once eaten.

When I read these accounts, I wonder: were the Lawrences as purely awful to one another as these stories seem to indicate, or was there something else going on? Maybe something *kinky?* Could it be that D. H. and Frieda were playing out some erotic power exchange that they both enjoyed, and that they were mischievously (and perhaps cruelly) enacting it in front of their unknowing friends? Is it further possible that they were into a version of cuckolding or hotwife and that Frieda's philandering took place with D. H.'s open—if complicated—encouragement?

Maybe. Or it could be that Lawrence was just a world-class asshole and his marriage to Frieda was totally toxic. We can never know for certain.

Therein lies the problem with historicizing kinky behavior. Since most of us—even those of us who write dirty literature—keep aspects of our private lives private, no one on the outside of a relationship can ever know exactly how it works. By their very nature, sexually non-normative relationships can *appear* suspect, unhealthy, weird, and alarming to others, since we live in a culture where it's understandably frowned upon to kick your partner, tie them up to a bedpost, pretend they're a dog, demand that they clean the bathroom, or fuck someone else on the side. When viewed through the lens of vanilla, monogamous relationship paradigms, such things sound ghastly, criminal, unhinged. And yet for most people who identify with one or more of the kinks and fetishes described in this book, those very behaviors—when done within a context of enthusiastic consent, trust, and good communication—are the things we hold most dear in our relationships.

I wish that every pervy person kept meticulous records of their escapades—and that those records were verified by their partners, so we could be sure no one was deluding themself. Because even with contemporary sources, when we're reading about taboo acts like physical beatings or emotional torment, it can be very difficult to gauge where someone has crossed a line from consensual kink to inappropriate behavior. When events are wrapped in the veil of history, they become even murkier, and as BDSM historian Peter Tupper wisely points out, for something to be kinky it must be consensual, and "consent . . . couldn't really exist until the creation of modern liberal ideas of personhood, self-determination and rights."

Not to mention the problem of how all sexual behavior is culturally specific, and so what might be considered totally freaky in one time or place can be quite commonplace in another. Were the orgies of ancient Rome as bizarre to people then as they seem to us now? They might have been scandalous and shocking, or they might have constituted a typical date night.

All that said, I find it deeply comforting—and exciting—to remember that the wild thoughts I have and the games I play with my lovers have been thought and played by others throughout history. It can be very lonely to be kinky. History, even as riddled with mysteries as it is, can provide some companionship and perspective: it brings me comfort and delight to know that over 150 years ago, the paying customers of French brothels were experimenting with whips, needles, electroshock equipment, strap-ons, and more—not to mention nun costumes!—just like my kinky friends do at events today. Which is why I've crafted this lovingly researched but nonetheless somewhat speculative attempt to place pervy behavior within a historic landscape.

But before jumping into the hot tub time machine of deviant sex, I want to acknowledge that, without question, some of the figures and stories that form the kinky canon were and are deeply problematic (I'm looking at you, Marquis de Sade!). Plus, as they say, history is written by the victors—otherwise known as the conquerors and colonizers. Like all other kinds of culture, the kinky sphere has been subject to marginalizing acts of appropriation, suppression, censorship, misinterpretation, and revision. Many colonizing forces throughout history and around the world have used sex-shaming as a way to keep people—especially BIPOC, trans, female-identified, and queer people—out of power. And perhaps no one is an easier target for sex-shaming than someone into kink. So let's bear in mind, as we read these accounts, that the sources that have survived may be quite tainted by whoever provided them and their personal motivations and agendas, and that, in Peter Tupper's words, the history of our sub-culture is "buried beneath layers of shame, secrecy and censorship."

ICONIC FIGURES AND MILESTONES IN KINK HISTORY

In this chapter, please note that I've chosen to focus on what seems, through our contemporary lens, to have been pleasurable kink: peo-ple having a good time with one another in ways that involve power exchange, impact play, group activity, and fetishistic behaviors. I have not included more normative sexual practices; homosexuality or gender-bending (which aren't categorically deviant, despite per-sistent and systemic homophobia and transphobia); sex work (which is an economic model, not a type of sexual desire); or examples of nonconsensual torture or sadism, which are sadly rampant through-out human history.

Ancient-times ritualistic group sex. Although it's hard to know ex-actly how before-the-Common-Era ("year zero") cultures got freaky, it's widely speculated that the ancient Egyptians celebrated the arrival of spring with fertility festivals that involved circle jerks into the Nile: reporter Mildred Europa Taylor wrote in *Face2Face Africa* in 2018 that this ritual could have come from the myth that the god Atum produced other gods by masturbating into water. And while it's still being debated as to whether or not the infamous Greek and Roman orgies happened the way they are often retrospectively depicted—as days-long celebrations in which wine and food were consumed to excess and everyone fucked in a big messy pile—the first-century Roman historian Livy claims that the Bacchanalia were indeed debauched as hell and involved all the cinematic moonlit dancing, feasting, drinking, animal sacrifices, and, yes, fornicating that one would expect. Such scenes are also depicted on many extant clay vessels.

Sacred, woman-centered sex in Mesopotamia. Scholar Louise Pryke wrote a 2018 piece for the website *The Conversation* in which she outlined how central sexual expression was to the peoples of the ancient Near East. She comments that "ancient authors of Sumerian love poetry . . . show a wealth of practical knowledge on the stages of female sexual arousal," as can be seen in a series of such poems from about 2000 BCE, in which the goddess Inanna and her shepherd lover share erotic fantasies that get her all wet. Inanna was also sometimes depicted wielding a whip that could throw a couple into a sexual frenzy. For the Sumerian, enthusiastically consensual sex that emphasized female pleasure was considered a cosmic force of good.

Rough sex in the Kama Sutra. Although mostly famous for its collection of myriad exciting positions for penis-in-vagina intercourse, this how-to book by Vātsyāyana, a second(-ish)-century Hindu Indian philosopher, also discusses the pleasures of erotic slapping, punching, hair-pulling, and biting. In a 2011 review for *The Guardian* of a translation of the book by A. N. D. Haksar, the British writer Hanif Kureishi called the tome, which was aimed at wealthy young men of its time, an "arch, comical and amazing . . . compendium" that contains etiquette and hygiene advice alongside its more esoteric sex instruction.

"Dream of a Fisherman's Wife." In Japan, during the Edo period (from 1600–1868), a genre of sex-positive erotic art called shunga ("pictures of spring") became popular. According to the art-collecting website Artsy, though shunga was banned off and on, the images are thought to have been widely distributed and enjoyed by people of all genders and orientations. The form has many examples of representations of orgasmic pleasure but is perhaps best epitomized through an 1814 woodblock print by the artist Katsushika Hokusai, whose work depicts a bestiality fantasy:

the woman is getting head from two amorous octopi, and in the accompanying text, one octopus is promising to whisk the lady off to an oceanic hideaway for further frolicking.

The Hellfire Club. This was a mid-1700s Dublin-based secret society of aristocrats whom Jonathan Swift deemed "monsters, blasphemers, and Bacchanalians" (making them sound like a pretty fun crowd). While other such clubs operated on the down-low throughout the English and Irish isles, this one was apparently extra raunchy, and according to a 2016 piece for the BBC by Nuala McCann, the Hellfire men originated the motto that has since been stolen by Las Vegas: "what goes on underground, stays underground." Members gathered at a tavern outside of Dublin, where they were often greeted by a stark-naked man, their host. The God-fearing community around them assumed the Hellfire guys were consorting with Satan, but most historians agree they were probably "freethinkers," not devil-worshippers. In the twentieth century, Midwestern BDSMers started the Chicago Hellfire Club—the CHC—as a nod to their hedonistic predecessors. (See below on the CHC; to find out more about the original clubs, you can refer to a few well-regarded books on the subject, including *The Hellfire Clubs: Sex, Satanism and Secret Societies* by Evelyn Lord and David Ryan's *Blasphemers & Blackguards: The Irish Hellfire Clubs.*)

Fanny Hill. Published in 1749, this notorious novel by English author John Cleland is a wall-to-wall fuckfest that puts to rest any notions that the "olden days" were wholesome and dull. Cleland's heroine gets up to all kinds of dirty adventures, including queer sex, group sex, cock worship, and an erotic beating with sharp rods, as well as obsessively fetishistic descriptions of spanking scenes and the equipment and costumes that bolster such fun. As writer Nicole Cliffe assures us in a piece for *The Awl:* "Make no mistake, this is a pornographic novel. It's not, oh, it's the 18th century, and he runs his hand over her heaving bodice, blah blah. It is *pure filth.*" This filthy novel is an important milestone not just for its content, but also because its publication resulted in the author's and publisher's arrest for "corrupting the King's subjects," according to a banned books site maintained by the Indiana University library. It also sparked one of America's first obscenity trials in 1821, when, as journalist Becky Little writes for the History Channel website, the Massachusetts Supreme Judicial Court prosecuted men who had been printing the book.

Marquis de Sade. The man who gave sadism its name, the marquis was a fascinating and truly debauched guy. In chapter 4, there is a section on this eighteenth-century French Revolutionary–era real-life pervert, criminal, and infamous novelist.

Hannah and Arthur Munby. The fascinating Victorian journals of Cambridge-educated barrister Arthur Munby (1828–1910) make it clear that the man had a fetish for the hearty working-class women of England: he sketched their rough hands and heavy boots, took notes about how they spoke, and wrote flowery odes to them. In 1854, Munby forged a loving and enthusiastically consensual Master/slave relationship with Hannah Cullwick, herself an avid diarist who role played at being his servant while also earning wages working in others' homes. Cullwick would return to Munby after a hard day's work to act as his bootblack and recount the grimy details of her day, which set him aflame. In her diaries, Cullwick addresses Munby as "Massa." She also wore a leather strap bracelet and a chain necklace with padlock—"the same as marriage to other folks"—which is perhaps the first re-corded use of a BDSM collar. Their kink wasn't limited to power exchange, either: they also did age play, with Munby acting as the baby. According to journalist and BDSM insider Peter Tupper, author of *A Lover's Pinch: A Cultural History of Sadomasochism,* Hannah and Arthur "built this little fantasy world all to them-selves, in private, and it gave them a great deal of pleasure." Eventually, they married in secret—Hannah called her husband "the truest, best, and handsomest man in my eyes that ever was born"—but ultimately, the class difference and burden of their closeted relationship was too much strain, and they separated, though they never stopped loving and wanting each other.

Leopold von Sacher-Masoch. Born in 1836 and coming into his own as a well-known figure in the late 1870s, this Victorian writer—and the unwilling namesake of masochism—pursued his desire to be dominated and whipped, as well as his serious fur fetish, both in his literary works and in his personal life. He may also have been the first person to ever devise a consensual BDSM contract for a lover. I discuss his legacy in the section in chapter 4 on sadism and masochism.

D. H. Lawrence. Born in 1885 and dying rather young in 1930, Lawrence wrote highly influential and controversial modernist fiction that depicts a wide array of kinky behavior, ranging from "gang rape [and] garment fetishism" to "naked wrestling, objectum-sexuality, [and] podophilia," as philosopher Stephen Alexander notes on his scholarly blog *Torpedo the Ark*. It seems likely that many of these kinks, along with garden-variety S/m and cuckolding, were things Lawrence enjoyed in his own life as well as in his art. What is not clear is how he felt about his outré sexuality: he was by all accounts a miserable, angry man, and even in his fiction, kinky urges are often depicted in complex and ambiguous terms that defy easy categorization. In widely banned novels such as *Lady Chatterley's Lover* and *Women in Love*, his work celebrates eros, but at the same time, his characters are usually punished for their desires with tons of angst and various tragic demises.

The cabarets of Weimar Germany. The fraught years between the two world wars saw a wild time in Germany, including a wonderfully sordid cabaret culture that has been oft-referenced since but never matched. I'm including it here not for any particular kink-related incidents but for a general and perhaps unprecedented zeitgeist of sex-positivity and cocaine-fueled hedonism by people of all walks of life. In a 2018 article for the History Collection website, staff writer D. G. Hewitt cites Weimar Germany's successful porn-movie industry; its on-premise sex clubs; its vibrant queer and trans communities, who published their own popular and widely available magazines and newspapers;

and a booming sex-work scene that catered to everyone from gay tourists and masochists to those with pregnancy, amputation, and "barely legal" fetishists. The cabarets themselves—there were almost nine hundred of them in Berlin alone—were the stuff of pervy legend. And in 1919, German sexologist Magnus Hirschfeld launched the Institute for Sexual Science, "the first such facility in the world to offer medical and psychological counseling" and "establish 'sexology' . . . as a topic of legitimate academic study and research," according to a 2014 article by Caroline Howe for the *Daily Mail*, who notes that the institute also housed a museum.

Tom of Finland. Every kinky person in a black leather harness, biker cap, or combat boots owes a debt to Tom of Finland, the pseudonym of midcentury artist Touko Laaksonen. His drawings of hunky gay men in tight jeans and leather caps became the inspiration for generations of leather Daddies to follow. First appearing in bodybuilding magazines, Tom of Finland's illustrations found their way to gay men hungry for erotic—and aesthetically beautiful—material. You can find more on him and his legacy in chapter 5.

Bettie Page. Just as Tom of Finland almost single-handedly created the signature look found the world over in gay bars and dungeons to this day, here in the USA his contemporary Bettie Page (born in 1923 and capturing hearts through the midcentury) crafted an iconic style still copied and beloved by strippers, fashion models, and hipsters. Born into poverty, pinup and fetish porn model Page worked her ass off, teaching herself to sew and do her hair and makeup. By all accounts (including the official Bettie Page website), and she was rather vanilla herself, Page first found success as a mainstream cheesecake model who posed in swimsuits and such for girlie magazines such as *Wink*, *Eyeful*, and, most famously, *Playboy* (she was the centerfold in January 1955). But Page is most remembered for the fetish work she did with "niche" photographer Irving Klaw, her glossy black bangs and painted mouth echoing the shiny leather corsets, silk stockings, and stilettos she wears as she cheerfully poses as either a whip-wielding Domme or a hog-tied sub.

Bizarre. Incredibly enough, according to Stephen K. Stein's history of BDSM, even the Edwardians had a fetish magazine: *Photo Bits* was published between 1909 and 1912 and featured fetish columns on topics from domination to rubber. *Bizarre* came a bit later but had a longer run. Published in North America from 1946 to 1959 by illustrator John Coutts, better known as John Willie, this magazine was positioned as a "fashion fantasia" to avoid obscenity charges. Willie himself was a shoe fetishist and bondage lover, as is evidenced by the gorgeous art he created, but his was an inclusive dirty magazine, and he tried to cover all the perverse bases. He also ran a letters column so that isolated midcentury kinksters—cross-dressers, submissives, rubber fetishists, and the like—had a place to turn in an era of enforced wholesomeness. According to Stein's research, *Bizarre* had over a thousand subscribers by the mid-1950s and was even sold on newsstands throughout the US and Canada. It and other similar magazines, such as the discipline-focused *Justice Weekly*, allowed folks to make covert contact with one another through ads and readers' letters, thus setting the stage for more organized BDSM communities in the 1970s. Writing about a reprint of *Bizarre* for *Out in San Antonio* in 2014, reviewer Joseph Green notes, "Life in the closet is mostly a life of pain. The idea that these folks were able to find a way to express themselves in this forum seems a very fine thing. And it also can lead to much amusing speculation about what exactly Ozzie and Harriet were up to during the commercial breaks." (The original midcentury magazine should not be confused with the British *Bizarre* magazine of the early 2000s, though both had pinup-girl covers.)

The Eulenspiegel Society, the Chicago Hellfire Club, the Society of Janus, and Samois. One of the oldest official kink clubs in the US, the Eulenspiegel Society, also known as TES, formed in 1971 when teacher Pat Bond posted personal ads in New York City newspapers seeking other masochists to form a kind of support/friendship group. Some folks answered and began meeting weekly in Bond's apartment; this group soon formalized into "the world's first publicly advertised BDSM organization," according to Stephen K. Stein. Soon thereafter, the Chicago Hellfire Club (CHC) was launched in the Midwest, and a group of San Franciscans formed the Society of Janus in 1974. As Stein notes, these groups were welcoming, low-cost, and allowed BDSMers to gather in person to learn techniques from each other and talk openly about their most secret desires while also building a vital "body of knowledge about [BDSM's] practices and codes of conduct emphasizing consent, negotiation and safety." The CHC even put on annual, invitation-only play events at which demonstrations in the finer points of rope, piercing, and enemas were offered, and which, according to Stein's research, may have been the birthplace of the "dungeon monitor" (often called a DM), a volunteer or staff member stationed to supervise play activities and keep things as safe as possible, a position that's still an important part of kink communities today. Though less well-known, it is also important to give a shout-out to Samois, the first women's BDSM organization, launched in 1978 amid a cultural moment when mainstream Second Wave feminism saw any such activity as oppositional to a liberatory agenda. As Stein notes, even more than the other organizations, Samois was in the position of having to continually assert and advocate for women's right to sexual expression to other feminists, and it was a vital godmother to the sex-positive feminist movement and other political activism that followed.

While there are certainly many more books, videos, and events available now than there were in the 1970s, one could argue that our current vast and crowd-sourced pool of information is no match for the intensive apprenticeship and camaraderie afforded by the kind of regular, intensive, intimate meetings hosted by these organizations. In the move online, we've gained plenty—easy access, a wealth of sources—but we've also lost something meaningful and sacred in the form of the (leather-culture originated) "apprenticeship" model that so much of the kink world has patterned itself after.

Mineshaft. New York City's Mineshaft was one of a wave of BDSM sex clubs that opened beginning in the 1970s to cater primarily to gay leathermen. (The Eagle's Nest, or simply Eagle, was another, and prompted other Eagle bars to open in many other cities, often with a strict leather dress code.) Mineshaft was immortalized in the BDSM erotica novel *Mr. Benson* by John Preston as "New York's heaviest leather bar" (see below for more on this novel); Stephen K. Stein describes the magical scene found in these clubs as full of "hot, sweaty men . . . who saw themselves as sexual outlaws." In other words, these were not the highly monitored, sanitized, well-organized dungeons you'd find at twenty-first-century events: these dark, sometimes dirty environs were meant for intense, often anonymous encounters, complete with special themed parties for mummification or electroshock, according to Stein's book *Sadomasochism and the BDSM Community in the United States.* These clubs also had gloryholes and all sorts of dank nooks for fucking, fisting, or just friendly chatting. Some became so infamous—"the stuff of legend," Stein writes—that celebrities tried to get in just to revel in the rough-and-tumble filthiness of it all. Many such clubs closed during the AIDS crisis and never reopened.

Catacombs. Started as a weekly basement house party in 1975, San Francisco's Catacombs boasted a notoriously restricted guest list, carefully curated playlists, and mood lighting to fit the party's theme. And whereas the Mineshaft scene was all cocks all the time, Catacombs was perhaps one of the first after-hours BDSM clubs to host a diverse clientele and foster an inclusive, welcoming environment emphasizing knowledge-sharing and intimacy. Stein writes that it was a place where "gay, lesbian and heterosexual BDSM populations mixed and learned from one another." Like Mineshaft and other sex clubs of the era, it was shuttered during the AIDS crisis.

Mr. Benson. Long before there was *Fifty Shades* for bored housewives, there was *Mr. Benson* for gay leather Daddies and their eager servants. First serialized in the gay magazine *Drummer* in 1979 and 1980, *Mr. Benson* is a novel by John Preston, which Stephen K. Stein describes as "the sexual adventures of Jamie, a young man who learns to love and serve" a stern M-type who teaches Jamie how to be the perfect BDSM s-type. While a work of fantasy (there is no adherence to "safe, sane, and consensual" in this book's sadistic romance), Preston's vivid descriptions of an extreme BDSM lifestyle did as much for the kinky gay community as *Story of O* or *Justine* did for heterosexuals interested in D/s, and it is still held up today as a kind of guidebook of a pure BDSM ideal. And notably, best-selling author Anne Rice was a good friend of Preston's, and through him learned enough about kink to write her own heterosexual BDSM novels, though through a much gauzier, more romantic lens.

Robert Mapplethorpe. Photographer Robert Mapplethorpe is just one of many artists throughout history whose images celebrate alternative sexualities, but because he came of age in the 1970s and captured the gay S/m and leather scenes flourishing then in NYC—and because those scenes were so horribly devastated by AIDS in the years immediately following—his work is especially influential and iconic. This alone might have secured Mapplethorpe's place in BDSM history, even if mostly in urbane, artsy circles. But the late 1980s saw Mapplethorpe become part of the American discourse, when the National Endowment of the Arts came under fire from conservatives for awarding grant money to a gallery that mounted a show of his "pornographic" photographs, which depicted, as Congressman Bob Dornan complained, "torture disguised as some sort of sexual thrill." Ironically, the attacks of then senator Jesse Helms and other figures of the religious Right helped catapult Mapplethorpe to stardom, but sadly the artist died of AIDS in 1989, the year after the Whitney Museum mounted a major retrospective of his work.

Bob Flanagan. Artist Bob Flanagan lived with constant pain due to cystic fibrosis and was one of the longest-living survivors of the illness: he died at age forty-three in 1996. In his own words, he was a "supermasochist" who "fought pain with pain" and turned his private sexual desires into performance art. While other kinky artists, such as Mapplethorpe, have folded their sexual deviancy into their art, few have made it the center of their life's work like Flanagan. As his friend and fellow writer Dennis Cooper details in his eulogy in *Artforum*, "gradually . . . sex, and in particular his unabashed enjoyment of submission, humiliation, and pain, were revealed as the true subjects of his work." By the mid-1980s, Flanagan had fallen in love with photographer Sheree Rose, who was also his dominatrix, and the relationship altered the course of his work. As Cooper puts it, "It wasn't unusual to drop by [their home] and find the place full of writers, artists, and people from the S/M community, all flying on acid and/or speed, Bob naked and happily enacting orders from the leather-clad Sheree." Later, the couple staged popular and increasingly extreme performance art pieces in Los Angeles, culminating in the work "Nailed," which, Cooper writes, "began with a gory slide show by Rose and concluded, after various, highly stylized S/m acts, with Bob nailing his penis to a wooden board." The work gained wide notoriety, and industrial music stars such as Nine Inch Nails began including Flanagan in their videos and concerts. His art gave voice to the complex pleasures behind masochism, offering, as Cooper writes, performances of "a highly estheticized, personal, pragmatic challenge to accepted notions of violence, illness, and death."

Annie Sprinkle. The BDSM world is blessed to have many brilliant sex workers among our ranks, but perhaps none has been as widely influential as Annie Sprinkle. Sprinkle had an illustrious career in porn and other sex work that spanned the early 1970s to the mid-1990s. In the late 1970s, Sprinkle's work began to morph into conceptual, Fluxus-art-inspired pieces such as the *Sprinkle Report* (a urophilia "newsletter"), and mail-order "Golden Shower Ritual Kits," which archivist Tom Garretson writes appealed both to fetishists and art collectors. Sprinkle then began touring as a feminist performance and multimedia artist whose queer, joyful, irreverent, and interactive works are also educational, political, and eco-minded: as she says in an *Interview* piece from 2019, these shows were among the "first full-on theatre piece[s] by a sex worker who plays herself," and Sprinkle would invite the audience to view her cervix and lead them in sex magic masturbation rituals. (Like Mapplethorpe, Sprinkle and her work became a target of Christian conservatives.) Although it was unusual at the time for a former porn star to gain so much traction on the university lecture circuit, there are signs that we are moving into an era where this is more common: other feminist sex educators who have worked as strippers, escorts, and porn stars—such as Jacq the Stripper, Madison Young, and Tina Horn—are now gaining mainstream respect, success, and outlets for their artistic voices. Sprinkle paved the way.

Kink.com. When Jon Mooallem at the *New York Times* wrote about Kink.com in 2007, it was the "country's most successful fetish porn company," with about sixty thousand paying subscribers—figures that seem laughably small to us now, but which represented a thriving and innovative business model at the time. Kink.com had the advantage of being helmed by Peter Acworth, a savvy, programming-minded entrepreneur who smartly headquartered his venture in San Francisco—a hotbed of both the tech boom and the BDSM scene. The actor James Franco made a documentary film about the company that came out in 2013. By the time Larissa Runkle wrote about Kink.com for *Hoodline* in 2017, it was "the world's largest"—and, one could argue, most lauded—"producer of BDSM porn," all of which was made with an eye toward providing an ethical, educational model. At the height of its glory, Kink.com purchased a historic building in the Mission district known as the Armory, which became a kind of upscale kink rec center. The Armory housed studios for its high-end porn shoots but also workshops, tours, cocktail hours, and sex parties, some of which were livestreamed. But the lines between professional pornography and community activity became blurred, and numerous scandals began to surface: Acworth was arrested on cocaine possession charges right after the Franco documentary came out, and—as reported in a 2014 article in *Dissent* and a 2017 article in *The Guardian*—there were also lawsuits around mistreatment of performers and incidents of sexual assault. These ongoing problems, combined with Bay Area gentrification and the proliferation of free online porn, led to the closure of the Armory. Kink.com has been up and down since then, but as of 2021, was back under Acworth's ownership as a space where he planned to "reimagine the company for a new, performer-centered fan market."

HOW THE WORLD WIDE WEB HAS MADE A WORLD OF DIFFERENCE—TO ME AND EVERYONE ELSE

With or without Kink.com, we are now firmly in the age of online kink. Before the rise of the Internet the work of kink artists, publishers, and organizers was truly trailblazing: without an easy way to identify and gather with like-minded others, the voices of these icons were often singular in their public championing of BDSM and fetish practices. Prior to the existence of sites like FetLife and Kink.com, concerted effort and genuine risk were required to find a dungeon, visit a fetishwear shop, or get your hands on niche erotica. That's why I feel that the earlier visionaries are so important for us to remember and honor, and why I harbor a deep fondness for *Bizarre* and other kinky media of days past.

My personal timeline overlaps with the shift from analog to digital kink. I'm of an age that when I first began to seek out fetish-related materials in the 1980s, it was nearly impossible to find resources on the subject: I remember getting rare access when a battered copy of an incest-themed porno paperback was passed around for laughs at a punk concert, and I discreetly and desperately pored through it in the dim light.

But just as I was hitting adulthood, things changed. In 1992, in the one-room computer lab at my college, I could use the school's Internet connection to access text-only Usenet forums. I quickly discovered alt.sex, a forum hierarchy that became a haven for people like myself eager to connect with others over our shared sexual deviancy: a 1993 survey by its creator, computer scientist Brian Reid, estimated that over 3.3 million readers were already clicking into alt.sex by that year. People who were paying attention to alt.sex could see how important it was in its moment. Critic Maureen Furniss wrote that "sexually-oriented boards act as a kind of support group, . . . especially for individuals whose sexual orientations are very marginalized." Alt.sex was organized by interest, with threads such as alt .sex.bondage, alt.sex.plushies, alt.sex.spanking, and the alt.sex.fetish hierarchy, which had myriad subcategories itself including alt.sex .fetish.feet, -jello, -motorcycles, -sleepy, and more. Because the world of the Internet was so small back then, people we now recognize as community experts—authors and educators such as Janet Hardy, Jay Wiseman, and Laura Antoniou—were weighing in on alt.sex, too.

As the 1990s wore on, home Internet access became more accessible and common (albeit slow and wonky), and we kinky types were off to the races. For a million reasons, private Internet access was a godsend—a marked departure from centuries of prevalent loneliness and isolation that sexually deviant folks had experienced prior. Suddenly, there was a place to have a conversation, to share fantasies and resources, to meet others like ourselves. There was even the possibility of connecting one-on-one with a potential sexual partner.

HOW I FOUND KINKY LOVE ONLINE IN THE MID-'90S

FUN FACT: Although I loved alt.sex and spent plenty of time there, I was a resourceful little bugger, and when I decided to seek out a hedonistic partner to fulfill my own fetishist fantasies, I posted on the "recreational" Usenet hierarchy rec.food.drink.beer, even though it was the furthest thing from a dating forum. I said that I was a girl "with otherwise only slightly-perverted fantasies" seeking a guy to tell me about his beer belly. "No kidding," I wrote, "this really turns me on!" And if you want to hear the craziest part, even though my post only got a handful of views, it worked, because twenty-five years and many twists and turns later, I'm married to the man who warily responded.

Beyond these obvious satisfactions, the rise of the web has brought other benefits for kinky people. Self-described "leather child of the Internet" Alexander Cheves recounts in a 2019 *Them* piece how he had his first D/s experience through the online gay dating app Scruff, bypassing the need to "call a number in the back of a leather magazine, as kink-minded people once did in decades past." Through the interviews he conducted for his piece, Cheves highlights some of the ways the digital age has changed kinksters' lives: access for a wheelchair-using puppy player who can't easily go to events but can stay digitally connected to the community; the fisting enthusiasts who can learn proper technique and safety tips from widely available online videos; and the ability of BIPOC folk to efficiently organize and call out racism within the community.

One of Cheves' interviewees, Jack Thompson, the first trans and Black person to be named International Mr. Leather, points out that the online age does have its drawbacks. Discovering kink through online fantasy versions can lead to unrealistic expectations that end in disappointment when the opportunity for IRL experiences finally arises. Thompson says, "When you learn by meeting people organically and in-person, you see all the messy and real parts of kink, and that's something vital."

KINK REPRESENTATION MATTERS

Yet even with all the highly specialized pornography now available, nuanced and positive representations of what it's like to have a non-normative sexuality are still few and far between. When Hollywood or other film and television industries do deign to give us depictions of kinky fuckers, we are likely to get something cliché-ridden, embarrassing, and damaging to the community, like *Fifty Shades of Grey*, which depicts a dynamic built on "bribery, coercion and emotional blackmail," in BDSM scholar Stephen K. Stein's words, rather than negotiation and enthusiastic consent.

Or, perhaps even worse, we get 1994's *Exit to Eden*. The source material, a novel by beloved writer and ally to the gay and BDSM communities Anne Rice (under the pseudonym Anne Rampling), centers on a luxurious D/s club. *Los Angeles Times* reviewer Carolyn See called the book a "cheerful novel of sadomasochism and bondage" that includes both "thrusting [and] grinding" and "hot chocolate and *beignets* at dawn," and therefore serves as "everybody's fantasy." Sadly, the movie version is a wacky buddy-cop comedy deemed by film critic Roger Ebert to be "dumb, ill-constructed, boring and tragically miscast." Even the directors and actors later said they thought it was terrible.

Why is it important to have good kink representation in movies? Because we need more than just porn, more than uncurated, crowd-sourced forums like FetLife. To combat shame, to feel like we have role models, to showcase diversity, and to acknowledge our very existence, it's vital that we see our sexualities depicted in well-crafted media that aims to do more than just arouse: we need to see our full selves reflected as people with relationships, families, jobs, anxieties, successes, health issues, hobbies, friends, and all the other elements that make up a complete life.

There are, luckily, some movies that do a halfway decent job of representing kinky life—not many, but *some*. To my mind, a good representation of kinky living involves not just a basic, well-informed understanding about what it's like to lust in this way, but also a certain level of artistry and style that goes beyond soft-core titillation. And although not every title on this top five list is completely kink-positive, they all at least operate from the standpoint that it's possible for a person to be kinky, happy, and healthy, rather than depicting kink as a bottomless pit of misery or harm, as in films like *Bitter Moon, Crash*, and *9½ Weeks*—or even higher-quality cult classics like *The Night Porter* and *The Piano Teacher*, which contain stereotypical portrayals of harrowing, tragic sadomasochistic dynamics borne out of deep trauma.

Number 5. *Professor Marston and the Wonder Women* (2017). The biopic of kink pioneer William Moulton Marston, who also created the Wonder Woman comics, with their rampant and juicy depictions of bondage. The film dramatizes the WWII-era life he made with both his wife and his lover, who all lived and raised children together. It isn't a particularly well-made movie, and the descendants of its characters say much of what it depicts isn't true. I'd also say that its portrayal of bondage isn't as complex or developed as its portrayal of polyamory, which is actually decent. However, I do absolutely love the scene in which the central threesome visit a lingerie shop in New York City. The shop owner ushers them into a back room to demo fetish gear for them and let them play dress-up. The shop owner's character is based on Charles Guyette, an underground erotica photographer who worked as a burlesque and theater costumer and created a sideline of custom-made boots, leather gloves, and other tools of the BDSM trade. Guyette was, according to Stephen K. Stein, "an important point of contact" for many members of the era's burgeoning kink scene. For me, the movie is worth seeing for the joys of picturing what it would have been like to happen upon a treasure trove of fetishwear in the backroom of a shop in 1940s America, and it reminds me of the fun one can have looking at corsets and paddles from vendors at kink events.

Number 4. *Maîtresse* (1976). Like *Belle de Jour* below, this film is ambiguous, a bit artsy, very French—and completely entertaining. It also contains some of the most graphic depictions of S/m in mainstream film. It's the vividly told story of Ariane, a successful dominatrix. (The filmmaker consulted with actual members of Paris' BDSM community; real-life masochists serve as extras, and a Pro Domme was on hand to handle some of the more sensitive play.) The evolution of Ariane's private life as she takes in Olivier—a brawny, hapless lover who only partially understands how she makes her money and how she feels about it—is shown to be messier than what goes on in her dungeon. Within their relationship, Ariane and Olivier play with consensual non-consent, power exchange, and other kink in ways I found realistic and nuanced. My biggest argument with this film is that sometimes too many fetishes are depicted in one client's session—how likely is it that a shoe fetishist is also a cross-dressing sadist into watersports, or that he'd ask for all these elements at once in his scene? Nonetheless, on multiple levels, it's an unusually on-target representation of nonnormative sexuality and worth watching for the deep dive into Ariane's dungeon setup—complete with a kinky medical play setup, a rack of latex costumes, and a bag of communion wafers.

Number 3. *Secretary* (2002). You knew you'd find this here, right? It's perhaps the most oft-cited BDSM movie after *Fifty Shades* and remains a cult favorite both in and outside of the kink community. It's a visually fascinating film with memorable and sexy performances by Hollywood stars, even if it's far from an ideal representation, and one which strays quite far from the much darker, less kink-friendly source material, a short story by Mary Gaitskill. On their bondage blog *Bound Together*, kinky couple Mimsy and Vagabond point out the key problem with the movie, which is that "the female lead's interests in submission are borne out of mental illness (a tired trope), and the beginning stages of her relationship with her boss are just plain abusive," which means that, despite its stylish approach, it sadly makes many of the same mistakes the far less interesting *Fifty Shades* makes. Nonetheless, the imagery is indelible and the consensually kinky relationship that the couple eventually forges is intricately portrayed, freaky, and exciting.

Number 2. *Belle de Jour* (1967). This masterpiece by Luis Buñuel is often described as a surrealist film about a bourgeois woman who secretly goes to work at an upscale brothel. While Catherine Deneuve's Séverine (probably named in honor of the protagonist in *Venus in Furs*) does do that, the even more titillating part is that she harbors deep and imaginative masochist fantasies of humiliation, torture, and being sexually "used," which her job allows her to explore. Like *Secretary* and *Fifty Shades*, there are hints that Séverine's kink comes from trauma or a mental disorder, but Buñuel's art-house treatment—and bizarre ending—renders everything more opaque and complex than a simple cause and effect. Plus it's just a gorgeous and wild film all the way through.

Number 1. *The Duke of Burgundy* (2015). Almost nobody has heard of this movie, much less seen it. This lesbian idyll is, in some ways, an acquired taste: slow-moving, ominous, and emotionally removed. (Also, the world that the male director depicts is entirely populated by women: there are no men ever shown on screen.) That said, if you can find the dark humor in this erotic and haunting film, you will find that it's also an unusually realistic portrayal of a loving, long-term 24-7 power exchange relationship between two interesting people. And it does a wonderful job of illustrating the topping-from-the-bottom, the ongoing negotiation complexities of such relationships, and the logistics of kink life. Where else can you find scenes that show how expensive and time-consuming it can be to custom-order your BDSM paraphernalia for home use, and how long you have to wait for it to arrive? Also, the 1970s-soft-core-horror-influenced production design is gloriously "high threadcount," in the words of *Guardian* film critic Jordan Hoffman.

I also want to give a brief shout-out to 2022's *Everything Everywhere All at Once*. It's an absolutely genius banger of a movie, and it also contains a subtle and brief instance of kink-positivity so powerful it made my partner burst into grateful tears (no spoilers—you'll have to see it for yourself and be on the lookout!). Hopefully, the years ahead will bring a much wider selection of realistic, nuanced portrayals of people who just happen to also be kinky, as in this shimmering moment from *Everything Everywhere*, as well as in a brief arc on the television series *Transparent*, in which one of the characters—a mom, no less—begins seeing a Pro Domme (played by an actual well-respected sex worker) for hot and therapeutic spankings. Given the fact that mainstream culture never seems to tire of the thrill of some hot BDSM action, I think it'd be a win-win for more movies and television shows to depict kink in compassionate, honest ways.

CHAPTER 10

THANK U 4 A FUNKY TIME

Forging Your Path and Community

*Resources for finding community—
can perversion really make you happy?*

W hen I watch the films discussed in the previous chapter, I experience more than just the joys of being entertained: I feel like I'm part of—or at least listening in on—important conversations about sexuality that I rarely get to have. I feel the same way when I go to kink events, where I can sit down at a picnic table with strangers over potato chips and watermelon and chat about the outré things we're into. It's a relief and a pleasure to be able to share stories about intimate feelings and experiences with other humans who really get it.

As we near the end of this book, my hope is that reading it has given you some of that same solace and spark. I also hope that these pages have provided you with ideas about where to go to find community—information, mentors, friends, and partners—to suit your tastes and interests. In the kink world, each person's sexuality and erotic path tends to be very particular. No one else is going to have exactly the same evolution, or require exactly the same resources, as you. You're going to have to forge your own journey and keep at it. With any luck, your quest will feel like an orgasmic yellow brick road: wild and beautiful, even as it twists and turns and presents challenges and obstacles.

WAYS TO FIND AND FORGE COMMUNITY

Forging supportive, meaningful communities of any kind can be a challenge, and finding and sustaining kink communities can be even harder, due to the underground nature of who we are and what we do. According to BDSM historian Stephen K. Stein, what we think of as the community—also known as the "scene" or "lifestyle"—has a very recent history, emerging from "scattered, loosely networked enthusiasts in the 1950s" and growing and evolving into a "cohesive subcultural" network of local organizations, conventions, clubs, magazines, and gatherings by the 1990s, only to become more diffuse and amorphous again via the Internet.

That said, there are a few all-purpose tools I can offer for you to pack in your kink basket next to Toto. What follows are some personally vetted sources of BDSM wisdom, expertise, and inspiration.

Podcasts

Podcasts were one of the first ways I started finding expert educational information about kink (as opposed to the crowd-sourced or unvetted material on websites). I love podcasts as a vehicle for exploring the kink world: the format guarantees an intimate, personal vibe that allows hosts and interviewees to delve deeply and explicitly into the subject, and you can listen to all sorts of raunchy stuff on your commute or while waiting at the auto shop and no one will be the wiser. Even podcasts that are no longer active tend to have their archives available, and you can pick and choose episodes most relevant to your interests.

Of course, anyone can make a podcast, so quality tends to vary. And a note of caution that even some of the more open-minded sexuality podcasts aren't as kink-aware as one would hope. Below are a few time-tested, well-made, kink-focused podcasts that are also some of my favorites. Note that all of these cover the full gamut of kink-related topics, but if you have a niche interest, there's probably a podcast for that (e.g., the *Rope Podcast* by Fox and Mya, or *Never Too Old for Agoodspankin*, hosted by Agoodspankin).

Why Are People Into That?! I've already sung Tina Horn's praises in this book: she's a brilliant writer and thinker who is also an experienced sex worker, porn star, and educator, so she's a veritable sensei of kink. Hers is one of the most thoughtful, in-depth, intelligent sex podcasts out there, to my mind, and it's *only* about kink, so it's a goldmine for readers of this book. (Tina Horn has her own book based on this podcast forthcoming, which is fantastic!)

Erotic Awakening. Some stars of the BDSM world can come off as pretentious or intimidating. The hosts of this podcast, Dan and dawn, a poly power exchange couple, sound like the approachable Midwestern middle-aged folks they are while also being seasoned presenters in the community. Even as their podcast delves deep into unusual fetishes or the intricacies of D/s, they remain accessible, sweet-natured, relatable, and a little goofy.

Sex Out Loud. Writer, educator, and porn director Tristan Taormino is an undisputed expert in the sex-positive community, and I love her candid but warm approach to teaching about and thinking through all aspects of sexual behavior, including kinky shit. She brings in wonderful guests from all over the sex world, from political theorists to novelists. This inclusive, intersectional podcast is an OG: it has been around since 2012.

Masocast. Axe, the s-type who hosts this show, has a definite leaning toward M/s and D/s, and the conversations he conducts with other kink-world luminaries are wry, smart, and a little snarky—proving once again that those of us who are submissive in the bedroom are often opinionated and assertive in the rest of our lives. It's maybe not the best podcast for beginners, since he doesn't always stop to explain the basics, but if you are already operating in this realm, the conversations on this podcast are terrific.

Savage Lovecast. Dan Savage has been doling out irreverent sex advice since the early 1990s, when he launched his newspaper column; at this point he's practically a household name. He is blunt and entertaining, and if you prefer your kink-related audio in bite-sized chunks, it's worth a listen. His podcast addresses all kinds of sexual topics with humor and frankness, though he's not always as well-informed as I'd like about less common subjects. (He is not a trained sex educator, and he tends to let his biases show: he's often made fat-phobic comments in his columns, and I will never forgive him for accusing a woman who wrote in with a weight-gain encourager fetish of "making it up.")

A few more podcasts you could check out: *American Sex*, hosted by married, poly, kinky couple Sunny Megatron and Ken Melvoin-Berg; *Sluts & Scholars*, hosted by licensed marriage and family therapist and sexologist Nicoletta Heidegger; and *Loving BDSM*, hosted by D/s couple John and Kayla.

Books

All media gets dated, and because books take longer to write and publish than, say, podcasts or social media posts, they can also age more dramatically. But of course I love books, and I cherish my library of kinky tomes, which occupy a discreet shelf in my back hallway. Thankfully, new kink books come out all the time: I recommend choosing ones published by larger, well-known publishing houses such as the Celestial Arts self-help imprint at Penguin Random House; such presses will have vetted and edited the work to make sure the information is solid and the writing clear. I also suggest combing the back catalogs of three BDSM-specific independent publishers, **Greenery Press** (founded by kink-education pioneer Janet Hardy), **Cleis Press**, and **Circlet Press** (which publishes "erotica for geeks"): these books have been reviewed and edited by those within the community. (Proceed with caution with self-published Amazon offerings: you have no idea what you'll find within those pages.)

Let's talk about some of the best-known kink books out there, starting with groundbreakers that started popping up in the mid-1990s. Three couples put out books that became BDSM bibles: John and Libby Warren published a smart and informative how-to, *The Loving Dominant* (and have since updated and republished it); Philip Miller and Molly Devon released the flawed but wonderfully-titled *Screw the Roses, Send Me the Thorns: The Romance and Sexual Sorcery of Sadomasochism*, complete with a big glossary, many appendices, and enticing illustrations; and academics William and Gloria Brame put out the well-researched and more erudite guide *Different Loving: The World of Sexual Dominance and Submission.*

Starting in about 2010, BDSM began gaining traction in the larger discourse, and a bunch of good new titles have appeared over the past decade. For those of you looking for more targeted information, check out Greenery's *Toybag Guide* series, which includes slender books on bondage, age play, foot worship, medical play, and more, all by the biggest names in these niche fields; I'm especially interested in Mollena Williams's *Toybag Guide to Playing with Taboo*. And I absolutely rejoiced when, just as I was kicking my own kink life into high gear after opening my marriage in 2012, Tristan Taormino's *Ultimate Guide to Kink* anthology was released. The chapters are written by different experts who discuss their kinky passions in a range of styles and voices, from personal memoir to academic study to hands-on instruction. Around the same time, Mollena Williams teamed up with another BDSM presenter I respect, Lee Harrington, to publish the how-to *Playing Well with Others.* Psychologist and journalist Jesse Bering's *Perv: The Sexual Deviant in All of Us* is well-researched while also being a fun read (though I find its perspective a bit vanilla).

Books published even more recently include the short fiction anthology *Kink: Stories* (friends tell me it's not all that kinky), edited by R. O. Kwon and Garth Greenwell and featuring notable authors such as Roxane Gay and Alexander Chee; the vividly masochistic deep dive *Hurts So Good: The Science and Culture of Pain on Purpose* by Leigh Cowart, which comes highly recommended by a D-type I know; and two books that have greatly enriched this one, *Sadomasochism and the BDSM Community in the United States* by Stephen K. Stein, which does the vital work of tracing the roots and current reality of what it means for kinky people to try to band together in meaningful ways, and *A Lover's Pinch: A Cultural*

History of Sadomasochism by Peter Tupper, a wonderfully readable work of in-depth research into evidence of consensual S/m activity throughout our species' timeline.

If you're more interested in one-handed reading and have already plowed through the classics, there are lots of good, contemporary kink erotica out there. Amazon lists a ton of self-published titles, but beware—those often include rampant typos and cringey sentences. Instead, I'd recommend sticking with some of the community's best-loved authors, folks who write with real wit and style, including groundbreakers such as **Samuel R. Delany** (a Black gay writer of sci-fi and fantasy whose work often champions consensually kinky relationships) and **Patrick Califia** (a former dyke and current trans man who writes leather and S/m-based smutty lit). Keep an eye out for work by **Laura Antoniou** (whose Marketplace novels chronicle high protocol D/s), **Cherise Sinclair** (for romance novels set in kinky dungeons), and **Cecilia Tan** (a self-described "Chinese-Filipino Irish Welsh bisexual" and BDSM insider who writes with a sci-fi bent and started Circlet Press, mentioned above) as well. I also recommend looking at anthologies of dirty fiction edited by lesbian activist **Susie Bright** (including the *Best American Erotica* series) and erotica writer **Rachel Kramer Bussel** (including her *Big Book of Submission* series and many anthologies of couples' and women's erotica). Finally, don't forget the dearly departed **Anne Rice**, mentioned in the last chapter: in addition to *Exit to Eden*, she also wrote the four-volume *Sleeping Beauty* series, which explores a supernatural D/s dynamic, and *Belinda*, a Lolita-inflected dark romance.

Places

Reading a book or listening to a podcast in the privacy of one's own home or earbuds is lovely, but it can be *wonderful* to visit a public space dedicated to the exploration of kink. There's something so exciting, so validating about it. "Sex tourism" usually refers to paying for sex work while on vacation, but my kind of sex tourism involves stopping at BDSM shops, clubs, museums, and gathering places when I travel to seek out a sense of camaraderie.

I even harbor a certain affection for a seedy, windowless adult bookstore where everyone looks slightly ashamed; however, such shops are not particularly woke or safe spaces. Luckily, most cities now have at least one feminist sex shop, the kind where the merchandise is clean and high-quality, and the people behind the desk are well-informed and make even your weirdest questions feel okay. Most sex shops carry at least some BDSM items—whips, handcuffs—but the **Pleasure Chest** and the **Stockroom** are meccas for kinksters. The Pleasure Chest is a trusted source that has been around since 1971; it carries harder-to-find kink items such as urethral sound kits and e-stim devices in its NYC, LA, and Chicago locations and its online shop. And I love browsing at LA's Stockroom, which caters exclusively to pervy folks and sells well-made fetishwear such as latex catsuits and leather harnesses along with the usual paraphernalia, all of which is also available through its website. I make it a point to support shops like these, which do so much to serve the larger community.

Don't need to fill your toy bag? Some educational institutions maintain museums or galleries that are open to the public: you can visit NYC's **Museum of Sex**, which also has an on-site retail shop and a fun bar; or Amsterdam's **Sexmuseum**, which houses impressive galleries of erotic art; or Chicago's **Leather Archives & Museum**, where admission to the library is free. In the virtual world, the websites of the Tom of Finland Foundation, the Center for Positive Sexuality, the National Coalition of Sexual Freedom, Canada's Centre for Sexuality, Berlin's Research Center for the Cultural History of Sexuality, the Kinsey Institute, and other sexuality research institutions make it easy to stay in the loop with the latest news and developments in the world of kink from wherever you are. Treat yourself to browsing through their sites or signing up for their newsletters.

As I write this, we are still in the throes of the COVID pandemic, and it feels like it's been forever since I got to gather with fellow perverts for a sex event. But I hope to do so again someday soon. One of the most well-run and lauded BDSM event producers is **Dark Odyssey**, which usually puts on three or more US-based events per year, each with an impressive roster of workshops and organized parties, plus plenty of high-end dungeon equipment. When I'm in the Bay Area, I always try to stop at **Wicked Grounds**, perhaps the world's only kink-centric coffee shop, where you can take classes, participate in a game night, buy stuff in the shop, or just hang out with a cup of tea. (On my first visit there, my partner and I watched an elderly couple in tweed coats stroll in with one of them attached to the other by a leash, and that has honestly been one of the highlights of my life.) San Francisco is America's BDSM hotspot, and for a while it boasted the after-hours version of Wicked Grounds at the **Armory Club**, an elegant and sexy cocktail lounge located in the downstairs space of the former Kink.com headquarters. Back on the East Coast, the NYC-based nonprofit **TES** (the Eulenspiegel Society, also mentioned in chapter 9), one of the scene's earliest groups, has been hosting meetings called "munches"—social gatherings for kinksters at restaurants and cafés, a term now used throughout the community—since 1971.

In nonpandemic times, you may be able to find a leather bar, meet-up, club, or munch within driving distance of your own location. FetLife has dedicated groups for most cities, states, and regions, often with calendar listings. In places with larger communities, one can find regular dungeon parties, leather club meetings, and general munches, as well as niche munches for spanking enthusiasts, Adult

---

STRANGERS IN THE NIGHT

A CAVEAT: Playing with someone you meet online can be a dicey proposition. Anyone can call themselves an experienced top or bondage expert, and you'd have to get multiple references to know whether or not this is true: they could be a novice, a charlatan, or just an asshole. Even if they are the most highly sought-after kinky person in their community—or a well-known kink-world educator or star—that doesn't mean they will be a perfect play partner for *your* needs. Proceed with caution. If you do decide to meet, meet them in a public, vanilla location such as a café for your first get-together; stay sober and alert; and always tell a trusted friend where you're going and how long you expect to be there. Better yet: don't go alone. When you feel ready to do nasty things together, meet the stranger at a kinky event space where you feel comfortable and safe and know there are people supervising, especially if you intend to engage in heavy play of any kind.

Babies, or twentysomething "TNG" ("the next generation") folks. Held in accessible public places, a munch can be a safe way to meet other locals and practice talking to friendly, kinky strangers who are glad to offer counsel and company.

Websites

One could easily fall into the black hole of kink on the interweb: there is no shortage of blogs, trainings, porn, and forums once you've figured out the best keywords to stick in your search box. So I'll only mention a few of the most obvious and important sites, such as **FetLife**, which is without question the premier social platform for the community; **Kink Academy**, a "comprehensive library" of on-demand, well-produced sex education videos on topics from fire play to protocol, featuring big names in the scene such as Princess Kali (one of my favorite presenters); and **Kink University** at Kink.com, a more porn-driven style of educational content. And because everyone deserves good-quality mental health care and legal services, I also want to plug the **Kink and Polyamory Aware Professionals** directory, hosted by the National Coalition for Sexual Freedom. The organization doesn't vet the practitioners listed, but it's an extremely useful first step when looking for an empathetic attorney, doctor, wedding officiant, or other professional who won't gasp in horror if you need to raise some unexpected issues.

CAN PERVERSION REALLY BRING YOU HAPPINESS?

You know that old saying that no matter where you go, there you are? The idea is that if you sow dissatisfaction in your daily life at home, or are miserable at your job, there's a good chance you will probably bring that misery along if you go on a luxury vacation or get a job someplace else. I believe that nothing—not even a fantastic and out-there sex life—can *make* a person happy, but that each of us can *aim* toward happiness through ongoing and intentional choices, decisions, and mindsets.

That said, while we all have different obstacles and challenges getting in the way of happiness, some of us have privileges and resources that make that path a lot smoother than it is for others. The way I am able to express myself through my nonnormative sexuality is a product, to a large extent, of my experience living as a white, middle-aged, partnered, cisgender person with a stable household income and secure housing, for example.

But no matter our circumstances, there are ways that kink-informed practices can nurture our inner strengths and deepen our satisfaction. I came across a piece by the D/s podcaster Kayla Lords on a self-help website called Happiness.com in which she describes some life lessons we can learn from practicing BDSM. I agree: when we do BDSM well, we cultivate important life skills. Specifically, we can learn how to be better at:

- communicating our wants and needs
- listening to the wants and needs of others
- reserving judgment and celebrating difference
- staying open and adventurous
- understanding and respecting consent
- taking care of each other

And at the same time, while we strive to be better citizens of the world and of our BDSM communities, we can also strive to keep the filth in the fun. This book has just laid out a whole slew of resources to help you learn the basics of kink and find your own community, but ultimately, kink is about sexual fantasy, and fantasies come from each of our weird, unique imaginations. Each of our fantasies are wonderfully, blissfully our own. Let us not allow our kink to become, in the words of erotica writer John Preston, "codified, measured and packaged," conforming to someone else's definition or an exact replica of something we saw or read elsewhere.

Moreover, let's make sure that kink never becomes too sterile, stagnant, or suburban. Stephen K. Stein's book quotes International Mr. Leather 1979 David Kloss as saying, "It's nice to be accepted, but I kind of liked that sense of the forbidden, too." As I say in chapter 3, kink without taboo is no longer kink. If we want to keep the dream of deviancy alive, we have to be willing to delve into some genuinely dirty ideas and celebrate and support the furthest reaches of our community. In Peter Tupper's history of sadomasochism, he quotes from a 2006 blog post by bondage expert Twisted Monk: "[BDSM history] was born in back alleys and leather bars by pornographers, queers and sexual outlaws. We should celebrate this rather than attempt to reimagine it."

Kink can be a space for deep subversion—many of us find this to be one of the most meaningful things about it. We can become another species, age, size, gender, creature; we can exist in any other time, or outside of time altogether. We can temporarily transmogrify our appearance, our personality, our material reality. Tupper says, "the pleasure to turn society upside down, to create a carnival-like setting—even if it [is] only in one room for one night—is the great pleasure of kink."

As Tupper writes, kink can be a space for "endless variation, innovation, experimentation [and] transformation." My wish for everyone—and especially for those who feel isolated, afraid, and lacking in options—is that this book will help you access your own pleasure through finding safe, sane, consensual outlets to experiment with and transform through your particular perversities. I hope that as you turned these pages, you have felt a little more understood, hopeful, informed, and inspired.

And aroused. Let's not forget that one.

WE'RE GOING DOWN TO ALPHABET STREET

An A-to-Z of Kinky Stuff

An abecedarium of gear, from anal hooks to zentai suits, including but not limited to blindfolds, collars, handcuffs, urethral sounds, and violet wands—alternately, #buynothing, an argument for psychological kink.

One of the most fun kink events I've ever attended was a mock trial held at an annual summertime gathering. Attendees could arrange ahead of time to accuse a friend or lover of some kind of sexual "crime" deserving of "funishment" in front of a delighted and raucous crowd, who stood around drinking beer and laughing while members of the community served as comic versions of attorneys, judge, and jury. Inevitably, when a particularly ridiculous accusation or defense was offered, such as "But my pants just *fell off!*," someone in the crowd would yell out, with faux pride, "'Merica!" and others would echo the satirically jingoistic chant.

I can think of nothing more 'Merican than the way in which we patriots have transformed even the intimate, underground pleasures of BDSM into big business. Here in the good old US of A, we seize any opportunity to take a hobby or passion and turn it into a reason to shop for more gear.

Don't get me wrong: I am as susceptible to this capitalist disease as anyone. So I try to choose lasting, quality items, and to channel my shopaholic tendencies toward small, local businesses—especially those owned by people of color, women, or queer folks. I love a feminist sex shop, a pervy Etsy seller, and the vendor's row at a kink event, not just because I like to bring home a special piece that will be well-used and loved, but also because it's such a joy to see others revel in access to the pervy items of their dreams.

The A-to-Z list below is meant to help get you up to speed on some of the BDSM gear most sought after and discussed. As many folks haven't yet seen or discussed such items in real life, it's useful to have a basic sense of what's available and what they're called. All of these items are hot topics at kinky conventions and on sites like FetLife, and I'm trying to cover ones that you are likely to run into but which haven't been thoroughly discussed elsewhere in this book and deserve a bit of explanation. This knowledge will make you a more informed kinkster: more prepared to enthusiastically consent—or not!—when someone brings up playing with shibari or a violet wand, and more ready to purchase the perfect sex toy when you make a pilgrimage to a good-quality BDSM store or website.

On a more introspective note, this list is also an incomplete but fun foray into all the *stuff* you can buy (or make yourself!) to outfit your boudoir or basement in a way that would shock the neighbors while simultaneously satiating your innermost fantasies. Mostly I'm writing about these things because they are wild, fun, interesting, and hold great potential for self-discovery: my hope is that this little alphabetical round-up might just spark an exciting new interest or awakening within your lascivious loins!

Finally, this list offers a glimpse into the kink world through the enterprises that have sprung up around it. I don't name specific vendors here, but in chapter 10 of this book, I list some long-standing, well-regarded shops and online sellers who carry most, if not all, of the products discussed here. For more in-depth advice, I recommend searching online for a review site geared to your specific kink or fetish, asking around at your local munch (kinky social event), or reading the forums on FetLife to find out what others think of particular brands and sellers.

Anal hooks. When I explain to friends just how freaky the kink world can get, I often tell this story: my partner and I once snuck off to an event's dungeon space to try wrestling on the gym mats there. It was the middle of the afternoon, when the dungeon is usually quite empty, and we were hoping for a goofy, relatively wholesome tussle in a quiet, well-padded space. Little did we realize that in the next station over was a workshop on anal hook suspension, complete with live demo! (Don't try this at home. Anal hooks are serious business, and suspending someone with one of them should be done only by experienced players who have learned—usually through apprenticing—about the delicate tissue of the back-door region. Even under the best circumstances, serious injury can occur.)

I put anal hooks under the category of "who thought this up and made it a viable reality?" But those who love them swear by both the physical sensation of the shiny hooks—which can range from small and subtle to large with a ridged steel ball at the end—as well as the psychological control they offer over the sub/bottom. The sub must remain rather still and follow the lead of whoever is handling the other end of the hook or the item (hair, spanking bench, rafter, outfit) to which the hook is attached. Believe it or not, you can buy a stainless-steel anal hook on Amazon if you want Jeff Bezos to profit from your desires, but I strongly urge you to make your purchase through a reputable and long-standing online BDSM seller or local feminist sex shop such as those mentioned in chapter 10. Your asshole (or that of your lover) is a delicate, sacred space, and it deserves the best-quality product available.

Boots. Boots are one of the most fetishized items of clothing, which makes sense if you think about their intrinsic value: from medieval times right up through contemporary cowboys, a pair of well-fitting leather boots can be one of the most valuable and well-used items in a wardrobe, and comfortably worn-in boots last for years. Plus, many boots are made of leather, which smells and tastes fantastic on its own and retains the smell of the feet they hold (if you're into that sort of thing). Then, of course, there is their strong association with dominance due to their inclusion in uniforms worn by authorities. It sounds super sexy to say you want to lick someone's boot; offering to slide your tongue up their sleeve or pants leg or hat just doesn't have the same seductive ring to it, does it?

Besides which, bootblacking—the practice of caring for boots through cleaning, buffing, and polishing, which comes from the bastion of traditional ritual that is the military—is perfect for those into high protocol and formal acts of service and submission. Over a century and a half ago, Victorian maid and diarist Hannah Cullwick documented her sexualized boot-cleaning services for her employer-husband-Master; the first International Mr. Bootblack competition was held at a leather convention in 1993. Many kink events now offer workshops on proper technique; a helpful website from the Phoenix Boys of Leather explains the multistep process, which traditionally employs a horsehair brush. A good leather kit, the Phoenix Boys tell us, should include over fifteen items, from saddle soap to toothbrushes, and when done properly, a good bootblacking can take "one to two hours."

Collars. On the recent Netflix comedy show *Bonding*, the Pro Domme is depicted wearing an O-ring collar—just like many other mainstream-media depictions of Dommes—and this annoys those of us in the BDSM community who know that collars are for submissives. Your collar can be a heavy, Rottweiler-appropriate industrial chain bought at a pet store, or a discreet golden anklet; you might have a "day collar" suitable for your professional life, brazen collars marked "SLAVE" for private use, and pretty ribbon-and-bell collars for kitten play. Many subs take our collars more seriously than our wedding bands: I wear my sterling padlock bracelet 24-7, more consistently than my engagement and wedding rings.

Most of the items in this abecedarium are either so rarified (such as anal hooks) or so normalized (such as boots) that you either can't bring them into your office job or no one would notice if you did. But the BDSM collar is a subtle yet unmistakable code that will be noticed primarily by other people in the kink community. In this way, they remind me of the wonderful but mostly lost art of the hanky code of the 1970s gay leathermen community, in which tucking a certain color bandana into one of your jeans' back pockets can signal the kind of play you're seeking while cruising at a bar or pier. Bright red, for example, can mean that you are into fisting—if you like giving it, you wear the hanky in your back left pocket, while receivers place the hanky in the back right. Likewise, when you wear a collar, you are "flagging" your sexual proclivities in public, but in a way that only those also in the know will recognize. (Note, though, that elaborate hanky codes indicating different meanings for fuchsia and magenta aren't particularly realistic: as BDSM historian Stephen K. Stein points out, the code can't work if it relies upon colors "impossible to differentiate in [the] dimly lit bars" where the code got started in the first place.)

Dildos (and strap-ons). The great thing about dildos is that they make penetration possible for everyone, no matter your orifices or other anatomy—and honestly, the act of penetrating an enthusiastically consensual partner is such an intensely intimate experience that I would encourage you to give it a go: it's really unlike anything else. And vice versa: if you are accustomed to being the penetrator, might you try spreading it for your lover?

Nowadays it's a brave new world that has such dildos in it. Gigantic, curved silicone anacondas! Petite and velvety pieces you can tuck in your pocket! Beautiful hand-blown (ha!) glass artifacts! Vibrating! Tie-dyed! Strapless strap-ons! You can find a dildo to wield in your hand, in a harness, or, with the right equipment, with one of your own orifices (though this can take practice to do well, so keep at it!). Just make sure to buy your dildo—and your harness, lube, cleaner, and other ancillary products—from a reliable source and brand, because sex toys are not regulated by the FDA, and you want anything you stick inside your fuck buddy to be safe. Look for dildos made of nonporous, nontoxic materials such as high-grade silicone, steel, or glass, all of which are easy to keep clean and don't have a nasty aftertaste or the ability to off-gas in your adorable holes. I highly recommend a trip to a helpful feminist sex shop—or an online chat with one—so that a wise staffer can help lead you to the best product for your particular body and desires. And research before you buy: these items can be pricey investments, and it sucks to spend $200 on a cute leather-harness-and-dildo combo only to find they aren't comfortable for you or your partner. Here, too, reading online reviews on designated kink-friendly sites, asking around on FetLife, or striking up a candid conversation with a good sex-shop staffer will be enormously helpful.

E-stim. Electrical-stimulation machines are used in physical therapy, sending pulses through electrodes placed on the skin to trigger healing. Incredibly, the ancient Egyptians used electricity-emitting fish to treat pain, and so did the ancient Greeks and Romans, "leveraging the electrical properties of fish like the electric ray to ease various ailments," according to the e-stim company Powerdot. By the mid-1830s, doctors and scientists were developing early electrical therapies to treat motor paralysis, and versions of our modern EMS machines came into use by the mid-1900s to ease various health issues.

One of the most well-known EMS machines is a TENS unit, a kind of e-stim specifically recommended for the nerves. This technology is now affordable and available for home use, so kinky folks have adapted it for our own nefarious purposes, skating the pleasure-pain continuum with an intense and unique set of sensations. Because the units can be controlled remotely, e-stim users often call themselves either "drivers" or "riders," conjuring up dirty images of one's erogenous zone as a toy car. E-stim is also popular for edging, in which one tries to stay as close to the brink of orgasm as possible for as long as possible without tipping over into it.

As "BDSM toy collector" Frederik of the website ToyTorture puts it, "There is no general rule [for] which intensity level to start with. . . . A level that [brings out] the grunting horny pain pig might [become] excruciating even after a short break because the body's pain memory and processing system calm down quite quickly." So proceed with all your RACK and PRICK protocols in place. Improper use of e-stim can lead to injury and should never be used on someone with a pacemaker or other electronic medical device.

Floggers. As with dildos, the variety of materials and styles for floggers are endless, and the field of study around the gear can be as intricate and geeked-out as for fly-fishing. What kinds you choose to wield or submit to are entirely up to your sensual preferences. Most impact players lean toward liking either a "thuddy" or "stingy" sensation (I'm Team Thud!), and you can choose your flogger accordingly: thicker, softer materials like cowhide tend to produce more thud, whereas stiff and thin materials such as rubber strands or metal chains produce more sting. Some materials—like deerskin—are so soft that the experience of being hit with them can be more relaxing than stimulating.

There are innumerable other kinds of impact play toys, of course, including whips and paddles. Most people I know who are into impact play don't own just one implement: they own a whole treasure chest of them, many of which are works of art, with intricate handles and hand-dyed strips available in every shade imaginable. The pomp and circumstance of showing off a beautiful flogger or similar weapon is often half the fun.

Gags. Certain kinky gear is just more visually arresting than others, and gags are one of those particularly stunning items that also provide a serious dose of psychological submissiveness. As with floggers, you can find a gag to suit your aesthetic. You can pony up (ha!) for a fancy leather bridle complete with bit. Or find an artisan vendor for a ball gag in the shape of a rose, dog bone, or heart. Or buy a ring gag that will keep that mouth open and ready, or get crafty at home with some silk or rope to keep it closed. In a pinch, a bandana, piece of cloth tied behind the head (called a cleave gag), or strip of duct tape will serve a similar purpose. Gagging is a subset of bondage, and one popular fantasy involves being gagged and bound together with another person, which provides a wonderful tease: you and someone sexy are intimately and physically connected to each other's bodies, but the ability to act on your attraction is kept at bay.

As someone who talks more than I need to in certain situations, a gag holds appeal for me because I like when BDSM helps with overall life skills such as learning how to stay silent when appropriate. (As mentioned in chapter 2, a nonverbal "safe word" is important in a scene where the bottom is unable to speak.) However, I find copious drooling only fun for so long and in certain situations (though I know others are into it). Which is just to say, if you are eager to try a gag, I hope you also like saliva.

Handcuffs. As with gags, the mere image of someone in handcuffs can be a shortcut to arousal: they just *look* so good, don't they? I'm especially partial to a shiny patent leather set with a pretty bow. Here, too, though, I recommend considering some practical concerns. If you really want handcuffs to be useful and not just decorative, you're going to want to think about type, fit, fastening, and material. Don't buy rabbit-fur cuffs for someone with an allergy. Don't get the kind that require a key if you want your lover to be able to wriggle out of them at the height of passion. If you're going to fly with them, maybe choose silk instead of something that will set off the metal detectors. And if you want to put your convict in them for a long time, consider a lightweight material—unless they are a heavy bottom.

The use of these restraints for punitive purposes goes back to antiquity, and as such, they have a sordid history connected with slavery and law-enforcement brutality. As clichéd and common as the sexy use of handcuffs is, it might be wise to have a serious conversation about them with your partner to make sure their real-life associations aren't triggering.

Inflatables. Why are inflatables—from balloons to beach balls to plastic blow-up dolls—such a turn-on? No one knows for sure, but it strikes me that these objects offer a complete sensory experience: vinyl and latex vessels that can be filled with (and released of) air, that have their own distinctive looks, smells, sounds, textures, and tastes. I can only imagine how exciting the recent surge in creatively shaped pool floats has been for inflatophiles: you can now inflate, deflate, or pop not just a ball or mattress but a giant translucent ice cream cone, glittery unicorn, or colorful cactus. And of course, it can be quite something to squeeze a fully pumped-up dolphin float between your knees. (If you are someone who would rather watch than participate, the Internet is full of inflatable-specific and utterly G-rated porn, featuring cute young women dressed in tank tops and shorts, making seductive faces while lying on deflating beach balls or jumping up and down in fairground bounce houses.)

On the kinky inflatables site Blow to Pop—which includes discussion forums and erotic writing—over 1,500 people have posted introductions, including a self-described "gay mature bloke" in the UK who is a "semi-popper." He "tends to 'loon' alone," checking himself into a hotel room for a private session of hugging and cuddling with balloons. He writes, "Love balloon-stuffing in my underwear, too!"

Japanese bondage. The terms "shibari" and "kinbaku" both refer to methods of decorative, highly photogenic rope-tying that originated in Japan. (Various types of rope can be used, so this entry refers more to technique that uses gear rather than the gear itself.) According to a FetLife post by licensed shibari instructor Nuitdetokyo, shibari means "to tie" and predates the introduction of the Chinese writing system in Japan; kinbaku is a much more recent word and implies more of a restriction of movement. Nuitdetokyo writes "there is no agreement, among Japanese people" about the difference between the two terms and that most Japanese rope artists simply choose one or the other term "depending upon the circumstances." (Heads up for your trip to Japan: he notes that Japanese rope porn tends to use the term "kinbaku.")

Autostraddle staffer and shibari educator Cee explains that Japanese erotic rope art "focuses on friction and wraps instead of knots," using repeated patterns to create shapes that hold and frame the body in a manner similar to, say, garters against a thigh or a leather harness against a chest. Alicia Joy, a writer based in Tokyo, points out that rope has been central to Japanese culture for thousands of years, used as belts for kimono and in spiritual Shinto practices. Most experts agree that using rope for shibari descends from the seventeenth- to nineteenth-century Edo-period martial arts used by the samurai to restrain prisoners, who were sometimes then put on public display while in bondage. After World War II, there was booming interest in Japanese culture in the United States and elsewhere, and one export was porn mags featuring fetish bondage photography.

What sets Japanese rope bondage apart from other methods is the emphasis on beauty and form. An article on the website run by sex shop Lovegasm says, "The importance of aesthetics doesn't end with beautiful rope patterns—the position of the restrained person is almost equally as important." Many practitioners find these arts more meditative or artistic than erotic, and, as with a Zen sand garden, the process is as cherished as the result.

Knives. Many people I found talking about erotic knife play in online BDSM forums and blogs used the same term to describe the appeal: the "mindfuck." There is just something both visual and visceral about wielding a knife over someone. More than a whip, more than a hand, the threat of a shiny blade is unmistakably and immediately terrorizing: think of all the knives, machetes, and the like featured on horror-movie posters (you don't picture Jason or Freddy with a gun!), and how etched into the public consciousness that scene from *Psycho* is, complete with fist clench and squealing music.

As one FetLife user put it, those into this kind of gear "love the potential for serious harm." They may also love the sound of a knife being flipped open, the feeling of cold metal on skin, the stinging sensation of being cut, the sight and sensation of blood, or the way knives can add a layer of mystery and gravity to ceremonial scenes. Knives are one of those things that deliver as much sensual input as psychological threat.

Latex. I once attended a kinky pool party on a humid summer day at an outdoor venue in a rustic, summer-camp-like setting. Everyone was barefoot, nude, sweating buckets, and splashing around to keep cool. Everyone, that is, except for a gorgeous young thing in full makeup, sky-high high heels, and a skin-tight black latex outfit who looked a gajillion times sexier and more elegant than all the butt-naked peasants around her. *That*, I thought, *is commitment.*

As someone who has always found dolphins and seals rather beautiful (who doesn't?!), I understand why someone would get into the sleek and shiny look and feel of latex clothing. But from what I've heard, it is notoriously hot, delicate, and expensive. It tears easily. Air bubbles can get stuck underneath it. Well-made, well-fitting gear can run into the hundreds of dollars per piece. And donning, removing, and maintaining latex clothing requires an intricate procedure involving baby powder, specialized polish, and immense patience and care. The whole thing sounds like an incredible hassle, but I think that's also part of the excitement of latex: it is so precious, so fragile, and so demanding. There's a built-in submissiveness involved, and it's a submission to the material itself.

Mummification. There's a popular and ancient method used to soothe babies called "swaddling." The newborn is wrapped tightly in a soft blanket, their arms pinned by their sides. The theory is that swaddling helps infants feel as cozy and snug as they did in the womb, and many people swear by it as a way to calm an unhappy little one.

My hunch is that kinky mummification works on the same principle: that wrapping a person from head to toe in material of some kind (but without the other intricacies of the ancient

Egyptian death practice!) can put them back in that dependent, infant-like mental space. As one FetLife user says, "Being mummified is the ultimate freedom. Someone else has taken away all control and responsibility. You have no decision to make, and you can't get anything wrong, because you can't *do* anything. You are free to meditate, sleep, feel at peace."

Most people in the FetLife mummification forums I read report enjoying an hour or so of "wrap time" per session, with careful attention paid to selecting the preferred mummifying materials (which can range from duct tape to plastic wrap to cotton sheets), using the right amount of tension, adjusting the room temperature, and accounting for circulation, hydration, bathrooming, and other safety issues. Others seek overnight experiences, which can be made more attainable through good pre-planning and gear, including custom-sized spandex sleeping bags marketed to people with sensory-processing issues.

Needle play. I try really hard not to let my own personal "squicks" (aka, things that turn me off) impact this book. But here's a place where I get a bit woozy just writing this. While I don't have a needle phobia, I'm the kind of person who needs to look away when getting a shot or blood drawn. So by my own design, this is not a kink I have researched heavily.

That said, I'm mostly aware of two kinds of needle play (which is also called play piercing): artistic and medical. The artistic kind, akin in some ways to shibari, is all about design. A skilled artist uses needles (and the subsequent blood, if desired) to create patterns on someone's body through temporary piercings; the needles are inserted through a pinch of flesh perpendicular to the body for a certain duration of time. (Just as most tattoo artists don't work on themselves, it's possible but difficult to make needle art on one's own body.) Typical patterns include angel wings, stars, corsets, and swirls. Medical play, on the other hand, is about role play, and often comes complete with props, costumes, and a "scene."

It goes without saying that you need to know what you're doing to engage in this kink, and you need to have supplies (disposable gloves, disinfectant) on hand. Those who work as professional piercers or nurses have a head start: I strongly recommend others take a class to learn proper technique. (I offer some resources for kink education in chapter 10 of this book.)

O-rings. I love a kinky toy that gets its name from a work of literature. O-rings—the circular hoops that hang from a steel or leather collar—are so named because something similar is worn by the submissive portrayed in the infamous and best-selling 1954 French BDSM novel *The Story of O* (*Histoire d'O*) by renowned literary translator Anne Desclos (pseudonym Pauline Réage). The book depicts the central character, O, as an extreme sub—a woman who is ritually disciplined, branded, routinely gangbanged, and otherwise thoroughly abjectified/objectified by members of an *Eyes Wide Shut*-like secret club that meets at a chateau. While such a depiction is wildly offensive to feminists who see pornography as inherently misogynist, the work actually has a feminist history: Desclos wrote it in defiance when her lover, a Sade fan, said that no woman could write like the Marquis.

In the novel, O's ring isn't dangling on the end of a collar: she has a specially designed signet ring on her finger to indicate that she has finished her submissive training. The O of the title could also refer to the ring of an enslaving, leash-style chain used on the protagonist. Or it could refer to the sub's wide-open orifices, taking all comers. Or to her status as an object (*objet*). But it has come to be the name for the most iconic accessory you can get on your collar, useful for being led around by a leash, being hog-tied, or simply to show the world that you're a wonderful pervert. (See Rihanna's "Work" video, in which she sports a thick pink spiked collar with an oversized O-ring. *Werk*, indeed.)

"Pervertibles." Every subculture has its own specific language: slang terms, acronyms, nicknames, and inside jokes that members of the community share to show that they belong, that they've been given the secret password to the tribe. "Pervertibles" is one of those bits of special language within the BDSM community.

It's generally held that this term was coined in the late twentieth century by gay leather activist David Stein, an all-around brilliant thinker and writer/editor. (He also originated the acronym SSC.) "Pervertibles" is a clever way to describe a fun activity: taking an object or item meant for something resolutely unsexual and transforming it, simply through imagination and use, into something depraved. Think, for example, of wielding a garden hose as a whip, or spanking someone with a hairbrush, or using electrical tape for bondage. Or come up with your own brand-new ideas! You can make sex toys out of things you find in the woods, at the hardware store or market, in the recycling bin, or lying around your apartment. Just remember, as sex educator Nadia Bello advises in a piece for the queer magazine *Xtra*, "the same rules about safety and sharing apply to pervertibles the same way they would to your more expensive goods: keep them clean and keep them separate."

Another great thing about pervertibles is that they remind us that nonnormative sexuality is a creative outlet, a way of viewing the world in a different and exciting light. And that, after all, is the most beautiful aspect of kink.

Queening. It's not easy finding words that start with the letter Q, so the entry here is a practice rather than a piece of equipment or object, and it's a practice that requires two willing—and physically able—bodies. Simply a fancier term for face-sitting, "queening" puts a majestic femme (or any queen-identifying person) where she belongs: sitting her ass down on a throne—which, in this case, is the countenance of her blissed-out partner. Queening is one of those multitasking activities that provides an array of louche sensory and psychological experiences all at once: the smell, taste, and mental satisfaction of ass or pussy worship; the dominance/submission vibes; the feeling of smothering or being smothered. Bonus: because it requires a prolonged, controlled squat or plié, it also doubles as a Barre workout.

Just keep both people's safety in mind. The queen should take breaks and shift positions to avoid cramping or fatigue, and some system should be devised so that the muffled bottom can indicate when they've had enough. Some wise D-types recommend giving the sittee (settee?) an object to hold, which they can drop when they are ready to stop—and which, in an emergency, would signal that a person has temporarily passed out from lack of oxygen.

Rope. I'd argue that before the rise of the Internet and its ability to transport all manner of individualized deviance into our lives, it was far less likely that a kinky trend would take hold: one sought out an underground community for one's particular interest—be that bootblacking or spanking or latex or what have you—and stuck within it. Or perhaps you made do with whatever debauched sexuality you could find access to. Back then, it was hard enough to find information or resources about even the most basic interests, much less more esoteric perversions.

But now we have kink websites, forums, e-commerce, and in-person gatherings whose details can be discovered online—as well as an expansive world of easily accessible professional and amateur porn. With access has come the ability for certain fetishes and predilections to gain popularity. And in my experience, rope and everything associated with it—from the intricate Japanese decorative bondage mentioned above to rigging and suspension—has recently become the X-rated equivalent of avocado toast or contouring makeup. Perhaps this is due in part to the rise in interest in and access to Japanese media, such as manga and anime, some of which heavily features bondage imagery? Or perhaps it's because rope combines so many different aspects of kink: power dynamics, S/m pain, arresting visual aesthetics, and—for the rope fetishist—specific smells, textures, and sounds. It also requires real skill, which can be practiced like an artistic hobby and can be combined with suspension, mummification, and other depraved add-ons. Not to mention that rope bunnies who love to be tied up often report an intense spiritual and emotional release from the experience.

No matter the reasons, in 2017, *Vice* called one form of rope bondage, *kinbaku,* "the latest trend." In my own experience, I've watched rope go from receiving as much attention and space at kink events as, say, flogging, to overtaking those other forms, becoming the most discussed topic at kink-convention workshops and online discussion boards. (I just checked FetLife while writing this, and I'm noticing an uptick in jeweled butt plugs and nipple clamps, so maybe those are the next big things?)

I'm not saying trendy kinks are any less legit or fun or hot than other kinks. I am merely curious about how and why such trends happen within our subculture. It will be interesting to see what happens to the interest in rope over the next couple of decades. In the meantime, you can easily find a wealth of articles, erotica, and forums devoted to rope pretty much anywhere within the kinky sphere, as well as online shops such as the one maintained by the Twisted Monk, which offers rope of various length, colors, and fibers, from hand-spun rainbow bamboo to glow-in-the-dark polyester, along with handy kits that come with an instructional DVD.

Spanking benches. Spanking is one of the more lo-fi, cost-efficient kinks out there: a hand works perfectly well, and if you prefer an implement, one can be improvised (perverted?) from a belt or hairbrush. But I wanted to give a special shout-out to the spanking bench, one of those BDSM-specific pieces of gear that make the specialists out there get all hot and bothered.

Could you use a chair, stool, or weight-lifting bench that you happen to have around the house? Sure. But a tailor-made spanking bench will offer accoutrements that give spanking the ritualistic refinement it deserves, while also making long sessions more comfortable for both the top and the bottom (heh heh), and provides an alternative to OTK (over-the-knee) sessions. I found spanking benches on Etsy that come with adjustable spreader bars, washable padded cushions, built-in ankle restraints—and even add-on vibrator attachments.

While some spanking benches are designed to look like vanilla furniture, most boldly reveal their purpose. And there's something arousing to me about investing in and storing a big, expensive, cumbersome piece of equipment in one's home that has been clearly devised to satisfy a wanton urge.

"Toys." This is catch-all term that folks into BDSM like to use to describe our gear. Anything that is commonly called a sex toy—vibrators, dildos, handcuffs, butt plugs—counts, but so do less common implements of pain and pleasure such as spreader bars, floggers, ball gags, and custom-made leather pony play tack.

Many of us keep our most-loved toys in a handy box or drawer by the bed for easy access, complete with sanitizer, gloves, condoms, and other safety equipment. Some kinky people assemble portable, comprehensive toy bags or toy chests that they can take with them on dates and to sex events. Even if none of those fun items end up being used, it can still be really sexy to lay out an array of beautiful play options from which a lover can choose.

Urethral sounds. I have zero expertise in and even less stomach for sounding, which is the practice of sticking some kind of thingy into your pee-tube (that's the technical definition). I was catheterized several times during the birth of my first child and there was nothing fun or sexy about it to me: I found it far less enjoyable than my five days of stop-start labor. But those who are into sounding—and their numbers seem to be growing—say that there is nothing like the sensation of masturbating while the urethra (inside either a penis or vulva) is stuffed with a metal rod (a "sounder"), small plug, or medical catheter. Some folks buy sets of increasingly thick, bumpy and/or long sounding devices to continually stretch the limits of their urethras, thereby also stretching the limits of their pleasure/pain sensory experiences. This is sometimes called "urethral training." For those with prostates, some sounds can stimulate that extremely sensitive spot, leading to mind-blowing orgasms.

Urethral sounding can be safe and can be an especially fantastic kink for those flying solo, but it does require careful sanitization, proper toys made from the right materials, lots of lube, practice, and good cleanup protocols; the website Sex Toy Collective offers a great beginner's guide, and I'm sure there are many others out there. You shouldn't try sounding if you're prone to urinary tract infections, so think about that before investing in a fancy steel sound/dilation set. I'd also recommend seeking out instructional videos from well-known sex educators before you begin (I found a good video from the YouTube channel of sex-toy company Lovehoney).

Violet wands. A relatively recent toy based on a century of people playing around with electrical currents, a violet wand is named for the purple glow that the device can take on when charged. It's a power supply instrument that looks a bit like an old car cigarette lighter; it plugs into an outlet and puts out electrical currents in the form of sparks, which then are transmitted through various kinds of electrodes or attachments to the skin and nerve endings. These attachments can range from glass rollers, swizzle sticks, and "mushrooms" to metal spurs to conductive steel rope so you can combine your electroshock fetish with your bondage fetish. And, as BDSM expert Stephen K. Stein points out, a violet wand's "buzzing sounds, . . . sparks, and glowing plasma [light] up dim rooms," which makes them especially fun at parties. Violet-wand kits are often packaged in a suitably steampunk leather chest for maximum aesthetic impact. If you can't quite envision what this all looks like, picture a mad scientist's lab from a low-budget 1950s film and you'll get the general idea.

In my opinion, while violet wands might win for the most romantically named kink gear, that very nomenclature presents some marketing issues, not to mention safety hazards. There is no one patented Violet Wand™. Any electrical buff can create—and even sell—their own contraption; these items are not regulated by the government. So when that eager-beaver Dom at your local dungeon bounces up to you with an offer of a violet wand pick-up play session, you don't really know what you're getting into. Be sure to proceed with caution and ask plenty of questions, such as what kind/brand of wand is being used, how much output it has, whether it's a less intense "solid state" circuit-board kit or an electromechanical device best suited for advanced or heavy players, what attachments are available, and what kinds of sensation they produce.

For a related kind of equipment, see the e-stim section above. One key difference between the two is that violet wands are built for and marketed solely to kinky people for erotic pleasure, whereas e-stim machines are "pervertible" medical devices.

Wax. There are a handful of kinks the notoriety of which we have pop star Madonna to blame—or thank. Wax is one of them. I personally can't think about wax play without thinking of the legendarily bad 1993 film *Body of Evidence*, starring the music icon as a femme fatale accused of killing her wealthy older lover. When she hooks up with her attorney, played by Willem Dafoe, they have the kind of sex that Hollywood thinks of as cinematically kinky, which in this case involves hot wax on genitals. (I haven't seen the movie and yet somehow I know about this scene, so deeply did it seep into the collective unconscious of Gen Xers.)

As entertainment reporter Joe Reid put it in a piece on the film's twenty-fifth anniversary for *Decider*, "Even the lightest kink is treated by this movie like a major transgression that ought to have you shunned from polite society." Reid himself, though, had never seen the movie until he wrote this piece, and as he says, he mostly wanted to watch it for the infamous wax scene. He writes, "I began to worry that . . . she would only pour the wax on his chest. . . . But just as I got scared that my childhood had been lied to, there Madonna was, dripping all that wax into Dafoe's (out-of-frame) genitals. If you think about it for half a second, it's not all that scandalous. . . . It's not even the worst thing that has been done to Willem Dafoe's genitals in a movie, which you'd know if you've seen *Antichrist*."

All of which is to say: You can drip hot wax on your lovers if that's a thing that appeals to you. You can buy special candles for this purpose, or you can use whatever candles you have around the house.

X-cross (a St. Andrew's cross). An X-cross is a dungeon staple also known as a St. Andrew's cross, or saltire cross. Supposedly, this saint was crucified on this kind of cross in Greece. Due to his martyrdom and his connection to St. Peter (his brother), he was canonized as a saint in 1320 by King Angus of the Picts as a way of currying favor with the pope, according to scholar Michael T. R. B. Turnbull. Turnbull writes that in medieval times, during a war in what is now Scotland, King Angus had a dream in which a cross appeared to him to foretell victory; the next morning, as he went into battle, he indeed reported seeing a "saltire cross" in the blinding light of the rising sun. After his army emerged triumphant, "Saint Andrew and his Saltire Cross were adopted as the national symbols for an emerging Scotland."

In any case, the X shape associated with him is seen on the flag of Scotland—and, somewhat randomly, on the Confederate flag as well. While searching for a symbol for their movement, the Confederate leaders considered various versions of the cross as well as variations on the stars and stripes already in use by the young American nation but landed on the St. Andrews' cross in part due to the popular "expressions of romanticized Scottish culture [that] permeated the antebellum South," according to Confederacy historian John M. Coski. (I think of how Scarlett in *Gone with the Wind* gives her daughter the Scottish name Bonnie.)

As dungeon equipment, the St. Andrew's cross is a person-sized wooden or metal X that usually comes with rings on which to attach various restraints, so it's the perfect tool for both bondage and impact play. As sub Kayla Lords writes in a piece for the website BDSM Training Academy, the cross offers wide potential for licentious play, including exhibitionistic fun. Lords points out that she can either be placed "on display," facing outward on the cross, or find privacy by facing toward the cross. "On the cross," she writes, "I'm at [my Dominant's] mercy. . . . While I could call it all off with a word, we both know I will pull and strain against my bonds in pain and pleasure instead. . . . With some toys, like whippy floggers or the dragon's tail, I can take more and longer impact at the cross than anywhere else. The cross helps us have a longer, better session."

You and your imagination. See next section.

Zentai suits. The Blue Man Group. Spiderman. *Deadpool.* If you can picture the costumes worn for these, you're picturing a zentai suit (also known as a morph suit): a stretchy, form-fitting, full-body suit usually made from spandex or Lycra. The suits were originally created for costuming and performances, but as they've become readily available and affordable, they have become—like many other kinks, via Japanese culture—fetishwear. Though somewhat restrictive in terms of sightline and temperature control, zentai suits still allow for movement and can be custom-made with handy holes or pouches for access to one's orifices and erogenous zones. Akin to latex and compression fetishes, the appeal of the zentai suit often has to do with an attraction to the smooth slickness of the material, the feeling of being tightly held by the fabric, and the anonymity and alien vibes of the look.

While researching zentai suits, I was delighted to come across a website called, amazingly, the ABCs of Kink, which, even more amazingly, turns out to be maintained by a one-time make-out partner of mine known as Creature. Here's how Creature describes their experience in a zentai suit: "The world is smaller. Emotions are clearer and sometimes more consuming." They go on to describe how the suit can help them feel "little and slow and soft," more open to giving and receiving gentle touch; they also find the sensory experience of "feeling your own body sleek and smooth and round and muscled and bony and fat" to be "a bit of a wonderland." In the suit, they say, "it was easy to be turned on, to just want to rub up against those closest to me."

SIMPLE AS ABC: AN ARGUMENT FOR MIND OVER MATTER

And on that lovely note, we end this little abecedarium of kinky shit you can make and buy. While much of the gear mentioned above requires shelling out some hard-earned cash—whether that's just a few bucks for some rolls of duct tape at the local hardware store or $750 for a bespoke latex dress from an independent designer—one does not need to participate in capitalist culture in order to be a proper deviant.

Whether you are a #buynothing type or are seeking to simplify your life by simplifying your perversion, I want to make the case for purely psychological kink. The truth is, no gear is required to make someone feel endangered, protected, humiliated, or otherwise in their preferred impure state of mind: you can just use communication.

The most basic version of this is one most of us recognize, and it's the ancient art of the seductive facial expression. My primary partner has this one look he gives me: chin lowered and unsmiling, he stares at me intensely from under his brows. The meaning is clear: he is a predator and I am his delicious prey. He conveys this feeling without props, without words, and he can do it whether we're on a hike or in the supermarket.

Psychological kink can also be used as an effective substitute for any of the gear above. Can't afford a crisp nurse's uniform? *Pretend* that you're wearing one: describe it to your lover while you run their hand over your body. Don't feel ready for actual knife play? Put a pencil between your teeth and do your best pirate imitation. Even bondage can be achieved by *telling* someone that they can't move. If all parties are GGG (Dan Savage's term: good, giving, and game), disbelief can be suspended and you too can be the owner of the most luxurious and elaborate sex toys in the world, even if only in your minds.

ACKNOWLEDGMENTS

I'm so fortunate to have a wide circle of dear friends and expert acquaintances who love to talk and think about the complexities of nonnormative sexuality as much as I do. Deepest gratitude for conversations, community, and shared experiences to Sinclair Sexsmith, Tina Horn, Kim Brooks, and the many writers and podcasters cited in this book whose own thinking informs mine; good friends including Roan, Carley, Marybeth, Brandon, Laura, Ames, Lindsey, Kelcy, and Hoa, who have furthered my perspective; my Oregon State University–Cascades MFA "girl gang" students, who wrote and laughed with me; the Dark Odyssey family I share with Mikey, including Emmanuel, Claire, Marta, Rachel, Mags, Ray, Noel, Capri, Kali, Tia, Danforth, Creature, Matt, and Frankie; and the kink educators, play partners, and fascinating folks I've met at BDSM events and online. Thanks, too, to the musicians and songwriters quoted here, who have provided my life's soundtrack. We all know what it really means to "rock 'n' roll."

Above all, my love and thanks to Mikey. I found him, against all odds, via kink; our relationship was forged in the furnace of deviant desire; and all these years later, here we are, still discussing, exploring, and sharing a life together that is erotic, wild, nourishing, and full. He is the fetish object of my wildest dreams, my Daddy, and also the thoughtful partner who made dinner alone many nights so I could keep working on this book. In a hundred ways, this book could not have been written without him.

WORKS CITED

INTRODUCTION: SHE'S A VERY KINKY GIRL: WHY I WROTE THIS BOOK

Rick James, "Super Freak," *Street Songs* (Gordy Records, 1981).

Audre Lorde, "The Uses of the Erotic: The Erotic as Power," in *The Selected Works of Audre Lorde*, ed. Roxane Gay (New York: W. W. Norton, 2020).

Peter Tupper, *A Lover's Pinch: A Cultural History of Sadomasochism* (Lanham, MD: Rowman & Littlefield, 2018).

Annaliese Griffin, "The Crucial Difference Between a 'Pervert' and a Predator," *Quartz*, November 16, 2017, https://qz.com/quartzy /1128392/is-louis-c-k-a-pervert-or-a-predator-or-both.

HRC Foundation, "Fatal Violence Against the Transgender and Gender Non-Conforming Community in 2021," Human Rights Campaign, https://www.hrc.org/resources, accessed September 5, 2022.

Elisabeth A. Sheff, "The Five Most Common Legal Issues Facing Polyamorists," Psychologytoday.com, January 18, 2014, https://www .psychologytoday.com/us/blog/the-polyamorists-next-door/201401 /the-five-most-common-legal-issues-facing-polyamorists.

Alex Abad-Santos, "The Perpetual Discourse over LGBTQ Pride, Explained," *Vox*, June 2, 2021, https://www.vox.com/the-goods/22463879 /kink-at-pride-discourse-lgbtq.

James Baldwin, "Here Be Dragons," in *The Price of the Ticket: Collected Nonfiction; 1948–1985* (Boston: Beacon Press, 2021).

Velvet Underground, "Venus in Furs," *The Velvet Underground and Nico* (Verve Records, 1967).

Michael Leigh, *The Velvet Underground* (New York: Macfadden Books, 1963).

Mike Brake, "The Skinheads: An English Working Class Subculture," *Youth & Society* (December 1974).

Charlotte's Web, dir. Charles A. Nichols and Iwao Takamoto (Hanna-Barbera, 1973).

Kendra Holliday [The Beautiful Kind, pseud.], "Gluttony Meets Lust, Part One: An Interview with Molly Ren," EdenFantasys.com, August 31, 2010, https://www.edenfantasys.com/sexis/sex/feederism-fetish -part-two-0831103.

Unorigin, comment on "So . . . When did you know you where [sic] a FA/FFA?," Curvage.org, March 11, 2013, https://curvage.org/forum /index.php?/forums/topic/460-sowhen-did-you-know-you-where -a-faffa.

CHAPTER 1: LET'S TALK ABOUT SEX, BABY: THE INS AND OUTS OF EROTIC DESIRE

Salt-n-Pepa, "Let's Talk About Sex," *Blacks' Magic* (Next Plateau and London Records, 1990).

"Most Popular Fetishes," FetLife.com, https://fetlife.com/fetishes/most _popular, accessed February 21, 2022.

Justice Anthony Kennedy, "Opinion of the Court in John Geddes Lawrence and Tyron Garner v. Texas," June 26, 2003, https://www.law .cornell.edu/supct/pdf/02-102P.ZO.

Amy Russell, *Clinician's Toolkit for Children's Behavioral Health* (London: Elsevier, 2020).

E. Pfeiffer, A. Verwoerdt, and G. C. Davis, "Sexual Behavior in Middle Life," *American Journal of Psychiatry* (April 1972).

Editors of Harvard Health Publishing, *Sexuality in Midlife and Beyond* (Boston: Harvard Health Publishing, 2019).

Emily Bolam and Samantha Jarvis, "The Language of Non-normative Sexuality and Genders" poster presentation, Western Washington University, 2016.

Elijah Wolfson, "The Chemistry and Chimera of Desire," *Healthline*, July 25, 2017, https://www.healthline.com/health/what-is-desire, accessed September 5, 2022.

Toni Morrison, *The Bluest Eye* (New York: Alfred A. Knopf, 1970).

Wolfson, "The Chemistry and Chimera of Desire."

Sarah Barmark, "The Misunderstood Science of Sexual Desire," *The Cut*, April 26, 2018, https://www.thecut.com/2018/04/the-misunderstood -science-of-sexual-desire.html.

David Buss and Cindy Meston, "Why Do People Have Sex?," UT News, July 31, 2007, https://news.utexas.edu/2007/07/31/why-do-people -have-sex-researchers-explore-237-reasons.

Carl Zimmer, "The Brain: The Dark Matter of the Human Brain," *Discover*, August 19, 2009, https://www.discovermagazine.com/mind /the-brain-the-dark-matter-of-the-human-brain.

Meredith L. Chivers, "A Sex Difference in the Specificity of Sexual Arousal," *Psychological Science*, November 1, 2004.

Katherine Angel, *Tomorrow Sex Will Be Good Again: Women and Desire in the Age of Consent* (New York: Verso, 2021).

Carrie Weisman, "7 Kinky Sex Ideas for Couples Looking to Spice Things Up," Fatherly.com, August 6, 2019, https://www.fatherly.com /love-money/kinky-sex-ideas-couples.

Madeline Howard, "20 Ways to Spice Up Your Sex Life, According to Sex Experts," *Women's Health*, October 15, 2021, https://www .womenshealthmag.com/sex-and-love/a19964722/spice-up-sex-life -with-kink.

Candice Jalili, "How to Spice Up Your Sex Life," *The Cut*, January 1, 2018, https://www.thecut.com/article/how-to-spice-up-your-sex-life.html.

Ayana Byrd and Samantha Lefave, "24 Ways You Can Immediately Spice Up Your Sex Life," *Redbook*, December 20, 2017, https://www.red bookmag.com/love-sex/sex/advice/g527/spice-up-sex-life.

Miranda Christophers, "10 Ways to Spice Up Your Sex Life," *Gentleman's Journal*, https://www.thegentlemansjournal.com/article/10 -ways-to-spice-up-your-sex-life, accessed September 6, 2022.

Regi George Jenarius, "This Kinky 30-Day Sex Challenge Will Spice Up Your Sex Life and Keep Your Relationship Fresh," *India Times*, May 23, 2018, https://www.indiatimes.com/health/tips-tricks/this-kinky -30-day-sex-challenge-will-spice-up-your-sex-life-and-keep-your -relationship-fresh-345990.html.

"How You Can Spice Up Your Love Life and Fulfil Your Fantasies," *Men's Health Australia*, May 2, 2021, https://www.menshealth.com.au /spice-up-your-love-life-and-fulfil-your-fantasies, accessed September 5, 2022.

CHAPTER 2: TAKE A WALK ON THE WILD SIDE: A PRIMER ON KINK, BDSM, AND FETISHES

Lou Reed, "Walk on the Wild Side," *Transformer* (RCA Records, 1972).

Samantha Cole, "This Man Invented a New Fetish as an Experiment, and It Worked," *Vice*, October 30, 2020, https://www.vice.com/en /article/bvx8aq/fedlegs-yellow-legs-fetish-weirdest-subreddit.

Peter Tupper, *A Lover's Pinch: A Cultural History of Sadomasochism* (Lanham, MD: Rowman & Littlefield, 2018).

Stefani Goerlich, *Kink-Affirming Practice: Culturally Competent Therapy from the Leather Chair* (London: Routledge, 2022).

Michael Aaron, "Growing Up Kinky: Research Shows How Kink Identity Is Formed," *Psychology Today*, May 30, 2018, https://www .psychologytoday.com/us/blog/standard-deviations/201805/growing -kinky-research-shows-how-kink-identity-is-formed.

Stephen K. Stein, *Sadomasochism and the BDSM Community in the United States: Kinky People Unite* (London: Routledge, 2021).

Mark McLelland, "'How to Sex'? The Contested Nature of Sexuality in Japan," in *The SAGE Handbook of Modern Japanese Studies*, ed. James Babb (London: SAGE, 2014).

Ogi Ogas and Sai Gaddam, "5 Things That Internet Porn Reveals About Our Brains," *Discover*, September 19, 2011, https://www.discover magazine.com/mind/5-things-that-internet-porn-reveals-about-our -brains.

Masters of Sex (Showtime, 2013–16).

Dan Savage quoting Jesse Bering, "Savage Love: Don't Judge the Fetish," LittleVillageMag.com, March 19, 2014, https://littlevillagemag.com /savage-love-dont-judge-the-fetish.

Jesse Bering, *Perv: The Sexual Deviant in All of Us* (New York: Scientific American/Farrar, Straus and Giroux, 2013).

Aaron, "Growing Up Kinky: Research Shows How Kink Identity Is Formed."

V. S. Ramachandran, *Phantoms in the Brain: Probing the Mysteries of the Human Mind* (Boston: Mariner Books, 1999).

Emma McGowan, "The Origins of Kink Are More Complicated than You Thought," *Bustle*, March 1, 2017, https://www.bustle.com/p /where-do-kinks-come-from-its-complicated-41467.

E. L. James, *Fifty Shades of Grey* (New York: Vintage Books, 2011).

S. Ten Brink, V. Coppens, W. Huys, and M. Morrens, "The Psychology of Kink: A Survey Study into the Relationships of Trauma and Attachment Style with BDSM Interests," *Sexuality Research and Social Policy*, February 18, 2020.

Midori, "The History & Myths of Japanese Bondage: Censorship, Sex Work and Othering in the World of Shibari," *Spectrum Journal*, https://spectrumboutique.com/journal/article/the-history-myths -of-japanese-bondage, accessed September 7, 2022.

Deadwood (HBO, 2004–6).

American Psychiatric Association, *Diagnostic and Statistical Manual of Mental Disorders, Fifth Edition (DSM-5)* (Washington, DC: American Psychiatric Association, 2013).

Evan Goldstein, "The Most Common Kinks and Fetishes in the U.S.," Future Method, https://futuremethod.com/blogs/the-future-edition /most-common-fetishes, accessed September 7, 2022.

N. J. Rinehart and M. P. McCabe, "An Empirical Investigation of Hypersexuality," *Sexual and Relationship Therapy* 13, no. 4 (1998).

The Abel Assessment for Sexual Interest (AASI-3), Abel Screening diagnostic tool for clinicians, 1995 and onward.

K. Freund, B. W. Steiner, and S. Chan, "Two Types of Cross-Gender Identity," *Archives of Sexual Behavior* 11 (1982).

M. P. Kafka, "Hypersexual Desire in Males: An Operational Definition and Clinical Implications for Males with Paraphilias and Paraphilia-Related Disorders," *Archives of Sexual Behavior* 26, no. 5 (1997).

Amanda Mannen, "6 Realities of Life When Your Fetish Is EXTREMELY Weird," *Cracked*, March 13, 2016, https://www.cracked.com/personal -experiences-2102-i-burn-myself-to-get-off-6-realities-extreme -fetishists.html.

Molly Young, "The Reigning Queen of Pandemic Yoga," *New York Times Magazine*, November 25, 2020.

Tupper, *A Lover's Pinch: A Cultural History of Sadomasochism.*

Becca Rothfeld, "Pleasure and Justice," *Boston Review*, September 20, 2021.

Amia Srinivasan, *The Right to Sex: Feminism in the Twenty-First Century* (New York: Farrar, Straus and Giroux, 2021).

Mia Schachter quoting Betty Martin, "Should Enthusiasm Be a Requirement for Sex?," ConsentWizardry.com, December 7, 2021, https:// consentwizardry.com/blog/2021/12/7/should-enthusiasm-be-a -requirement-for-sex.

Rothfeld, "Pleasure and Justice."

Stein, *Sadomasochism and the BDSM Community in the United States.*

Gary Switch, "Origin of RACK: RACK vs. SSC," The-Iron-Gate.com, https://www.the-iron-gate.com/essays/138, accessed September 7, 2022.

Adrienne Westenfeld, "Inside the Necessary Work of Intimacy Coordinators, Who Make Hollywood Sex Scenes Safe," *Esquire*, July 13, 2020, https://www.esquire.com/entertainment/tv/a33232977/what -is-an-intimacy-coordinator-sex-scenes-i-may-destroy-you-normal -people-ita-obrien-interview.

Rothfeld, "Pleasure and Justice."

CHAPTER 3: HEAVEN HELP ME FOR THE WAY I AM: TABOOS AS THE HEART OF KINK

Fiona Apple, "Criminal," *Tidal* (The WORK Group, 1996).

Pink Flamingos, dir. John Waters (Dreamland, 1972).

Jillian Keenan, "Can You Really Be Fired for Being Kinky? Absolutely," *Slate*, October 28, 2014, https://slate.com/human-interest/2014/10 /the-jian-ghomeshi-case-echoes-many-kinksters-worst-fear-being -outed-and-fired.html.

William Faulkner, "A Rose for Emily," in *Collected Stories of William Faulkner* (New York: Vintage, 1995).

Nell Frizzell, "Heartbreak Is Hard, Even When Your Lover Is the Eiffel Tower," *Vice*, January 13, 2015, https://www.vice.com/en/article /nnqpnm/breaking-up-with-the-eiffel-tower.

Amy Marsh, "Love Among the Objectum Sexuals," *Electronic Journal of Human Sexuality* 13, March 1, 2010, http://www.ejhs.org/volume13 /ObjSexuals.htm.

Blade Runner, dir. Ridley Scott (Warner Bros., 1982).

Her, dir. Spike Jonze (Warner Bros., 2013).

James Kincaid, "Hunting Pedophiles on the Net," *Salon*, August 24, 2000, https://www.salon.com/2000/08/24/cyber_menace.

Diana Tourjée, "Most Child Abusers Are Not Pedophiles, Expert Says," *Vice*, April 4, 2016, https://www.vice.com/en/article/mgmzwn/most-child-sex-abusers-are-not-pedophiles-expert-says.

Brian D. Erp, "Pedophilia and Child Sexual Abuse Are Two Different Things—Confusing Them Is Harmful to Children," blog post on the *Journal of Medical Ethics*, November 11, 2017, https://blogs.bmj.com/medical-ethics/2017/11/11/pedophilia-and-child-sexual-abuse-are-two-different-things-confusing-them-is-harmful-to-children.

CHAPTER 4: CHAINS AND WHIPS EXCITE ME: ON SADOMASOCHISM

Rihanna, "S & M," *Loud* (Def Jam Records, 2010).

Susan Sontag, "Fascinating Fascism," *New York Review of Books*, February 6, 1975.

Peter Tupper, *A Lover's Pinch: A Cultural History of Sadomasochism* (Lanham, MD: Rowman & Littlefield, 2018).

Zaria Gorvett, "Why Pain Feels Good," BBC, October 1, 2015, https://www.bbc.com/future/article/20151001-why-pain-feels-good.

Barry Komisaruk et al., "Women's Clitoris, Vagina, and Cervix Mapped on the Sensory Cortex: fMRI Evidence," *Journal of Sexual Medicine* 8, no. 10 (July 2011).

Barry Komisaruk, Carlos Beyer-Flores, and Beverly Whipple, *The Science of Orgasm* (Baltimore: John Hopkins University Press, 2006).

Paul Rozin et al., "Glad to Be Sad, and Other Examples of Benign Masochism," *Judgment and Decision Making* 8, no. 4 (July 2013).

Maria Cohut, "When and Why Is Pain Pleasurable?," *Medical News Today*, June 7, 2019, https://www.medicalnewstoday.com/articles/325419.

Cara Dunkley et al., "Physical Pain as Pleasure: A Theoretical Perspective," *Journal of Sex Research* 57, no. 4 (2020).

Gorvett, "Why Pain Feels Good."

Sigmund Freud, *Three Essays on the Theory of Sexuality*, trans. James Strachey (New York: Basic, 2000).

Lissa Rankin, "What Is a Masochistic Person? 10 Traits & Behaviors of a Masochist," *Mind Body Green*, July 29, 2022, https://www.mindbodygreen.com/0-22868/10-ways-to-spot-a-masochist.html.

Richard von Krafft-Ebing, *Psychopathia Sexualis*, trans. Franklin S. Klaf (New York: Arcade, 2011).

Marquis de Sade, *The 120 Days of Sodom*, trans. Will McMorran (Oxford: Oxford University Press, 2021).

Marquis de Sade, *Justine*, trans. John Phillips (Oxford: Oxford University Press, 2013).

Tony Perrottet, "Who Was the Marquis de Sade?," *Smithsonian Magazine*, February 2015, https://www.smithsonianmag.com/history/who-was-marquis-de-sade-180953980.

Leopold von Sacher-Masoch, *Venus in Furs*, trans. Joachim Neugroschel (New York: Penguin, 2000).

Sean K. Kelly, "Leopold von Sacher-Masoch and Human Rights," *Modern Austrian Literature* 43, no. 3 (2010).

Gilles Deleuze, "Coldness and Cruelty," trans. Jean McNeil, in *Masochism* (Princeton: Princeton University Press, 1991).

Catherine Sauvat, *Man in Furs* (Seattle: Fantagraphics, 2021).

Gloria Brame, William Brame, and Jon Jacobs, *Different Loving: The World of Sexual Dominance and Submission* (New York: Villard, 1996).

Zachary Zane, "If You're Topping from the Bottom, You're Doing BDSM Wrong," *Men's Health*, May 11, 2021, https://www.menshealth.com/sex-women/a36396905/topping-from-the-bottom-bdsm.

Alexander Cheves, "How 6 Kinksters Found Their Kinks," *Them*, February 14, 2019, https://www.them.us/story/how-kinksters-found-their-kinks.

CHAPTER 5: LET'S PLAY MASTER AND SERVANT: ON DOMINANCE AND SUBMISSION

Depeche Mode, "Master and Servant," *Some Great Reward* (Mute Records, 1984).

Larissa Pham, "Why Do We Like BDSM?," *Complex*, May 5, 2016, https://www.complex.com/life/2016/05/who-likes-bdsm-and-why.

National Sexual Violence Resource Center, https://www.nsvrc.org/statistics, accessed September 8, 2022.

Joseph Critelli and Jenny Bivona, "Women's Erotic Rape Fantasies: An Evaluation of Theory and Research," *Journal of Sex Research* 45, no. 1 (2008).

Susan Brownmiller, *Against Our Will: Men, Women and Rape* (New York: Bantam, 1976).

Margaret Mitchell, *Gone with the Wind* (New York: Macmillan, 1936).

"Just Fucking Fuck Me, Already," Craigslist.org, February 3, 2008, https://www.craigslist.org/about/best/sea/561877622.html.

Anna North, "Why Women Really Like '*50 Shades of Grey*': It's About Being Served," *BuzzFeed*, May 14, 2012, https://www.buzzfeed.com/annanorth/why-50-shades-of-grey-is-less-about-submission-a.

Noah Berlatsky, "When Rape Is a Fantasy," *The Atlantic*, June 17, 2013, https://www.theatlantic.com/sexes/archive/2013/06/when-rape-is-a-fantasy/276933.

Nancy Friday, *My Secret Garden: Women's Sexual Fantasies* (New York: Trident, 1973).

Critelli and Bivona, "Women's Erotic Rape Fantasies."

Paul Joannides, "Rape Fantasy or Pseudo Rape Fantasy?," *Psychology Today*, June 13, 2008, https://www.psychologytoday.com/za/blog /you-it/200806/rape-fantasy-or-pseudo-rape-fantasy.

Justin J. Lehmiller, *Tell Me What You Want: The Science of Sexual Desire and How It Can Help You Improve Your Sex Life* (New York: Hachette, 2020).

Jennifer Billock, "When Rape Survivors Have Rape Fantasies," *Vice*, January 29, 2018, https://www.vice.com/en/article/3k5gey/when-rape -survivors-have-rape-fantasies.

Alesandra, "Total Power Exchange Relationships: Ultimate Guide," *Dom Sub Living*, https://domsubliving.com/total-power-exchange -relationships-guide.

Vice Staff, "Cash Slaves: Inside the Dystopian Fetish of Financial Domi- nation," *Vice*, October 22, 2015, https://www.vice.com/en /article/7bde84/cash-slaves-817.

Kayla Lords, "24/7 D/S Realities: What You Need to Know," *Loving BDSM*, October 18, 2021, https://lovingbdsm.net/2021/10/18/247 -ds-realities.

Sinclair Sexsmith, "View from the Top: Coming and Crying; Master and Slave," *Autostraddle*, July 19, 2016, https://www.autostraddle.com /view-from-the-top-master-and-slave-345554.

Sinclair Sexsmith, "On Stepping Away from M/s Language," *Sugarbutch Chronicles*, July 24, 2020, https://www.sugarbutch.net/2020/07/ms -statement.

Hayley Jade, "Mastering the Art of Financial Domination Fetish Is Harder Than It Looks," *Vice*, March 28, 2018, https://www.vice.com /en/article/mbxg8a/mastering-the-art-of-financial-domination-fetish -is-harder-than-it-looks.

"Inside the Kink of Financial Domination," *Vice*, February 1, 2022, https:// video.vice.com/en_us/video/inside-the-kink-of-financial-domination.

Vice Staff, "Cash Slaves: Inside the Dystopian Fetish of Financial Domination."

Russell J. Stambaugh, "Leopold Ritter von Sacher-Masoch," *Elephant in the Hot Tub*, May 21, 2016, https://elephantinthehottub.com/2016 /05/leopold-ritter-von-sacher-masoch.

Stephen K. Stein, *Sadomasochism and the BDSM Community in the United States: Kinky People Unite* (London: Routledge, 2021).

Sinclair Sexsmith, to author, personal interview, December 1, 2021.

Valentine Hooven II, Tom of Finland Foundation, https://www.tomof finland.org/about-tom-of-finland/#1, accessed September 7, 2022.

Scorpio Rising, dir. Kenneth Anger (Puck Film Productions, 1963).

Jesse Monteagudo, "A Short History of Physique Magazines," *South Florida Gay News*, February 14, 2011, https://southfloridagaynews.com/Jesse-Monteagudo/a-short-history-of-physique-magazines.html.

Steve Hogan and Lee Hudson, *Completely Queer: The Gay and Lesbian Encyclopedia* (New York: Henry Holt, 1998).

Stein, *Sadomasochism and the BDSM Community in the United States.*

Jack Fritscher, "CMC Carnival: The World's Best Annual Gay Party," *Drummer*, no. 20 (January 1978).

Durk Dehner, "Tom of Finland: A Personal Remembrance," *World of Tom of Finland*, http://www.worldoftomoffinland.com/foundation/durks.html, accessed September 7, 2022.

Paul Welch, "Homosexuality in America," *Life*, June 26, 1964.

"60s Photos Put SG GLBT Community on Map," ABC7 San Francisco, June 25, 2010, https://abc7news.com/archive/7521577.

"Leather Culture," Leatherpedia, http://www.leatherpedia.org/leather-culture, accessed September 7, 2022.

Sinclair Sexsmith, to author, personal interview, 2021.

Larry Townsend, *The Leatherman's Handbook* (Beverly Hills, CA: L T Publications, 1972).

Kassie, "David Stein on 'Defining Leather,'" *Leatherati*, September 8, 2011, https://leatherati.com/david-stein-on-defining-leather-6c5d7ce1c718.

Phoenix Boys of Leather, September 21, 2022, http://phoenixboysofleather.com.

Sinclair Sexsmith, to author, personal interview, 2021.

Matt Baume, "Inside the Changing Leather Scene," *Rolling Stone*, August 18, 2017, https://www.rollingstone.com/culture/culture-features/inside-the-changing-leather-scene-202707.

"Leather Culture," Leatherpedia, http://www.leatherpedia.org/leather-culture, accessed September 7, 2022.

"Dirty Looks on Location—Cuffs," event posting, Bluf, https://bluf.com/events/2557, accessed September 9, 2022.

International Mr. Leather, https://www.imrl.com, accessed September 9, 2022.

Stein, *Sadomasochism and the BDSM Community in the United States.*

"Queer 1950s Household," FetLife Group, https://fetlife.com/groups/12202, accessed March 13, 2022.

CHAPTER 6: SHE'S GOT LEGS: ON FETISHES

ZZ Top, "Legs," *Eliminator* (Warner Bros. Records, 1983).

FetLife, https://fetlife.com/fetishes/most_popular, accessed January 24, 2022.

Merriam-Webster Dictionary, s.v. "fetish (n.)," https://wwwmerriam-webster.com/dictionary/fetish, accessed September 8, 2022.

Roy Ellen, "Fetishism," *Man* 23, no. 2 (1988).

Mikelle Street, "Here's Everything You Need to Know About Water-sports," *Out*, March 7, 2019, https://www.out.com/sex/2019/3/07 /everything-need-know-about-watersports-golden-showers.

The Spanko (Charlotte Tyran, 2012).

Jaimee Bell, "What Is Plushophilia?," *Sofia Gray*, June 29, 2020, https:// sofiagray.com/blog/what-is-plushophilia.

Elise Nezir, "A Brief History of Quentin Tarantino's Foot Fetish," *Volta*, February 7, 2020, https://voltamagazine.wordpress.com/2020/02/07 /a-brief-history-of-quentin-tarantinos-foot-fetish.

C. Scorolli, S. Ghirlanda, et al., "Relative Prevalence of Difference Fe-tishes," *International Journal of Impotence Research* 19 (February 15, 2007).

Emily Leibert, "What It's Like to Have Odontophilia—a Fetish for Teeth," *Men's Health*, October 25, 2021, https://www.menshealth .com/sex-women/a37974716/teeth-fetish-odontophilia.

Aleks Kang, "How I Came to Terms with People Fetishizing My Disabil-ity," *Vice*, March 24, 2016, https://www.vice.com/en/article/vdxa34 /how-i-came-to-terms-with-people-fetishizing-my-disability.

Sophie Saint Thomas, "A Beginner's Guide to Balloon Fetishes, Straight from an Actual Looner," *Allure*, May 22, 2019, https://www.allure .com/story/balloon-fetish-guide-what-is-a-looner.

Alex, "Into the Rubber World: What Is a Latex Fetish?," LaidTex, https://laidtex.com/blogs/news/into-the-rubber-world-what-is-a -latex-fetish, accessed June 24, 2022.

Sandra Song, "The Art of Tickle Torture," *Paper*, March 26, 2019, https://www.papermag.com/tickle-sluts-bdsm-sex-dominatrix -torture-2632850926.html.

Tierney Finster, "That's My Fetish: Cigarette Smoking," *MEL Magazine*, January 8, 2016, https://medium.com/mel-magazine/that-s-my-fetish -cigarette-smoking-a7403e9af577.

Monica Heisey, "I Had a Food Fight with a Food Fetishist," *Vice*, Sep-tember 30, 2013, https://www.vice.com/en/article/av4zy4/i-had-a -food-fight-with-a-food-fetishist.

J. G. Ballard, *Crash* (London: Jonathan Cape, 1973).

Zadie Smith, "Sex and Wheels: Zadie Smith on JG Ballard's *Crash*," *The Guardian*, July 4, 2014, https://www.theguardian.com/books/2014 /jul/04/zadie-smith-jg-ballard-crash.

Ed Wood, *When the Topic Is Sex*, ed. Bob Blackburn (Albany, GA: Bear-Manor Media, 2022).

Jesse Bering, "I Don't Mean to Be Forward, but Please Park on My Face?," *Scientific American*, September 3, 2013, https://blogs.scientific american.com/bering-in-mind/i-done28099t-mean-to-be-forward -but-please-park-on-my-face.

Tina Horn, "Why Are People into Fluids?," *The Establishment*, April 17, 2017, https://medium.com/the-establishment/why-are-people-into -fluids-b996a48d9ea1.

The Great British Sex Survey, Channel 4 (UK), 2016.

Street, "Here's Everything You Need to Know About Watersports."

Raymond Denson, "Undinism: The Fetishization of Urine," *Canadian Journal of Psychiatry* 27, no. 4 (1982).

Horn, "Why Are People into Fluids?"

CHAPTER 7: I WILL BE YOUR FATHER FIGURE: ON ROLE PLAY

George Michael, "Father Figure," *Faith* (Columbia Records: 1987).

Bill Amend, "Roger's Gambit," *Foxtrot*, December 27, 2020, https://fox-trot.com/2020/12/27/rogers-gambit.

Aly Walansky, "7 Hottest Role Play Ideas," *Bustle*, May 4, 2015, https:// www.bustle.com/articles/80707-7-hottest-role-playing-ideas-because -your-imagination-may-be-the-key-to-better-sex.

Roleplaying Group, FetLife.com, accessed December 28, 2020.

Stephen K. Stein, *Sadomasochism and the BDSM Community in the United States: Kinky People Unite* (London: Routledge, 2021).

Mollena Williams-Hass, www.Mollena.com, accessed February 24, 2022.

Mollena Williams-Hass, "Stop, Drop and Role! Erotic Role Playing," in *The Ultimate Guide to Kink*, ed. Tristan Taormino (Jersey City, NJ: Cleis Press, 2012).

Anna North, "When Prejudice Is Sexy: Inside the Kinky World of Race-Play," *Jezebel*, March 14, 2012, https://jezebel.com/when-prejudice-is -sexy-inside-the-kinky-world-of-race-5868600.

Catherine Scott, "Thinking Kink: Playing with Race in BDSM," *Bitch*, August 2012, https://bitchmedia.org/post/thinking-kink-the-right -to-play-with-race-feminist-magazine-bdsm-sex (no longer posted but now available at https://sexuality646.rssing.com/chan-21180250 /all_p1.html).

Zachary Woolfe, "A Composer and His Wife: Creativity Through Kink," *New York Times*, February 23, 2016.

Sunny Megatron and Ken Melvoin-Berg, hosts, "Midori: Erotic Role-play & Finding Your Dominance," episode 42, *American Sex* (pod-cast), https://americansex.libsyn.com/midori-erotic-roleplay-finding -your-dominance-ep-42.

Stein, *Sadomasochism and the BDSM Community in the United States*.

Tykables, Elk Grove Village, IL, https://support.tykables.com, accessed December 29, 2021.

Little Baby Boo Nursery, Palmdale, CA, https://www.littlebabyboo nursery.com, accessed December 29, 2021.

Amy Martin, "What Is a Little?," *Beautifully Broken Submissive*, July 31, 2016, https://beautifullybrokensubmissive.com/2016/07/31/what-is-a-little.

Sassafras Lowrey, "Slaying Fear, Being Out & Rise of the Guardians," December 4, 2012, http://sassafraslowrey.com/2012/12/slaying-fear-being-out-rise-of-the-guardians.

Lolita, dir. Stanley Kubrick (MGM, 1962).

Lolita, dir. Adrian Lyne (Samuel Goldwyn Company, 1997).

Pretty Baby, dir. Louis Malle (Paramount, 1978).

Poison Ivy, dir. Katt Shea (New Line, 1992).

American Beauty, dir. Sam Mendes (DreamWorks, 1999).

Lana Del Rey, https://www.lanadelrey.com, accessed January 12, 2022.

Martin, "What Is a Little?"

Chicago Ageplay Convention, CAPCON, https://www.capcon.club, accessed January 11, 2022.

Melanie Martinez, https://www.melaniemartinezmusic.com, accessed January 11, 2022.

Eartha Kitt, "My Heart Belongs to Daddy," *That Bad Eartha* (RCA/Victor, 1953).

Beyoncé, "Partition," *Beyoncé* (Parkwood/Columbia, 2013).

Storey Sisters, "Sweet Daddy," single (Cameo, 1958).

The Waitresses, "I Know What Boys Like," *Wasn't Tomorrow Wonderful?* (Polydor, 1982).

Charli XCX, "Babygirl," *Number One Angel* (Asylum, 2017).

Hartman's Heartbreakers, "Give It to Me, Daddy," *Give It to Me, Daddy!* (Bluebird, 1937).

Mark Armstrong, liner notes for Hartman's Heartbreakers, "Give It to Me, Daddy," *Give It to Me, Daddy!* (Bluebird, 1937).

The Runaways, "Cherry Bomb," *The Runaways* (Mercury, 1976).

Julie London, "Daddy," *Julie* (Liberty, 1961).

gordonskene, "The Bobby Troup Trio with Julie London," blog post on *Past Daily*, https://pastdaily.com/2021/01/10/the-bobby-troup-trio-with-julie-london-live-at-the-cameo-room-1956-past-daily-downbeat, accessed September 9, 2022.

The Neighbourhood, "Daddy Issues," *Wiped Out!* (Columbia, 2015).

Lana Del Rey, "You Can Be the Boss" (unreleased, 2010).

James Michael Nichols, "Get a Glimpse into the World of Puppy Play," *HuffPost*, October 2, 2016, https://www.huffpost.com/entry/puppy-play-zak-krevitt_n_57ed6f4ae4b082aad9ba2ae6.

Ponies on the Delta, The Wizard of Odd TV/iWonder, https://www.youtube.com/watch?v=PFEvlc9QdQ8, accessed January 14, 2022.

George Gurley, "Pleasures of the Fur," *Vanity Fair*, March 2001.

John Metcalfe, "Where the Furries Are," *Bloomberg*, March 9, 2015, https://www.bloomberg.com/news/articles/2015-03-09/a-reddit-user-created-a-worldwide-heat-map-of-furries.

Furmap, https://furmap.net, accessed July 12, 2022.

Anthrocon, https://www.anthrocon.org, accessed July 12, 2022.

Glow (Netflix, 2017–19).

Dylan Matthews, "9 Questions About Furries You Were Too Embarrassed to Ask," *Vox*, March 27, 2015, https://www.vox.com/2014/12/10/7362321/9-questions-about-furries-you-were-too-embarrassed-to-ask.

CHAPTER 8: CAUGHT UP IN YOU: ON THE KINKS OF ATTENTION AND NEGLECT

38 Special, "Caught Up in You," *Special Forces* (A&M Records, 1982).

Animotion, "Obsession," *Animotion* (Mercury, 1984).

John Fowles, *The Collector* (London: Jonathan Cape, 1963).

Natalie Angier, "A Scientific Reckoning of the Sex Drive," *New York Times*, April 10, 2007.

Sex, Lies and Videotape, dir. Steven Soderbergh (Miramax, 1989).

"Voyeur," *Kinkly*, May 18, 2022, https://www.kinkly.com/definition/10281/voyeur.

American Psychiatric Association, *Diagnostic and Statistical Manual of Mental Disorders, Fifth Edition* (*DSM-5*) (Washington, DC: American Psychiatric Association, 2013).

"Voyeurism: What It Is," WebMD, https://www.webmd.com/sex/what-is-voyeurism, accessed September 20, 2022.

Kayla Kibbe, "How to Have Sex Outside, Which Is in Your Human Nature," *Inside Hook*, July 1, 2021, https://www.insidehook.com/article/sex-and-dating/have-sex-outside.

Alyssa Girdwain, "The Ultimate Guide to Having Sex in Public—Because You Should," *Women's Health*, August 10, 2019, https://www.womenshealthmag.com/sex-and-love/g28581400/sex-in-public-places.

Coco McPherson, "Public Sex and the Standard Hotel," *New York*, June 11, 2009, https://nymag.com/intelligencer/2009/06/standard_hotel.html.

Elizabeth Rosner and Ruth Brown, "Residents Fuming over Sex-Crazed Hotel Guests," *New York Post*, August 1, 2017, https://nypost.com/2017/08/01/residents-fuming-over-sex-crazed-hotel-guests.

Swing Lifestyle (SLS), https://www.swinglifestyle.com, accessed November 18, 2021.

Stuart Nugent, "Why Is Cuckolding a Popular Fantasy," Lelo.com, September 4, 2020, https://www.lelo.com/blog/cuckolding.

"Take My Wife, Please! All About Cuckolding," Pornhub.com Insights, November 28, 2016, https://www.pornhub.com/insights/cuckold.

Charlotte Shane, "Do U Even Hotwife?," *MEL Magazine*, July 13, 2016, https://medium.com/mel-magazine/do-u-even-hotwife-1e3b30a0f6a6.

"11 Types of Hotwives—What Type Are You?," *Cuckold Club*, https://cuckoldclub.net/2021/04/23/11-types-of-hotwives-what-type-of-hotwife-are-you, accessed September 20, 2022.

Haley Lyndes, "Experts Explain Why Edging May Be the Greatest Way to Elevate Your Orgasms," *Popsugar*, September 18, 2022, https://www.popsugar.co.uk/love/what-is-edging-get-meaning-tips-from-sex-expert-48417136.

Albrecht Classen, *The Medieval Chastity Belt: A Myth-Making Process* (London: Palgrave Macmillan, 2008).

Dainis Graveris, "5 Best Chastity Cages of 2022," SexualAlpha, June 5, 2021, https://sexualalpha.com/best-chastity-cage.

"Mummification Bondage Master Guide—Learn How to Wrap Safely," Lovense, June 6, 2019, https://www.lovense.com/sex-blog/kink-bdsm/mummification-bondage.

E. J. Dickson, "The Bimbo Is Back. Like, for Real!," *Rolling Stone*, November 23, 2020, https://www.rollingstone.com/culture/culture-features/bimbo-reclaim-tiktok-gen-z-1092253.

Max Bliss, "Make Your Sex Life Limitless with Hypnosis," *Medium*, April 15, 2020, https://medium.com/hypnotic-erotica/make-your-sex-life-limitless-with-hypnosis-ebce45b2a1ce.

Arielle Richards, "Bimbofication Is Taking Over. What Does That Mean for You?," *Vice*, February 2, 2022, https://www.vice.com/en/article/4aw4kd/bimbofication-is-taking-over-what-does-that-mean-for-you.

Rowan & Martin's Laugh-In (NBC, 1967–73).

Hee Haw (CBS, 1969–97).

Josie and the Pussycats (CBS, 1970–72).

Dickson, "The Bimbo Is Back. Like, for Real!"

Mary Poppins, dir. Robert Stevenson (Walt Disney Productions, 1964).

Buildabhm, post on Tumblr, 2020, accessed January 3, 2022, since deleted.

CHAPTER 9: SUPERFREAKY: KINK HISTORY AND ICONS

Rick James, "Super Freak," *Street Songs* (Gordy Records, 1981).

Corinna Honan, "DH Lawrence's Steamiest Story of All? His Wife's," *The Daily Mail*, May 14, 2021, https://www.dailymail.co.uk/news/article-9580981/DH-Lawrences-steamiest-story-wifes-sexual-adventures.html.

Peter Tupper, *A Lover's Pinch: A Cultural History of Sadomasochism* (Lanham, MD: Rowman & Littlefield, 2018).

Mildred Europa Taylor, "The Sacred Mystery of Public Masturbation Ceremonies in Ancient Egypt," *Face2Face Africa*, May 3, 2018,

https://face2faceafrica.com/article/the-sacred-mystery-of-public
-masturbation-ceremonies-in-ancient-egypt.

Louise Pryke, "In Ancient Mesopotamia, Sex among the Gods Shook Heaven and Earth," *The Conversation*, April 22, 2018, https://the conversation.com/in-ancient-mesopotamia-sex-among-the-gods -shook-heaven-and-earth-87858.

Hanif Kureishi, "Kama Sutra: A Guide to the Art of Pleasure, Translated by AND Haksar," *The Guardian*, March 25, 2011, https://www .theguardian.com/books/2011/mar/25/kama-sutra-pleasure-haskar -review.

"What Is Shunga?," *Artsy*, September 24, 2013, https://www.artsy.net /article/editorial-what-is-shunga.

Nuala McCann, "Digging Up the Truth about the Notorious Hellfire Clubs," BBC, October 12, 2016, https://www.bbc.com/news/uk -northern-ireland-37609835.

Evelyn Lord, *The Hellfire Clubs: Sex, Satanism and Secret Societies* (New Haven, CT: Yale University Press, 2010).

David Ryan, *Blasphemers & Blackguards: The Irish Hellfire Clubs* (Newbridge, Ireland: Merrion Press, 2012).

John Cleland, *Fanny Hill* (New York: Penguin Classics, 1986).

Nicole Cliffe, "*Fanny Hill*: Weapons of Pleasure," *The Awl*, June 1, 2011, https://medium.com/the-awl/fanny-hill-weapons-of-pleasure -2ab51138b070.

Becky Little, "When the Supreme Court Had to Read an 18th Century Erotic Novel," History, January 23, 2019, https://www.history.com /news/fanny-hill-banned-book-supreme-court-case.

Tupper, *A Lover's Pinch: A Cultural History of Sadomasochism*.

Stephen Alexander, "Thoughts on D.H. Lawrence: in Conversation with David Brock," *Torpedo the Ark*, June 27, 2016, http://torpedotheark .blogspot.com/2016/06/thoughts-on-d-h-lawrence-stephen.html.

D. H. Lawrence, *Lady Chatterley's Lover* (New York: Signet, 2011).

D. H. Lawrence, *Women in Love* (New York: Penguin Classics, 2007).

D. G. Hewitt, "17 Reasons Why Germany's Weimar Republic Was a Party-Lovers Paradise," *History Collection*, October 18, 2018, https:// historycollection.com/17-reasons-why-germanys-weimar-republic -was-a-party-lovers-paradise.

Caroline Howe, "Berlin Was a Liberal Hotbed of Homosexuality and a Mecca for Cross Dressers and Transsexuals Where the First Male -to-Female Surgery Was Performed—Until the Nazis Came to Power, New Book Reveals," *Daily Mail*, November 25, 2014, https:// www.dailymail.co.uk/news/article-2847643/Berlin-liberal-hotbed -homosexuality-mecca-cross-dressers-transsexuals-male-female -surgery-performed-Nazis-came-power-new-book-reveals.html.

"About Bettie Page: Biography," *Bettie Page*, https://www.bettiepage.com/about, accessed February 20, 2022.

Stephen K. Stein, *Sadomasochism and the BDSM Community in the United States: Kinky People Unite* (London: Routledge, 2021).

The Complete Reprint of John Willie's Bizarre, ed. Eric Kroll (Cologne, Germany: Taschen, 2005).

Joseph Green, "Dear John Willie: The Complete Reprint of John Willie's *Bizarre*," *Out in San Antonio*, December 12, 2014, https://outinsa.com/dear-john-willie-complete-reprint-john-willies-bizarre.

Stein, *Sadomasochism and the BDSM Community in the United States*.

John Preston, *Mr. Benson* (Jersey City, NJ: Cleis Press, 2004).

Bob Flanagan, *The Pain Journal* (Los Angeles: Semiotext(e), 2000).

Andrea Juno, *Bob Flanagan: Super Masochist* (San Francisco: RE/Search, 1993).

Dennis Cooper, "Flanagan's Wake," *Artforum*, April 1996.

Tom Garretson, "The Sprinkle Story: The First 25 Years," AnnieSprinkle.com, 2003, https://anniesprinkle.org/the-sprinkle-story.

Nadja Sayej, "Annie Sprinkle Isn't Covering Anything Up," Interview, September 30, 2019, https://www.interviewmagazine.com/culture/annie-sprinkle-show-tell-new-exhibition.

Annie Sprinkle, *Post-Porn Modernist: My 25 Years as a Multimedia Whore* (Jersey City, NJ: Cleis Press, 1998).

Kink Network, Kink.com, accessed October 21, 2022.

Jon Mooallem, "A Disciplined Business," *New York Times*, April 29, 2007, https://www.nytimes.com/2007/04/29/magazine/29kink.t.html.

Kink, dir. Christina Alexandra Voros (MPI Media Group, 2013).

Larissa Runkle, "Ironing Out the Kink: The Armory Reboots as Live Event Venue," *Hoodline*, December 29, 2017, https://hoodline.com/2017/12/ironing-out-the-kink-the-armory-reboots-as-live-event-venue.

Melissa Gira Grant, "For the Love of Kink," *Dissent*, Spring 2014, https://www.dissentmagazine.org/article/for-the-love-of-kink.

Sam Levin, "End of an Era: Porn Actors Lament Loss of Legendary San Francisco Armory," *The Guardian*, January 25, 2017, https://www.theguardian.com/culture/2017/jan/25/porn-bdsm-kink-armory-closing-san-francisco.

Brian K. Reid, "Usenet Readership Summary Report," News.lists on Usenet, July 1993.

Maureen Furniss, "Sex with a Hard (Disk) On: Computer Bulletin Boards and Pornography," 15, no. 2 (1993).

Alexander Cheves, "Four Perspectives on How the Internet Has Changed Kink," *Them*, July 10, 2019, https://www.them.us/story/how-the-internet-has-changed-kink-bdsm-leather.

E. L. James, *Fifty Shades of Grey* (New York: Vintage Books, 2011).

Stein, *Sadomasochism and the BDSM Community in the United States.*

Anne Rice [writing as Anne Rampling], *Exit to Eden* (New York: Avon Red, 2007).

Exit to Eden, dir. Garry Marshall (Savoy Pictures, 1994).

Carolyn See, "A Sexual Fantasy That Romps to a Happy Ending," *Los Angeles Times*, October 27, 1986.

Roger Ebert, "*Exit to Eden*," *Chicago Sun-Times*, October 14, 1994, https://www.rogerebert.com/reviews/exit-to-eden-1994.

Bitter Moon, dir. Roman Polanski (Canal+, 1992).

Crash, dir. David Cronenberg (Columbia Tristar, 1996).

9½ Weeks, dir. Adrian Lyne (MGM/UA, 1986).

The Night Porter, dir. Liliana Cavani (Ital-Noleggio Cinematografico, 1974).

The Piano Teacher, dir. Michael Haneke (MK2 Productions, 2001).

Professor Marston and the Wonder Women, dir. Angela Robinson (Annapurna Pictures, 2017).

Stein, *Sadomasochism and the BDSM Community in the United States.*

Maîtresse, dir. Barbet Schroeder (Gaumont, 1976).

Secretary, dir. Steven Shainberg (Lionsgate, 2002).

James, *Fifty Shades of Grey.*

Mary Gaitskill, "Secretary," *Bad Behavior: Stories* (New York: Simon & Schuster, 2009).

Mimsy and Vagabond, "The Only Kinky Movies You'll Ever Need to See," *Bound Together*, January 5, 2019, https://bound-together.net/kinky-movies.

Belle de Jour, dir. Luis Buñuel (Allied Artists, 1968).

The Duke of Burgundy, dir. Peter Strickland (Curzon Artificial Eye, 2014).

Jordan Hoffman, "*The Duke of Burgundy*: Filthy and Fraught with Genuine Emotion," *The Guardian*, September 7, 2014, https://www.theguardian.com/film/2014/sep/07/duke-of-burgundy-review-toronto-film-festival.

Everything Everywhere All at Once, dir. Dan Kwan and Daniel Scheinert (A24, 2022).

Transparent (Amazon, 2014–19).

CHAPTER 10: THANK U 4 A FUNKY TIME: FORGING YOUR PATH AND COMMUNITY

Prince, "Darling Nikki," *Purple Rain* (Warner Bros. Records, 1984).

Stephen K. Stein, *Sadomasochism and the BDSM Community in the United States: Kinky People Unite* (London: Routledge, 2021).

Tina Horn, host, *Why Are People Into That?!* (podcast), September 22, 2022, http://whyarepeopleintothat.com.

Dan and dawn, hosts, *Erotic Awakening* (podcast), September 22, 2022, https://www.eroticawakening.com/.

Tristan Taormino, host, *Sex Out Loud* (podcast), September 22, 2022, http://tristantaormino.com/sex-out-loud/about.

Axe, host, *Masocast* (podcast), October 3, 2022, https://www.masocast.com.

Dan Savage (host), *Savage Lovecast* (podcast), September 22, 2022, https://savage.love/lovecast.

Cleis Press, September 21, 2022, https://cleispress.com.

Circlet Press, September 21, 2022, https://www.circlet.com.

John Warren and Libby Warren, *The (New and Improved) Loving Dominant* (Emeryville, CA: Greenery Press, 2008).

Molly Devon and Philip Miller, *Screw the Roses, Send Me the Thorns: The Romance and Sexual Sorcery of Sadomasochism* (Fairfield, CT: Mystic Rose Books, 1995).

Gloria Brame, William Brame, and Jon Jacobs, *Different Loving: The World of Sexual Dominance and Submission* (New York: Villard, 1996).

Mollena Williams, *Toybag Guide to Playing with Taboo* (Emeryville, CA: Greenery Press, 2010).

The Ultimate Guide to Kink, ed. Tristan Taormino (Jersey City, NJ: Cleis Press, 2012).

Lee Harrington and Mollena Williams, *Playing Well with Others: Your Field Guide to Discovering, Exploring and Navigating the Kink, Leather and BDSM Communities* (Emeryville, CA: Greenery Press, 2012).

Jesse Bering, *Perv: The Sexual Deviant in All of Us* (New York: Scientific American/Farrar, Straus and Giroux, 2013).

Kink: Stories, ed. R. O. Kwon and Garth Greenwell (New York: Simon & Schuster, 2021).

Leigh Cowart, *Hurts So Good: The Science and Culture of Pain on Purpose* (New York: PublicAffairs, 2021).

John Preston, "What Happened?," in *Leatherfolk: Radical Sex, People, Politics, and Practice*, ed. Mark Thompson (New York: Alyson Books, 1991).

Stein, *Sadomasochism and the BDSM Community in the United States.*

Peter Tupper, *A Lover's Pinch: A Cultural History of Sadomasochism* (Lanham, MD: Rowman & Littlefield, 2018).

Pleasure Chest, https://thepleasurechest.com, accessed September 22, 2022.

Stockroom, https://stockroom.com, accessed September 22, 2022.

Museum of Sex, https://www.museumofsex.com, accessed September 22, 2022.

Sexmuseum, https://sexmuseumamsterdam.nl, accessed September 22, 2022.

Leather Archives & Museum, https://leatherarchives.org, accessed September 22, 2022.

Tom of Finland Foundation, https://www.tomoffinland.org, accessed September 22, 2022.

Center for Positive Sexuality, https://positivesexuality.org, accessed September 22, 2022.

National Coalition of Sexual Freedom, https://ncsfreedom.org, accessed September 22, 2022.

Centre for Sexuality, https://www.centreforsexuality.ca, accessed September 22, 2022.

Centre for Research on the History of Sexual Science, https://magnus -hirschfeld.de/forschungsstelle/center, accessed January 13, 2023.

Kinsey Institute, https://kinseyinstitute.org, accessed September 22, 2022.

Dark Odyssey, http://darkodyssey.com, accessed September 22, 2022.

Wicked Grounds, https://wickedgrounds.com, accessed September 22, 2022.

The Eulenspiegel Society, https://www.tes.org, accessed September 22, 2022.

FetLife, https://fetlife.com, accessed September 22, 2022.

Kink Academy, https://www.kinkacademy.com, accessed September 22, 2022.

Kink University, https://www.kink.com/channel/kink-university, accessed September 22, 2022.

Kink and Polyamory Aware Professionals directory, https://www.kap professionals.org, accessed September 22, 2022.

Kayla Lords, "How Writing and Teaching BDSM Brought Me Balance," *Happiness*, https://www.happiness.com/magazine/inspiration -spirituality/writing-teaching-bdsm-balance, accessed September 22, 2022.

Sue-Ellen Case, *The Domain-Matrix: Performing Lesbian at the End of Print Culture* (Bloomington: Indiana University Press, 1997).

Stein, *Sadomasochism and the BDSM Community in the United States.*

Tupper, *A Lover's Pinch: A Cultural History of Sadomasochism.*

APPENDIX: WE'RE GOING DOWN TO ALPHABET STREET: AN A-TO-Z OF KINKY STUFF

Prince, "Alphabet Street," *Lovesexy* (Gordy Records, 1988).

FetLife, https://fetlife.com, accessed September 22, 2022.

Autumn Stanley, *Diaries of Hannah Cullwick, Victorian Maidservant* (New Brunswick, NJ: Rutgers University Press, 1984).

International Mr. Bootblack, https://www.imrl.com/bootblack-contest, accessed September 22, 2022.

Phoenix Boys of Leather, http://phoenixboysofleather.com, accessed September 22, 2022.

Bonding (Netflix, 2018–21).

Stephen K. Stein, *Sadomasochism and the BDSM Community in the United States: Kinky People Unite* (London: Routledge, 2021).

"The Science and History Behind EMS," *Powerdot*, https://www.powerdot .com/blogs/training/the-science-and-history-behind-ems, accessed September 22, 2022.

ToyTorture, https://www.toytorture.com, accessed September 22, 2022.

"Introductions" forum, Blow to Pop, https://blowtopop.net, accessed September 22, 2022.

Shibari group, FetLife, https://fetlife.com, accessed September 22, 2022.

Cee, "Shibari 101: Single- and Double-Column Ties," *Autostraddle*, May 10, 2018, https://www.autostraddle.com/shibari-bondage-101-single -and-double-column-ties-350776.

Alicia Joy, "A Brief History of Kinbaku: The Art of Japanese Bondage," *Culture Trip*, March 2, 2017, https://theculturetrip.com/asia/japan /articles/a-brief-history-of-kinbaku-the-art-of-japanese-bondage.

"Shibari: The Ancient Art of Japanese Bondage," *Lovegasm*, https:// lovegasm.co/blogs/kink/shibari-the-ancient-art-of-japanese-bondage, accessed September 22, 2022.

Psycho, dir. Alfred Hitchcock (Paramount Pictures, 1960).

FetLife, https://fetlife.com, accessed September 22, 2022.

Anne Desclos writing as Pauline Réage, *The Story of O* (New York: Ballantine, 2013).

Eyes Wide Shut, dir. Stanley Kubrick (Warner Bros., 1999).

Rihanna, video for "Work" (Roc Nation, 2016).

Mistress Matisse, "Pervertibles," *The Stranger*, January 10, 2002, https:// www.thestranger.com/columns/2002/01/10/9742/control-tower.

Nadia Bello, "Alabama Slammer," *Xtra*, August 18, 2004, https://xtra magazine.com/love-sex/alabama-slammer-41182.

Marnie Sehayek, "A Brief History of Japanese Rope Bondage," *Vice*, February 14, 2017, https://www.vice.com/en/article/8qka45/kinbaku -japanese-rope-bondage.

The Twisted Monk, https://www.twistedmonk.com, accessed September 22, 2022.

J. C. Ways, "Urethral Sounding—A Guide to This Extreme Fetish," Sex Toy Collective, August 22, 2019, https://sextoycollective.com /urethral-sounding.

"Beginner's Guide to Urethral Sounding" video, *Lovehoney*, May 2, 2017, https://www.lovehoney.com.au/blog/what-is-urethral-sounding.html.

Stein, *Sadomasochism and the BDSM Community in the United States*.

Body of Evidence, dir. Uli Edel (MGM, 1993).

Joe Reid, "Body of Evidence at 25: Is the Razzie-Winning Sex Thriller as Bad as Its Reputation?," *Decider*, January 15, 2018, https://decider .com/2018/01/15/body-of-evidence-25th-anniversary.

Michael T. R. B. Turnbull, *Saint Andrew: Scotland's Myth and Identity* (Edinburgh: St Andrew Press, 1997).

John Coski, *The Confederate Battle Flag: America's Most Embattled Emblem* (Cambridge, MA: Harvard University Press, 2006).

Kayla Lords, "Why I Love the St. Andrew's Cross," BDSM Training Academy, https://bdsmtrainingacademy.com/why-i-love-the-st -andrews-cross, accessed September 22, 2022.

Creature, "Z Is for Zentai," ABCs of Kink, June 13, 2014, https:// abcsofkink.com/?s=zentai.

INDEX

Abad-Santos, Alex, 5
ABCs of Kink, 229
abusive relationships: and child
    molesters, 39, 68–69, 72–73;
    consensual power exchanges vs.,
    62–63, 98, 104, 110; identifying,
    110; National Domestic Violence
    Hotline, 104
acronyms, common, 56–57
activity fetishes, 131
Acworth, Peter, 190–91
Adore, Ava, 95
Adult Babies and diaper lovers
    (ABDL), 144–46
aftercare, 95–96, 105
agency: addressing inequities and
    traumas, 98, 101, 110, 120;
    and bimbofication, 173; and
    power, self-empowerment, 8, 69,
    110–11, 173; and white privilege,
    4, 110. See also consent
age play: about, 144; Adult Babies
    and diaper lovers (ABDL),
    144–45; Daddy/girl age play mix-
    tape, 149–52; finding partners,
    148; Littles, 145–46; Hannah and
    Arthur Munby's, 182; pedophilia
    vs., 148
AIDS crisis: impact on clubs and
    venues, 187; Mapplethorpe's
    death from, 188; role of leather
    families during, 117
Alesandra, 105
Alexander, Stephen, 183
allosexual people, 17

Allure magazine, article on 'looners,
    130
alt.sex forum, 191–92
Amen, Adam MC, 166–67
American Journal of Psychiatry, car-
    crash fetish description, 134
American Sex podcast (Megatron
    and Melvoin-Berg), 201
amputee fetishists, 129, 134
amygdala, 21
anal hooks, 16, 211
Andrew (smoking fetishist),
    131–32
Angel, Katherine, 26
Anger, Kenneth, 115
Angier, Natalie, 159
animals, anthropomorphized, 154.
    See also furries, furry community;
    plushies
animals, sex with: as always non-
    consensual, 68–69, 79; Hokusai's
    fantasy, 180
anterior insula, 21
Antoniou, Laura, 203
Armory Club, San Francisco, 205
armpit fetishes, 48, 64, 129
Armstrong, Mark, 150
arousal: complexity of, 20; involun-
    tary, 50–51; nonlinear nature of,
    20. See also lust; orgasm/climax
Artforum, Cooper's Bob Flanagan,
    189
asexual people, 16–17, 27, 79
AMSR (autonomous sensory merid-
    ian response), 132

association/conditioning theory of kink, 44, 128, 212. *See also* triggering, avoiding

attraction: complexity of, 21–22, 42; involuntary, 73–74; mutual, 71, 100; and the myth of "true love," 158; personal understanding, 29, 41; societally determined vs. our own, 20, 23, 72; specific, fetishes as, 124, 128; and taboos, 61–62, 68

authority: exchange dynamics, 38, 105, 106, 116; and leather culture, 114–15; norms about, upending, 103. *See also* BDSM

Autostraddle online magazine: on D/s vs. M/s dynamics, 107; on Japanese erotic rope art, 218

Avatar (leather club), 118

The Awl magazine, article on *Fanny Hill*, 181

Axe, *Masocast* podcast, 200

"Babygirl" (Charli XCX), 150

Babygirl/Lolita role, 147

Bacchanalia, 179–80

Baldwin, James, 7

Ballard, J. G., 134

balloon fetishists ('looners), 130

Barmak, Sarah, 20, 32

Basson, Rosemary, 20

Baume, Matt, 117

BDSM (bondage and discipline, dominance and submission, and sadism and masochism): accessibility of, 77; aftercare, 95–96, 105; anal hooks, 211; boots, 211–12; capitalism and, 209; celebrating, 207–8; and closeness/trust, 80; collars, 212; common associations with, 76; contracts, 88–90; diversity of, 16, 130; dungeon monitors, 186; erotic knife play, 218–19; e-stim machines, 214–15; events and event producers, 204–5; gear associated with, 210, 215–16, 221, 224–25; inflatables, 217; leather culture, 113, 116;

life lessons from, 207; media portrayals, 76, 193; *Mr. Benson* as guidebook to, 188; Hannah and Arthur Munby, 182; origins of the term, 81; "pervertibles," 221–22; pleasure-pain continuum, 78–80; power exchanges, 104–13; public events, 154; queer 1950s household events, 121; rape role play, 102; rope bondage, 46, 223–24; as sexual theater, 39; *shibari* and *kinbaku*, 217–18; as a subcategory of kink, 38; support groups/sex clubs, 185–87; "topping from the bottom," 94; upending norms through, 103; as voluntary play, 52, 91–92; X-cross (St. Andrew's cross), 228. *See also* D/s; sex toys; S/m

BDSM Training Academy website, 228

Beautifully Broken Submissive blog, 147

being drugged or impaired, 68–69

Bell, Jaimee, 127–28

Belle de Jour (Buñuel), 196

Bello, Nadia, 222

Bering, Jesse, 42, 134, 202

Berlatsky, Noah, 101

Berlin, Germany, cabarets, 183–84

Beyoncé, 149

BHM (big handsome man) encouragers, 175

Billock, Jennifer, 102

bimbofication, 172–74

BimboTok, 173–74

Bitch magazine, article on living fearlessly, 143

Bivona, Jenny M., 99, 101–2

Bizarre magazine: importance, 185, 191; pet-play photography in, 153

Black people: and children's belief in inferiority, 19; and the experience of enslavement, power abuses, 103, 107, 110, 216; violence against, 3

Bliss, Max, 174

Blow to Pop website, 217
The Bluest Eye (Morrison), 19
body fluid fetishes, 135
Body of Evidence (movie), wax scene in, 227
Bogdanoff, Fanny Pistor, 88–89
Bolam, Emily, 18
Bond, Pat, 185–86
bondage. *See* BDSM
Bonding (Netflix comedy), 212
books, kink-positive, 201–3
boot fetishes, 50, 64, 211–12
"bottoms"/bottoming, 82–83, 94
Bound Together blog, 196
the brain: and nonnormative sexuality, 42–45; response to arousal, 21, 78–79; as a sexual organ, 64
Brake, Mike, 9
Brame, Gloria and William, 92–93, 202
Bright, Susie, 203
Brownmiller, Susan, 99
Buñuel, Luis (*Belle de Jour*), 196
Buss, David, 21
Bussel, Rachel Kramer, 203
Bustle magazine, role play article, 138

Cafee, Mike, 116
Califia, Patrick, 203
California Motor Club Carnival, 1977, 115
camping, sex while, 163
CAPCON (Chicago Ageplay Convention), 148
car-crash fetish, 134
cars, sex in, 162
cartoons, kiddie: fetish porn in, 11, 127; and furries, 154; and Littles, 146
cash slaves, 109–10
Catacombs BDSM club, San Francisco, 187
Charli XCX ("Babygirl"), 150
Charlotte's Web (cartoon), 11–12
chastity belts, 169
"Cherry Bomb" (the Runaways), 151
Cheves, Alexander, 95, 192–93

Chicago Hellfire Club (CHC), 181, 186
children: defining, 74; pedophiles, molesters, 39, 68–69, 72–73; power abuses, 103; sexual activity in, 17. *See also* Littles
Chinese Han dynasty, kinky sex practices, 39
Chivers, Meredith, 22
Chlapecka, Chrissy, 173–74
Christian sex-negative cultures, 40
Circlet Press, 201, 203
Classen, Albrecht, 169
Cleis Press, 201
Cleland, John (*Fanny Hill*), 181–82
Cliffe, Nicole, 181
climax. *See* orgasm/climax
Clinician's Toolkit for Children's Behavioral Health (Russell), 17
cock cages, 169–70
cockteasing, 150
Cohut, Maria, 80
collars, 108, 212
The Collector (Fowles), 157
colonialism, and kink, 179
color codes, 213
combat boots. *See* boot fetishes
communication: asking permission, 53–54; backing off quickly, 54; of changing needs or desires, 53; consent without enthusiasm, 54–55; of interest, etiquette of, 54; of likes and dislikes, importance, 26–30; between long-term partners, 56. *See also* consent
compassion, 2, 16, 31, 197
compatibility, sexual: complexity of, 26, 33; matching desires and needs, 30–31
Completely Queer: The Gay and Lesbian Encyclopedia (Hogan and Hudson), 115
consensual non-consent (CNC), 102–3, 195
consent: BDSM contracts, 88–90, 195; communicating needs and desires clearly, 26; and consensual non-consent (CNC), 102–3;

enthusiastic, challenges of, 55; fundamental importance, 60; GGG (good, giving, and game), 230; importance, 34, 52; and involuntary arousal, 51; limits of, 56, 68; listening, 52–53; matching needs and desires, 175; modern ideas of personhood and self-determination, 178; as mutual attraction and interest, 55, 100; for nonmonogamous sex, 167; objectophiles, 70–72; power vs. abuse, 67, 110–11; pXe protocols, 81; during role playing, 141; reverent objectification, 171–72; self-control, 62, 68–69, 72–73; sexual predation, 51–52; tops and bottoms, 38, 82–83, 94; and variability of response within an encounter, 20, 53. *See also* agency; communication; relationships

Cooper, Dennis, 189

Coski, John M., 228

Cowart, Leigh, 202

Craigslist posting about desire for sex, 100

Crash (Ballard), 134

Creature, 229

Critelli, Joseph W., 99–102

crossed wires theory of kinkiness, 43–44

Cuckold Club, 166

cuckolding, 41, 164–67

cuddling, 16, 106, 146, 217

Cullwick, Hannah, 182, 212

cum. *See* orgasm/climax

Cupid. *See* eros

Currie, Cherie, 151

The Cut magazine: article on Basson, 20; sex advice, 32

"Daddy" (Troup), sung by Julie London, 151

"Daddy," as a pet name, 149

Daddy/girl age play mixtape, 149–52

"Daddy Issues" (the Neighbourhood), 151

Daily Mail newspaper: Honan article on D. H. and Frieda Lawrence, 176–77; Howe article on the Institute for Sexual Science, 184

Dan and dawn, 200

Dark Odyssey BDSM event producers, 204

dark role play: ABDL players, 145; and acting out unethical fantasies, 141

Deadwood (TV series), "specialists," 47

decision fatigue, 111, 113

degradation, desire to experience, 99, 165

Dehner, Durk, 114

Delany, Samuel R., 203

Deleuze, Gilles, 87

Del Ray, Lana, 151–52

demeanor, role in the erotic, 9–10

deMorrow, Betty Lou, 150

Deneuve, Catherine, in *Belle de Jour*, 196

Denson, Raymond, 135–36

Des Barres, Michael, 157

Desclos, Anne (Pauline Réage), 221

desire. *See* lust

"deviant," as a term, 3

DeviantArt website, 37

Devon, Molly, 202

Dickson, E. J., 173

Different Loving: The World of Dominance and Submission (Brame and Brame), 93–94

Different Loving: The World of Sexual Dominance and Submission (Brame and Brame), 202

dildos and strap-ons, 213–14

disempowering situations, 103–4

domestic violence/abuse: and abusive power relationships, 104; and money, 109; power exchanges vs., 63

Dominix Deluxe cock cage, 170

Domly Dom, Sir, 52

Dom Sub Living blog (Alesandra), 105

Donahue, Patty, 150

dopamine, 20
Dornan, Bob, 188
"Dream of a Fisherman's Wife,"
    180–81
Drummer magazine: Fritscher's work
    for, 116; *Mr. Benson* in, 187–88
D/s (dominance and submission):
    activities involved in, 90;
    bimbofication, 173; dominants
    (d-types, doms, dommes), 1,
    82, 105; exchanging authority
    and roles, 38, 91; and money,
    109; physical markers, 108;
    psychological power dynamic,
    83; Sacher-Masoch's contract
    template, 88–90; the "stability
    fetish," 111–13; surrender-
    ing control, 172–73; tops and
    bottoms, 82–84, 94; use of fetish
    objects, 90–91
DSM-5 (*Diagnostic and Statistical
    Manual of Mental Disorders, Fifth
    Edition*): on paraphilia and para-
    philiac disorder, 47; voyeuristic
    disorder, 160
Dublin, Ireland, the Hellfire Club, 181
The Duke of Burgundy (movie),
    196–97
dungeons: dungeon monitor (DM),
    58, 69–70, 186; in *Maîtresse*,
    195; Sade's, 85; tools associated
    with, 6, 169, 204; X-cross (St.
    Andrew's cross), 228

edging (orgasm control/denial, teas-
    ing), 59, 168–69, 214
Egypt, ancient, fertility festivals, 179
Eiffel, Erika, 70–71
elder abuse, 103. *See also*
    gerontophilia
Ellen, Roy, 124
employees, sex with, 68–69
endorphins, 66, 78, 108
enslaved peoples, 97–98
eros, 18, 183
Erotic Awakening podcast (Dan and
    dawn), 200
erotic experience. *See* lust

Erp, Brian D., 73–74
escape-pod adventure, 31–32
The Establishment magazine, article
    on body fluid fetishes, 135
e-stim (electrical stimulation) ma-
    chines, 214–15, 226–27
ethical non-monogamy, 30, 32, 41,
    160
the Eulenspiegel Society (TES),
    185–86, 205
Everything Everywhere All at Once
    (movie), 197
exhibitionism, 161–62, 164. *See also*
    voyeurism (liking to watch)
Exit to Eden (Rice), 193–94

Face2Face Africa, Taylor article on
    Egyptian masturbation, 179
Fanny Hill (Cleland), 181–82
fantasies. *See* imagination, fantasies
fat women, 41
Faulkner, William, 68
the Fedleg fetish, 36–37
feederism, 9, 12–13
feminism: the appeal of kink, 172;
    bimbofication, 174; rape fantasies
    as patriarchal conditioning, 99;
    self-empowerment, 120, 143;
    sex-positivity, 186, 190; viewing
    porn as misogynist, 221
feminist sex shop, 1, 204, 210–11, 214
fertility festivals, 179–80
"fetish," as a term, 47–48, 123
fetishes: fetish objects, 90–91; group
    events, 153–54; historical per-
    spectives on, 177–79; individual/
    personal nature, 8–12, 23–24, 29,
    47; involuntary arousal, 50–51;
    pedophilia vs., 72–74; power
    of, 49; problematic, character-
    istics, 126; psychological and
    physical manifestation, 36, 123,
    127–28; reverence for, 11, 48;
    specificity of, 9–10, 48, 127–28,
    131–32; spectrum of, 124–25; as
    a subcategory of kink, 38, 123;
    surrendering control, 173. *See
    also specific fetishes*

fetishists: active vs. passive preferences, 130; behaviors of, 49–50; changing intensity of desire, 126; defining, 1, 33, 38–39; disturbing fantasies, 68; marginalizing/stereotyping of, 53, 122; Rule 34, 9–10; and truth telling, 136

FetLife website: community building, 141–42; daily top 100, 15–16; kink gear info, 211; on knife play, 218–19; localized resources, 205–6; the "Most Popular" top fifty, 122; on mummification, 220; popularity of, 15; queer 1950s household, 119–21

Fifty Shades of Grey (James), 44, 100, 187

finding a partner. *See* partners

findom (financial domination), 109–10

Finkelhor, David, 73

Finster, Tierney, 131–32

Flanagan, Bob, 188–89

floggers: buying, 46; types and purpose, 215

flogging: as impact play, 92, 95–96; as kink-adjacent play, 46–47

Folsom Street Fair (San Francisco), 118

foot fetish, 48, 51, 128–29

foreplay, 20–21, 24

Fowles, John, 157

Franco, James, 190

freaks, as a term, 7, 127

Frederik, 215

Freud, Sigmund, 81–82, 84, 160

Friday, Nancy, 101

Fritscher, Jack, 115–16

Furmap.net, 155

Furniss, Maureen, 192

furries, furry community, 1, 153–56

gags, 215–16

gaining/feeding/encouraging fetish, 9–11, 172–75, 201

game playing: and consent, 67, 95, 105; mind games, 137; nonconsensual activities, 68, 112. *See also* psychological kink; role play

gang bangs, 164, 167

Garretson, Tom, 189

gay men: animal role play, 152; and gaining, 175; in the military, 114; persecution risk, 3; and piss play, 135; rejections of effeminacy, 116; turn ons, 22. *See also* leather culture

gerontophilia, 64–65

Girdwain, Alyssa, 162–63

"Give It to Me, Daddy" (Hartman's Heartbreakers), 150

Goerlich, Stefani, 38

"Golden Shower Ritual Kits," 189

Gone with the Wind theory, 100

Gorvett, Zaria, 78, 81

Graveris, Dainis, 169–70

Green, Joseph, 185

Greenery Press, 201

Greenwell, Garth, 202

Griffin, Annaliese, 3

group sex, 40, 179

Gurley, George, 154

Guyette, Charles, 195

Haksar, A. N. D., 180

handcuffs, 76, 204, 216

Happiness.com website, 2–7

hardwired theory of kinkiness, 42–43

Hardy, Janet, 192, 201

Harrington, Lee, 202

Hass, Georg Friedrich, 143

Hawke, Chris, 126, 135

hedonic reversals, 79–81

hedonism, 9, 86, 174–75, 181, 183

Heidegger, Nicoletta, 201

Heisey, Monica, 133–34

the Hellfire Club, 181

Helms, Jesse, 188

heteronormative cliches, 40, 119–21

Hewitt, D. G., 183–84

higher consciousness, search for, 77–78

high heels fetish, 122, 124, 219

hippocampus, 21

Hirschfeld, Magnus, 184

Hoffman, Jordan, 197

Hogan, Steve, 115

Hokusai, Katsushika, 180–81
Hollywood portrayals of kink, 20, 23, 59, 193, 196, 227
Holy Trainer V4 cock cage, 170
Honan, Corinna, 176–77
Hoodline magazine, article on Kink .com, 190
Hooven, Valentine, 114–15
Horn, Tina, 10, 135, 200
hotwife kink, 164–67
"How to Sex'? The Contest Nature of Sexuality in Japan" (McLelland), 40
Hudson, Lee, 115
Hughes, Samuel, 38–39, 42–43
Human Rights Campaign, 3
120 Days of Sodom (Sade), 85
Hurts So Good: The Science and Culture of Pain on Purpose (Cowart), 202
hyper-masculinity, 114–15
hypnosis, erotic (hypno-kink), 172–74

"I Know What Boys Like" (The Waitresses), 150
imagination, fantasies: applying to cuckolding, 166; and cost-free kinks, 93; as individually unique, 37, 207; *My Secret Garden*, 101; negative, controlling, 68–69; objects as focus of, 70–72; pervertibles, 222; as private, 66–67, 166, 180; psychological kink, 93, 229–30; Sade's, 86; sharing/ acting on, cautions, 66–67; as unlimited, 141. *See also* psychological kink; rape fantasy; role play
impact play: accessibility, 77; and consent, 56; and the diversity of sensory experience, 130; and pain, 65–66; types and characteristics, 92
incest role play, 138–39
inflatables, 217
injustice, systemic, 97, 106–7, 179, 216
Institute for Sexual Science, founding, 184

intense stimulation, 92–93
International Mr. Leather conference, 118, 193
Internet connections: alt.sex forum, 191; dating apps, 192–93; fetish porn, 126–27; kink-positive podcasts, 199–201; and unrealistic expectations, 193; variety of, 37, 154–55, 191; websites and newsletters, 204, 206
intimacy coordinators, 58–59
Isa (@subversivenotbasic), 174
iWonderTV, interview with Ponies on the Delta player, 153

Jade, Hayley, 109
James, E. L., 44, 100
Japan: kink culture, 40; shibari and kinbaku, 46, 217–18, 223; zentai suits, 229
Jarvis, Samantha, 18
Jezebel magazine, Williams-Haas interview, 143
"Jim" (Fedleg fetish), 36
Joannides, Paul, 101
Johanna (rape victim), regaining agency, 101
John, on sadist experience, 95–96
John and Kayla, *Loving BDSM* podcast, 202
Johnson, Virginia, 20, 42
Journal of Sex Research: article on rape-fantasy, 99; "Physical Pain as Pleasure" article, 80
Justice Weekly magazine, covert connections using, 185
Justine (Sade), 85

Kama Sutra: kinky sex practices, 39; rough sex in, 180
Kang, Aleks, 129
Keeler, Martin, 134
Kennedy, Anthony, 15
kiddie shows, kink in, 11–14
kinbaku rope typing, 223
Kincaid, James, 73
kink: as affectionate and playful, 63; celebrating, 208; as a creative

outlet, 222; cultural taboos about, 39, 62, 193–94; defining, 38–39; and exploring the idea of obsession safely, 158; and fads, 46; fetishes as a subcategory of, 165; as a form of escape, 137; historical perspectives on, 177–79; identifying and communicating with partner, 29; as an identity, 1, 33; in Japan, 40; negative associations with, 37; and nonmonogamy, 164–65; as nonnormative sex, 39–40; nonsexual behaviors, 156; and objectification, 171–72; origins, 42–45; and pain, 65–66; and playfulness, 2, 133; and power, 62–63, 97–98; psychological exchanges/games, 63–64; putrid games/exchanges, 64; queer 1950s household, 119–21; and loneliness, 178; and sex in public, 161; as sexual theater, 39; and "spicing up" sex, 32–33, 66–67; as a superpower, 14; vs. vanilla sex vs., 23–24; and voyeurism, 160. *See also specific kinks and fetishes*

Kink Academy website, 206
kink-adjacent experience, 46
Kink and Polyamory Aware Professionals directory, 206
Kink.com, 190–91
kink community: and the apprenticeship model, 186; common acronyms, 56–58; creating and participating in, 198; early clubs, function, 185–86; events and venues, 205; fictional accounts, 203; finding, 199–201; importance, 2, 191–93; podcasts, 199–201; risks, 4; safe words, 58; sex shops, 204; and systemic injustice, 106; websites and newsletters, 204
kink-shaming, 41
Kink: Stories (ed. Kwon and Greenwell), 202

Kink University at Kink.com, 206
Kinsey Institute, Indiana University, 42, 204
kissing, 16
Kitt, Eartha, 149
Klaw, Irving, 184–85
Kloss, David, 207
"knee-chest" masturbation, 8
knife play, 218–19
Komisaruk, Barry, 79
Kraft-Ebbing, Richard von, 84, 86, 88
Krevitt, Zak, 153
Kureishi, Hanif, 180
Kwon, R. O., 202

Laaksonen, Touko (Tom of Finland). *See* Tom of Finland
language about sex, 3, 18. *See also specific terms*
latex: as fetishwear, 33, 131, 195, 204, 219; and inflatables, 48, 217
LaudTex commerce site, 131
Lawrence, D. H., 176–77, 183
Lawrence, Frieda, 176–77
Leather and Lace (leather club), 118
Leather Archives & Museum, Chicago, 204
Leatherati blog, Stein interview, 116–17
leather culture: authority exchanges, 116; boots, 211–12; diversity of, 118; kinks associated with, 116–17; and the leather bar, 115, 187; leather families, 113–14, 117; leather fetish, 122, 131; physique magazines, 115; queer-centered spaces, 117–18; stability and rules, 117; as a subculture, 113, 116; Tom of Finland, 114–15, 184; and WWII, 114
The Leatherman's Handbook (Townsend), 116
Leatherpedia, 116
legal age for consent, 39
Lehmiller, Justin, 102
Leigh, Michael, 7

lesbians: BDSM among, 113, 187; *The Duke of Burgundy*, 196; erotica, 203; nonnormative sexuality, 40
LGBTQ+ people and kink at pride parades, 5, 119
libido, 26
Life magazine on leather bar culture, 115
listening, importance, 105, 198, 207
listening to partner, importance, 52
Little Becky, 182
Littles, role play involving, 1, 145–47, 156
Livy, 179–80
London, Julie, 151
long-term relationships: and the complexity of sexuality, 33–34; finding partners, 129; power-exchanges, 196–97; and self-awareness, 111; talking openly about sex, 56, 103
Lorde, Audre, 2
Lords, Kayla, 106, 207, 228
Lovense web site, Robyn on sensory deprivation kinks, 171
A Lover's Pinch: A Cultural History of Sadomachism (Tupper), 77, 182, 202–203
Loving BDSM podcast (John and Kayla), 202
The Loving Dominant (Warren and Warren), 202
lust: and being desired, 158; as a bodily function, 19; commonalities, 37; embracing fully, 9–10; fantasies about desirability, 99–100; handling incompatibilities, 30–31; identifying and accepting needs, 26–27; idiosyncratic and complicated nature, 11–12, 19–20; and limits of consent, 56; need to be desired, 100–101; power of, 2, 11; as a promise of what is to come, 19; and sexual minorities as super-heroes, 14; talking about with a partner, 27–30, 34–35

Lyndes, Haley, 168–69
Madonna, 227
Maîtresse (film), 195
Man2Man magazine, 116
Man in Furs (Sauvat), 87
Mannen, Amanda, 51
Mansfield, Katherine, 176–77
Mapplethorpe, Robert, 116, 188
Marley, Mistress, 109
Marsh, Amy, 71
Martin, Amy, 147
Martinez, Melanie, 148, 152
Masocast podcast (Axe), 200
masochists/masochism: benign masochism, 79; characteristics, 82–84; definitions and complexity, 1; origins of the term, 7; and self-denial, 168; and sensation, 38; "topping from the bottom," 94–95. *See also* BDSM; Sacher-Masoch, Leopold von; S/m
massage, 16, 82
Master of Sex (television show), 42
Masters, William, 20, 42
Master/slave (M/s) relationships, 106–7, 110,·182
masturbation: communal, 179; forced, 93; frequency, 27, 30; to porn and fantasies, 25, 70, 132; Sprinkle's sex magic rituals, 190; in young children, 8, 17; watching others, 27, 159
Matthews, Dylan, 155
McCann, Nuala, 181
McDaniel, Rena, 43
McLelland, Mark J., 40
McPherson, Coco, 162–63
Medium magazine, article on erotic hypnosis, 174
Megatron, Sunny, 201
MEL Magazine: article on healing from infidelity, 165 interview with smoking fetishist, 131–32
Melvoin-Berg, Ken, 201
Mesopotamia, sacred woman-centered sex in, 180

Meston, Cindy, 21
Middles, role play involving, 146–47
Midori: on race play, 144; on shibari, 46
mild paraphilia, 50
Miller, Philip, 202
Mimsy and Vagabond, 196
Mineshaft sex club, 187
minors, sex with, 75, 148, 162
MiscAlleneous, 131
moderate paraphilia, 50
money, fetishes associated with, 109–10
monogamy, 41, 177
Monteagudo, Jesse, 115
Mooallem, Jon, 190
Morrison, Toni, 19
Morse, Emily, 169
movies: Hollywood portrayals of kink, 20, 23, 59, 227; intimacy coordinators for, 58–59; negative representations of kink, 193–94; positive representation of kink in, 194–97
Mr. Benson (Preston), 187–88
Muir, Kate (@bimbokate), 174
mummification, 16, 170, 220
Munby, Hannah and Arthur, 182
Museum of Sex, New York City, 204
"My Heart Belongs to Daddy" (Porter), 149
My Secret Garden (Friday), 101

"Nailed" performance art (Flanagan and Rose), 189
National Coalition for Sexual Freedom, 206
National Domestic Violence Hotline, 63, 104
needle play, 56, 220–21
the Neighbourhood, 151
New York City, Mineshaft sex club, 187
New York Magazine, "Public Sex and the Standard Hotel," 162–63
New York Times: Angier on impact of sexual imagery, 159; Mooallem

article on Kink.com, 190; Williams-Haas interview, 143
Nine Inch Nails, 189
non-damaging pain, 79
nonmonogamy, 28, 41, 164–65
nonnormative sexuality: celebrating difference, 2–3, 37–38; and community, 164, 198; as a creative outlet, 222; as culturally defined, 17, 19–20; and happiness, 206–7; and isolation, 191; in Japan, 40; kink as, 39; language about, 18; nuanced and positive representations of, 193. See also nonmonogamy; polyamory; swingers; specific kinks and fetishes
normative sexual behavior. See vanilla sex
Nugent, Stuart, 164
Nuitdetokyo, 217–18

objectification, reverent, 171–72
objectophiles, 70–72
obsession, 158. See also fetishes
"Obsession" (Animotion), 157
omorashi fetish, 136
online kink, 191
oral sex, 15, 40
orgasm/climax: benefits of, 8; and delight/glee, 175; denial, 168–70; female, 40; as a goal, 20; hands-free, 174; hormonal-physical response, 78–79; and pain, 66; urethral training, 225; at young age, 8. See also arousal; edging; specific kinks and fetishes
O-rings, 221
Out in San Antonio, article on Bizarre magazine, 185
Out magazine, watersports article, 125–26
overeating fetish. See gaining/feeding/encouraging fetish

Page, Betty, 184–85
pain-pleasure continuum: as common in sexual encounters,

66; differing types of pain, 79; hormonal-physical response, 78–79; inflicting or experiencing, 65–66, 80; mind-body connections, 81; non-damaging, 79; psychology of, 80. *See also* BDSM

pansexual behavior, 17

pantyhose/stockings fetish, 122

Paper magazine, article on tickling fetish, 131

paraphilia (fetishism), definition, 47–48. *See also* fetishes; fetishists

partialist fetishes, 128–29

"Partition" (Beyoncé), 149

partners: connecting with, 37; establishing consent, 51–52; finding, 5, 26, 148, 192, 199–200, 205; long-term relationships, 129; and matching needs and desires, 27–30, 33–34, 52–53; as multi-layered and complex, 33–34; respecting and caring for, 62–63. *See also* communication; consent

pedophilia, 72–74, 148

penetrative sex, 24, 40, 90

Perrottet, Tony, 86

Perv (Bering), 134

pervert, as a term, 3, 6–8

pervertibles, 221–22

Perv: The Sexual Deviant in All of Us (Bering), 42, 202

pet play, 152–54. *See also* furries, furry community; plushies

Pham, Larissa, 98

pheromones, 20

Phoenix Boys of Leather group, 117, 212

Photo Bits magazine, 185

"Physical Pain as Pleasure: A Theoretical Perspective" (*Journal of Sex Research*), 80

physique magazines, 115

pick-up play, 53, 55–56, 226

Pink Flamingos (Waters), 64

Play, Kenneth, 94, 161

Playing Well with Others (Williams and Harrington), 202

the Pleasure Chest, NYC, LA and Chicago, 204

plushies, 130, 192

podcasts, kink-positive, 199–201

polyamory, 28–29, 164, 194, 206

Ponies on the Delta event, 153

Popsugar magazine, article on edging in, 168–69

porn: ASMR videos and podcasts, 132; child porn, 74; children's cartoons as, 11; *Fanny Hill*, 181–82; fetish porn, 9–10, 126–27; Rule 34, 37, 65; unintentional sources of, 51; and voyeurism, 159. *See also* the Internet

PornHub, 1, 165

Porter, Cole, 149

power exchange (pXe): abusive relationships vs., 62–63, 110; and agency, 110–11; benefits, 98, 107–8; combining D/s with, 104; complexity of, 105–6; and consent, 56, 67, 107; and D/s contracts; and kink, political context, 97–98; and money, 109; and nonconsensual relationships, 69; and nonsexual power abuses, 103; physical markers of, 108; and psychological commitment to play, 81; stability fetish, 111–13; varieties and diversity of approaches, 104–8. *See also* role play

preference, sexual, 22–24

Preston, John (*Mr. Benson*), 187–88, 207

pretending. *See* imagination, fantasies

PRICK (personal responsibility, informed consensual kink) protocols, 57–58, 215

Pride parades and respectability politics, 5, 118–19

privacy: and ASMR videos, 132; in-home, 4–5, 144–45; and scene names, 14; violating consent, 51

Pro Dommes, 109, 195, 197, 212

Professor Marston and the Wonder Woman (movie), 194–95
Pruke, Louise, 180
psychological kink, 63, 93, 131, 229–30
"The Psychology of Kink: A Survey Study into the Relationships of Trauma and Attachment Style with BDSM Interests" (*Sexuality Research and Social Policy*), 44–45
Psychopathia Sexualis (Kraft-Ebbing), 86, 88
public sex, 161
putrid games/exchanges, 64

queening, 222–23
queer 1950s household, 119–21
queer people, 5, 42–43

race play, 142–44
RACK (risk-aware, consensual kink) protocols, 56–57, 215
Ramachandran, V. S., 43
Rankin, Lissa, 83
rape culture, 69–70, 73
rape fantasy: as effort to find healing, 102; and openness to sexual experience, 98–99; and role playing ravishment, 93–94, 99–101; theories about sources for, 99; and violence, 103
rec.food.drink.beer recreational Usenet, 191–92
"red" (safe word), 58
Reid, Brian, 191
Reid, Joe, 227
relationships: mutually respectful vs. abusive, 104; negotiating, challenges of, 29, 41; nonconsensual game playing, 112; and the "stability fetish," 111–12. *See also* communication; consent; partners
Ren, Molly, 13–14
respectability politics, 5, 118–19
Reubens, Peter Paul, 88
Rice, Anne, 188, 203
Richards, Arielle, 173–74

The Right to Sex (Srinivasan), 55
Robyn on sensory deprivation kinks, 171
role play: age play, 144–45, 148; bimbofication, 173; and consent, 56; as creative and freeing, 35, 101, 137–40; cuckolding, 165–66; deep kink versions, 138; encouragers, 175; flexibility, 140–41; getting into, 139; incest role play, 138–39; nonsexual, term needed for, 156; pet play, 152–54; popular scenarios, 138; props and accoutrements, 140; safe words, 58; in semi-public places, etiquette, 144
Rolling Stone magazine: article about BimboTok, 173; article about leather families
rope bondage, 46, 223–24
Rose, Sheree, 189
"A Rose for Emily" (Faulkner), 68
Rothfeld, Becca, 54–55, 60
rough sex, 77, 93, 180
Rozin, Paul, 79
Rule 34, 37, 65. *See also* porn
Rumelin, Angelika Aurora, 87
the Runaways, 151
Runkle, Larissa, 190
Russell, Amy, 17
ryōki (curiosity hunting), 40

Sacher-Masoch, Leopold von, 7, 86–88, 183
Sade, Hugues de, 86
Sade, Marquis de, 84–86, 182
Sadomasochism and the BDSM Community in the United State (Stein), 39, 187, 202
safer sex practices, 117
safe words, 58, 216
Saint Thomas, Sophie, 130
Samois, 186
San Francisco, California: as a BDSM hotspot, 205; Catacombs BDSM club, 187; Kink.com, 190; Tool Box bar, 115–16
Sassafras, 146

Satyrs, Los Angeles, 115
Sauvat, Catherine, 87
Savage, Dan, 42, 200–201, 230
Savage Lovecast podcast (Savage),
    200–201
scene names, 14
Schachter, Mia, 55, 58
scopophilia (voyeurism), 159
Scorpio Rising (film, Anger), 115
*Screw the Roses, Send Me the Thorns:
    The Romance and Sexual Sorcery
    of Sadomasochism* (Miller and
    Devon), 202
Secretary (film), 195–96
self-awareness: and exploring kinky
    interests, 1–2; of needs and
    desires, identifying and commu-
    nicating, 27–30; of needs and
    desires, importance, 26–27; and
    self-empowerment, 173; through
    experiencing deviant desires, 2
semi-public locations for sex, 162
sensory deprivation kink, 168,
    170–71
sensory fetishes, 130–33
serious paraphilia, 50
Serling, Ricky, 163
seven deadly sins/gluttony fetish, 10
sex: and aging, 17–18; consensual,
    importance, 14; culturally
    determined options, 178; desire
    for sensation and connection,
    16–17; escape-pod adventures,
    31–35; as an event, 93; factors
    promoting intimacy, 20–21; as
    a form of escape, 137; impor-
    tance and power of, 2; kinky,
    ethical requirements, 52–53;
    legal risks of non-normative
    behaviors, 4; normal, on the
    FetLife top 100, 16; personal
    importance, 27; and ravishment
    fantasies, 100; sex parties, 163;
    sexual adventuring, 91; talking
    about, challenges, 26–35, 42,
    52; underwhelming, moving be-
    yond, 55; variability of response
    within, 20. *See also* imagination,

fantasies; orgasm/climax; shame
    and secrecy about sex and *specific
    kinks and fetishes*
sex clubs, 163, 183, 187
sexiness, cultural norms for, 17, 23,
    40–41
Sexmuseum, Amsterdam, 204
sexology field, creation of, 184
Sex Out Loud podcast (Taormino),
    200
sex-shaming, 179
Sexsmith, Sinclair, 106–7, 116–17
sex toys: ancient Egyptian, 39;
    cock cages, 169–70; dildos and
    strap-ons, 213–14; e-stim ma-
    chines, 214–15; floggers, 46, 215;
    gags, 215–16; handcuffs, 216;
    imaginary, 230; inflatables, 217;
    knives, 218; "pervertibles," 222;
    rope, 223–24; sex shops, 203–4;
    shibari and *kinbaku*, 217–18;
    spanking benches, 224–25; vari-
    ety of, 225; violet wands, 226–27
sexual compatibility: and adventur-
    ousness, 28, 99; and changing
    preferences, 23; chemistry, 20;
    complexity of, 26–27, 29, 33;
    frequency/time of day prefer-
    ences, 27–28; handling incom-
    patibilities, 30–31; making
    kinks clear, 29; power dynamics,
    29–30; preferred sex acts, 28;
    preferred tone, 28; questionnaire
    for determining, 27–30
sexual development, myths about,
    17–18
sexual identity: coming out as
    deviant, 5–6, 33, 14; cultural/
    politicized features, 21–23;
    orientation vs. preference, 22;
    and persecution, 3–4, 41, 67
sexuality research, 3, 41–42, 44–45
sexual predation, 51–52
sex workers: abusing, 85; Annie
    Sprinkle, 189–90; Mistress
    Marley, 109; Pro Dommes,
    109, 195, 197, 212; screen
    names/pseudonyms, 14; as sex

educators, 190; sex tourism, 203; as superheroes, 14; Tina Horn, 200; in Weimar Berlin, 184

shame and secrecy, 41, 127, 129, 135, 138, 160–61

shamelessness, eroticism of, 10–11, 13, 37

Shane, Charlotte, 165

Sheff, Elisabeth A., 4

shibari (Japanese art of knot binding), 46, 217–18

shunga (Japanese erotic art), 180–81

Simon, Anne, 87

Sinclair, Cherise, 203

Sluts & Scholars podcast (Heidegger), 201

S/m (S&M, sadomasochism): accessibility, 77; activities involved in, 82, 90; impact play, 77, 92; and intense stimulation, 38, 92–93; and mutual respect, 83–84, 95–96; non-consensual, non-erotic, 83; origins of the term, 81–82; pain-pleasure continuum, 65–66; psychological torture, 93; role exchanges, 91; rough sex, 93; safety and consent, 95. *See also* BDSM

Smith, Stephen K., 213

Smith, Zadie, 134

smoking fetish, 131–32

Society of Janus, 186

Sofia Gray blog, 127

somnophilia, 133

Song, Sarah, 131

Sontag, Susan, 76

sounding, 225–26

spanking: popularity, 23–25; sex toys, 46, 215; spanking benches, 224–25; spanking fetishists, 24–25; spankos, 91, 125–26; toys for, 91

The Spanko (film, Tyran), 125–26

spectrum of fetishistic tendency, 49–50

Sprinkle, Annie, 189–90

Sprinkle Report, 189

Srinivasan, Amia, 55

SSC (safe, sane and consensual), 56–57

stability fetish, 111–13, 117

Stamburgh, Russell J., 110

Standard Hotel, New York City, 162–63

Stein, David, 116–17, 222

Stein, Stephen K.: on the emergence of biker-culture, 115; on the Eulenspiegel Society, 185–86; on *Fifty Shades of Grey*, 193; on Guyette's importance, 195; on kink at pride marches, 119; on leather as an identity, 113; on *Photo Bits* magazine, 185; *Sadomasochism and the BDSM Community in the United States* (Stein), 202; on sexual theater, 39; the SSC acronym, 57, 222; on taboos and race play, 142; on violet wands, 226

the Stockroom, Los Angeles, 204

"Stop, Drop and Role! Erotic Role Playing" (Williams-Haas), 143

Storey Sisters, 150

The Story of O (*Histoire d'O*; Desclos), 221

students (yours), sex with, 68–69

style, Brake's definition, 9

submissives (s-types): and aftercare, 105; and collars, 212; and consent, 56; definitions, 82–83; and findom, 109–10; and latex clothing, 219; "topping from the bottom," 94–95. *See also* BDSM; D/s; S/m

"subvert," non-sexual meanings, 7

Sugarbutch Chronicles (blog), on Master/slave terminology, 107

Sumerian love poetry, 180

support groups, 185–86

swaddling, 219–20

"Sweet Daddy" (Storey Sisters), 150

Swift, Jonathan, 181

Swinger Lifestyle (SLS), 163

swingers, 28, 32, 54, 163–64, 166

taboos, cultural: appeal of exploring, 142; and body fluid paraphilia, 136; and kink, 62, 64–65, 207; and pain, 65–66; and the putrid, 64; and role playing, 138, 143–44
talismen, 124
Tan, Cecilia, 203
Taormino, Tristan, 200, 202
Taylor, Mildred Europa, 179
teenagers: in age play scenarios, 146–47; identification as Littles, 148; sex among, 74–75
Tell Me What You Want: The Science of Sexual Desire and How It Can Help You Improve Your Sex Life (Lehmiller), 102
Templeton (rat in *Charlotte's Web* cartoon), 12–13
TENS units, 214
TES (the Eulenspiegel Society), 205
textile fetishes, 130–31
Them magazine: article on Scruff dating app, 192–93; interviews with perverts in, 95
Thompson, Jack, 193
tickling fetish, 131
Tom of Finland, 114, 184
Tomorrow Sex Will Be Good Again (Angel), 26
Tool Box bar (San Francisco), 115–16
"topping from the bottom," 94–95
"tops"/topping, 82–83, 94
Torn, Cherry, 109
Torpedo the Ark blog, 183
Townsend, Larry, 116
toxic masculinity, 99, 165
Toybag Guide series (Greenery Press), 202
ToyTorture website, 215
Transparent (TV series), 197
trauma experiences: sharing with partner, 27; trauma/abuse theory of kink, 98; ubiquity and diversity of, 45
triggering, avoiding, 216
Troup, Bobby, 151

Tupper, Peter: on appeal of S/m, 52–53, 77; on BDSM as ritualistic, 38; on celebrating kink, 208; on Hannah and Arthur Munby, 182; on the history of kink, 178–79; *A Lover's Pinch: A Cultural History of Sadomasochism*, 77, 182, 202-3
Turnbull, Michael T. R. B., 228
Twisted Monk blog, 208
Twisted Monk store, 224
Tyran, Charlotte, 125–26

The Ultimate Guide to Kink (anthology), 143, 202
urethral sounding, 225–26
uromasochism, 136
urophilia (pee play), 125, 135–36, 189–90
Usenet forums, and connection with other deviants, 191–92
"The Uses of the Erotic: The Erotic as Power" (Lorde), 2

vanilla sex: kink or fetish vs., 23, 25; and mutual consent, 55; rough sex, 77; as a societal paradigm, 177; as a term, 16; and watching others become aroused, 159–60. *See also* nonnormative sexual activity
Vanity Fair magazine, article about furries, 154
Vātsyāyana, 180
Velvet Underground, 7
Velvet Underground (Leigh), 7
Venus in Furs (Sacher-Masoch), 86–87
Vice magazine: article by an amputee, 129; article on bimbofication, 173–74; article about kink financial domination, 109; article on WAM fetishes, 133–34; the Fedleg fetish, 36; video on cash slaves, 109–10
violet wands, 226–27
vore fetish, 51, 68

voyeurism (liking to watch): commonness of, 159; and exhibitionism, 161–62; as a term, 160; types and characteristics, 160–61
voyeuristic disorder, 160

Walansky, Aly, 138
WAM (wet and messy) fetishes, 133–34
Warren, John and Libby, 201
Waters, John, 64
watersports fetishes, 135
wax play, 227
weight gain fetish. *See* gaining/feeding/encouraging fetish
Weimar Germany, kink in, 183–84
West, Xan, 98
Westenfeld, Adrienne, 59
whisper fetish, 132
white privilege, 4, 6
Why Are People Into That? (podcast, Horn), 200

Wicked Grounds coffee shop, San Francisco, 204–5
Williams, Mollena (Mollena Williams-Haas): expertise on role play, 143; on living fearlessly, 143; *Playing Well with Others*, 202; role play origins, 143; *Toybag Guide to Playing with Taboo*, 202
Willie, John (John Coutts), 153, 185
Wolfson, Elijah, 19
Women's Health, 162
Wood, Ed, 134

X-cross (St. Andrew's cross), 228
Xtra magazine, safety rules, 222

"yellow" (safe word), 58
"You Can Be the Boss" (Del Ray), 151–52

Zane, Zachary, 94
zentai suits, 229

ABOUT THE AUTHOR

A rielle Greenberg speaks about kink and ethical non-monogamy at universities and on such podcasts as *Dear Sugar*, *Why Are People into That?!*, and *Sex Out Loud*. She is the author of several books of poetry and creative nonfiction. A former tenured professor in English at Columbia College Chicago, she has spent over twenty years as a scholar and academic, writing about cultural studies and literature and teaching undergraduate and graduate students, as well as in the community. She identifies as a life-long sexual fetishist.